ROUTLEDGE LIBRARY EDITIONS: AGING

I0130935

Volume 41

OLD AND ALONE

OLD AND ALONE

A Sociological Study of Old People

JEREMY TUNSTALL

Routledge
Taylor & Francis Group

LONDON AND NEW YORK

First published in 1966 by Routledge & Kegan Paul

This edition first published in 2024
by Routledge
4 Park Square, Milton Park, Abingdon, Oxon OX14 4RN

and by Routledge
605 Third Avenue, New York, NY 10158

*Routledge is an imprint of the Taylor & Francis Group, an informa
business*

British Library Cataloguing in Publication Data
A catalogue record for this book is available from the British
Library

ISBN: 978-1-032-67433-9 (Set)
ISBN: 978-1-032-70187-5 (Volume 41) (hbk)
ISBN: 978-1-032-70198-1 (Volume 41) (pbk)
ISBN: 978-1-032-70197-4 (Volume 41) (ebk)

DOI: 10.4324/9781032701974

Publisher's Note
The publisher has gone to great lengths to ensure the quality of this
reprint but points out that some imperfections in the original copies
may be apparent.

Disclaimer
The publisher has made every effort to trace copyright holders and
would welcome correspondence from those they have been unable
to trace.

OLD AND ALONE

A sociological study of old people

JEREMY TUNSTALL

LONDON
ROUTLEDGE & KEGAN PAUL

First published in 1966
by Routledge and Kegan Paul Ltd
Broadway House, 68-74 Carter Lane
London, EC4V 5EL
Reprinted 1971

Reproduced and Printed in Great Britain by
Redwood Press Limited
Trowbridge & London

ISBN 0 7100 2205 0

CONTENTS

v

Contents

Contents

Contents

TABLES

ix

Tables

Acknowledgements

This book would never have happened but for the generosity
of the United States Public Health Service. Peter Townsend
and Dorothy Cole Wedderburn have directed a national study
of old people in Britain (as part of a cross-national study with
colleagues in U.S.A. and Denmark). They originally conceived
my study as a follow-up piece of research about one minority
group of old people. In practice it developed a fairly autono-
mous life of its own – but it took place under the umbrella of
their study. I am indebted to them for permission to use evidence
from their national survey, although the presentation and interpretation of these 'national' tables is my own responsibility. As
a newcomer to social research about old people, I was particularly fortunate during the first year of my study to share an
office at the London School of Economics with Peter Townsend.
His advice and encouragement have been of the greatest value.

My thanks are due also to the sixteen doctors (and their
partners) in Harrow, Northampton, Oldham and South Norfolk who provided me with random lists of old people's names.

The screening interviews were most efficiently conducted by
Joyce Arkley, Anne Bromley, Paul Bridge, Lydia Cole, Ruth
Jefferies and Brenda Swann.

Maurice Coutts undertook the large task of typing the interview commentaries. Daphne Partos, Sheila Benson, Wendy
Morgan and Katie Pringle performed the other typing labours.

The following read the book in draft and provided invaluable
advice : Sheila Benson, Sylvia Korte, Ann Lapping, Denis Levy,
Anthony Rees, Michael Sissons, Kathleen Slack, Peter Townsend, Brian Tunstall, Peter and Phyllis Willmott.

Finally and obviously my greatest debt is to the old people
themselves who answered my questions.

The title 'Old and Alone' was previously used in an article
I wrote for the *New Statesman*. Other pieces based on the same
survey have appeared in *Twentieth Century*, *The Observer*, and
New Society.   J.T.

xi

Chapter One
INTRODUCTION AND
SUMMARY

Introduction

Old people are eight times more likely to live alone than are people aged under 65. About 1,300,000 people aged 65 and over in Britain today live alone. A larger number, about 1,600,000, in reply to a question will say they are lonely (a quarter of these being 'often' lonely). About a million old people in Britain are socially isolated.[1] About a million are anomic. Half a million old people have been widowed within the last five years; half a million have been housebound for at least six months; seven-tenths of a million are single.

Another group of nearly 400,000 are residents in institutions of various sorts – Residential Homes, Psychiatric and other hospitals, nursing-homes and so on.

Nevertheless the total number of men and women aged 65 and over in Britain in 1963 was about 6,200,000. Of these only 6 per cent are temporary or permanent residents in institutions. The remaining 94 per cent live in private households; of this total group 78 per cent do *not* live alone, 72 per cent say they are *'never'* lonely. The majority are not socially isolated and not anomic. The great majority of old people can move about outside their home. About half of all old people are married and most of the other half have been widowed for over five years.

Those who are old and alone are thus a minority of all old people. The size of the minority depends upon which kind of 'aloneness' is being discussed.

---

[1] These terms are defined below, pp. 17–21.

Introduction and Summary

I. THE MAJORITY OF OLD PEOPLE

Old people in this study are defined as being aged 65 and over. This is the age in Britain at which State contributory pensions become payable to retired men,[2] although women can receive their retirement pensions from the age of 60 onwards. Public interest in old age has tended to revolve around retirement and retirement pensions. During the present century a dramatic increase has taken place in the proportion of old people in the population of Britain and other developed countries.

PERCENTAGE OF POPULATION OF ENGLAND
AND WALES AGED 65 AND OVER[3]

Year	Men	Women	Both sexes
1841	4·2%	4·7%	4·4%
1871	4·4%	5·0%	4·7%
1901	4·2%	5·1%	4·7%
1931	6·7%	8·1%	7·4%
1961	9·4%	14·3%	11·9%

Academic research on all aspects of old age has also developed significantly. The first International Congress of Gerontology took place in 1948. In the same year J. H. Sheldon published his pioneering Wolverhampton study *The Social Medicine of Old Age*. Since then studies in Britain and elsewhere have shown that the *majority* of old people are mobile and think their health is fairly good. Another major focus of social research has been on retirement – especially the rather abrupt retirement experienced by most men. A number of studies have supported Sheldon's finding that the majority of old people are in intimate and regular contact with their close kin, especially their children.

Various research workers have reported that popular stereotypes of old age as a period of unrelieved gloom and despair are wildly exaggerated. The tone of much sociological research on old age has been basically optimistic. However, more recently there has been an increased realization that while the

[2] The standard contributory retirement pension for a single or widowed person aged 65 was £3 7s. 6d. during the interviewing stage of this study in 1963–4.
[3] Registrar General 1961 Census.

2

The Importance of the Alone Minority

majority of old people may be reasonably contented, there are *minority* groups of old people who constitute important exceptions. Research has pointed to the existence of unmet medical needs and unmet need for State financial assistance. Peter Townsend's *The Last Refuge* has shown in painstaking detail the inadequacy of many Homes for old people.

The present study follows this recent tendency, and concentrates on another minority group of old people.

2. THE IMPORTANCE OF THE ALONE MINORITY

Old people who are 'alone' in one or more ways are important from several points of view. *Firstly*, an adequate sociological understanding of the human life-cycle requires a theory of the process of ageing; some preliminary attempts have been made in this direction. But these studies have tended to emphasize the majority group of socially integrated old people; a more complete theory must also take account of the alone minority.

Secondly, social isolation is a social condition which affects not only old people but also some in younger age-groups. Old people, however, probably represent the most extreme examples of social isolation, and studies of them may help to throw some general light on the subject.

Thirdly, old people in general are becoming increasingly important from the point of view of social policy. Matters like hospital planning or the organization of general medical practice cannot be discussed without reference to the needs of old people. In the provision of housing and the adaptation of the supply of housing to the changing requirements of people at different stages in the human life-cycle, the situation of old people is again vitally important. The whole question of social insurance and pension provision – with its ramifications in such fields as savings and capital investment – revolves primarily around the problem of how society should provide for old age. Automation and technical innovation are likely to have their biggest impact among older workers, perhaps in the long run lowering the age of retirement from work and thus in effect expanding the size of the 'elderly' group. Financial provision for people living in what society chooses to define as poverty also centres upon the elderly. For such reasons politicians and

3

administrators seem likely to become even more concerned about old people; and among the elderly, the alone minority includes many of those towards whom that concern will be especially directed.

3. FOUR-AREA AND NATIONAL SURVEYS

The present book reports on only one of a series of studies of old age which have been generously financed during the past few years by the United States Public Health Service.[4] The principal study is of people aged 65 and over living in private households. The Government Social Survey interviewed 4,000 old people in Britain in 1962 – 2,500 in the first stage – and roughly the same number as in this first stage were also interviewed in the United States and Denmark during April to July 1962. A basically common questionnaire was used in all three countries and the research teams met frequently to co-ordinate methods and concepts. The British part of this international project is referred to in the present book as the *national* survey.

A second study was also conducted throughout Britain into the circumstances of old people living in three types of institution – Residential Homes, Psychiatric hospitals, and non-Psychiatric hospitals and nursing-homes; this is referred to hereafter as the *institutional* survey. An interim report of these studies has been published.[5]

The third study is reported in the following pages. Originally it was hoped to draw from the main national sample a sub-sample of old people who were isolated or alone and to re-interview them. But unfortunately the Government Social Survey felt unable to pass on the names and addresses of old people from the main survey. Consequently another system of

[4] By the National Institute of Mental Health and later the Community Health Services Division, Bureau of State Services of the United States Public Health Service. (British grant numbers being MH–05511–02 and CH 0053–02.) The cross-national study was directed in Britain by Professor Peter Townsend (University of Essex) and Mrs. Dorothy Cole Wedderburn (Department of Applied Economics, Cambridge University), in U.S.A. by Dr. Ethel Shanas (University of Chicago) and in Denmark by Dr. Henning Friis (National Institute of Social Research, Copenhagen).

[5] Peter Townsend and Dorothy Wedderburn, *The Aged in the Welfare State* (1965).

Four-Area and National Surveys

sampling had to be employed and since there is no available national register of old people in Britain this was a serious problem. As in some other field surveys the Government Social Survey had drawn a sample of all households and rejected approximately two-thirds which contained no old person. Any study of a minority group of old people involves rejecting in turn the majority of old people. The inevitably high expense of such a procedure made this sampling method impracticable. Thus it was decided to conduct the study in a small number of local areas and to draw a sample of old people from the lists of general medical practitioners. (The national survey indicated that of old people in private households only 1 in 500 is not registered with a doctor.) Names of people aged 65 and over were drawn at random from the lists of sixteen general practices in four contrasted areas of England.

Screening interviewers were employed to visit the old people and conduct a short interview; 538 of these screening interviews were completed. Old people who came into one of the minority groups with which the study was concerned were re-interviewed by the author; 195 of these follow-up interviews were completed, each lasting a median of 1 hour 45 minutes. (There was a failure rate of 10·8 per cent at the screening stage and 10·1 per cent at the follow-up stage – including non-contacts and people too ill or deaf to be interviewed.)[6]

To distinguish it from the *national* survey of old people in private households and the *institutional* survey, the smaller investigation with which this book is primarily concerned is referred to as the *four-area* survey. The areas are Harrow, Northampton, Oldham and South Norfolk. Harrow and Oldham are part of the large conurbations of London and Manchester; Northampton is a smaller urban area, but with a strongly industrial character. South Norfolk is a completely rural, farming area. Oldham and Northampton are mainly manual working class; Harrow is suburban and more white collar middle class.

The 538 old people interviewed in the four-area survey compare fairly closely in terms of sex, marital status and age with the figures for the 1961 Census in England and Wales. The main difference is that the four-area survey includes somewhat

[6] See Appendix 1.

5

Introduction and Summary

too many widows and widowers – and there is a partly related over-weighting in the age-group 70–74. Some of this difference is due to the fact that in the four-area survey separated old people are placed with the widowed (and divorced) whereas the Census includes them with the married.[7]

		[7] *1961* *England and* *Wales*	*1963–4* *4 Area* *Survey*
Women as proportion of all people 65 and over		61·7%	61·0%

Male			
Married		70·3	68·1
Single		7·6	5·7
Widowed/Divorced		22·2	26·2
		100	100

Female			
Married		34·3	31·1
Single		15·6	14·0
Widowed/Divorced		50·2	54·9
		100	100

Male			
Age 65–69		39·0	35·2
70–74		28·5	33·8
75–79		18·5	16·2
80+		14·0	14·8
		100	100

Female			
Age 65–69		34·1	32·0
70–74		27·8	31·7
75–79		20·0	16·2
80+		18·1	20·1
		100	100

4. THE FOUR AREAS

Harrow is a large sprawling suburban area about ten miles from Central London, with a population of over 200,000. It was built up mainly between 1918 and 1939; most of the old people who live there were born nearer to the centre of London, but some

6

The Four Areas

can remember the predominantly rural nature of the area before 1914. Harrow is known for a famous public school, and there are a number of other schools in the area. School teachers abound but are outnumbered by the white-collar workers many of whom commute into London to work in offices and shops. Harrow itself is a shopping and office centre; it also employs many manual workers in printing, at the Kodak factory, and on the railways. All three Harrow constituencies were Conservative in 1964. A characteristic view contains a row of redbrick semi-detached houses, a railway line near by and the green of Harrow hill in the distance.

Northampton was once a market town, and still has a cattle market. It is thirty-one miles from Coventry and close to the London–Birmingham motorway. Much of the housing dates from the late nineteenth century. Before the First World War the leather and boot and shoe industries played a dominant part in the town and many old people report that there was little other real choice of employment. More recently a number of new firms have entered the town, and Northampton now has strong light and heavy engineering elements. The population is over 100,000 and there are a number of new housing estates. Northampton voted Labour in 1964. The air is clearer than in many industrial towns and it is usually possible to see from one of the outlying housing or industrial estates to the centre of the town, with the dull red brick of the shoe factories on the skyline.

Oldham is a relic of the industrial revolution and the Lancashire cotton industry. It is about seven miles from the centre of Manchester and sprawls up and down the foothills of the Pennines towards the Yorkshire border. Oldham's housing is extremely bad even by the low standards of the Manchester area, and during the 1950's the situation continued to get worse. Since then substantial slum-clearance projects have been started near the centre of the town. Before the first war the cotton-spinning industry dominated Oldham with the support of some coal-mining. More recently the cotton industry has shrunk severely and many of Oldham's citizens now work in the electronic and aircraft industry, or at factories in Manchester. Both the Oldham constituencies voted Labour in 1964. The characteristic view of Oldham looks up a hilly street of mean

7

dirt-encrusted houses to where out of the industrial smog and drizzle looms the grim four-square hulk of an old cotton mill. Two important features of Oldham are its long tradition of married women going out to work and its excellent record in providing welfare services for old people.

South Norfolk is a flat farming area of scattered small villages and disused airfields, about a hundred miles from London. It varies between ten and thirty miles from the county town of Norwich. This is one of the most prosperous farming areas in Britain, with big farms, large fields, few hedges, much machinery and a highly unionized force of farm workers. Loss of population has continued since 1945, and some of the picturesque cottages in the village-centres are standing empty. However, many people still live in bad housing conditions. Before the First World War the area concentrated on grain farming, and the old people often report how they started work as children scaring crows or picking stones off the fields. Now there has been a switch to sugar-beet, poultry farming and growing peas and other vegetables on contract for freezing. In some villages small canning or processing factories provide new employment. Growing prosperity and declining population have led to severe restriction of the bus and train services. Old people without their own transport often find it quite impossible to visit a relative only a few miles away. South Norfolk voted Conservative by a narrow margin in 1964. The typical view looks across a huge open expanse of field to a large stone church dominating a row of raw brick Council houses, with a line of tall trees in the far distance.

5. THE FOUR-AREA INTERVIEWS

The main object of the screening interview in the four-area survey was to discover old people who came into one of the categories with which the study was primarily concerned. In the planning of the survey four ways of being alone were defined:

1. Living alone
2. Social isolation
3. Loneliness
4. Anomie

The Four-Area Interviews

Previous evidence indicated that three groups of old people were particularly likely to fall into one or more of these 'alone' categories. These groups at risk were defined as:

1. The single
2. The recently widowed
3. The housebound

Any old person who was single, recently widowed or housebound was re-interviewed – using a common schedule with special questions (of an open type) for people belonging to one of the 'at risk' categories. In addition all old people who were 'socially isolated' or those who said they were 'often lonely' were also re-interviewed. Old people who were either living alone or anomic were not re-interviewed unless they came into one of the special 'at risk' categories as well.

The design of this piece of research thus produces a series of categories each of which overlaps to a greater or lesser extent with other categories. The precise design adopted is by no means the only one possible; for instance it might have been desirable to re-interview all those who lived alone or were anomic regardless of whether they were single, recently widowed or housebound, or came into none of these 'at risk' categories. But some sort of overlapping research design seems inevitable.

A danger of this sort of research design is that the reader is continually told of correlations between one category and another, but may lose sight of the old person as a whole. To counteract such a danger reports on interviews with individual old people are included in the text.

Although there is a big literature on the methodology of designing and carrying out empirical social research, much less has been written as to how the social scientist should select from his material when he comes to writing his report. In even such a comparatively small study as the present one, apart from the 538 three-page screening schedules and 195 sixteen-page follow-up schedules there are about 410,000 typed words of the author's notes on the follow-up interviews. How does one select from such a mass? Many research reports spice the statistical information with paragraph-long quotes from interview notes. But how does one select one section of a particular interview from, say, 100 interviews with isolated old people?

9

Introduction and Summary

One object of including much larger reports on individual interviews in the present book is to illustrate the point that there are no 'typical cases'. On the whole the ten interview reports in the text are selected for being somewhat extreme examples of the different ways of being alone – or not being alone, despite being 'at risk'.

However, the reader is also enabled to compare each individual interview with the general sample on certain basic criteria. At the beginning of each interview details are listed of whether the old person lives alone or with others, and of his social isolation (or higher social contact score), his self-ascribed loneliness, his anomia score, whether he is single or recently widowed and whether he is housebound. Each of these categories is explained in turn in the text of Part I and II. One further score is included for each interview, namely 'incapacity' for self-care; this score derives from the follow-up interview and is based on the old person's capacity to do such things as climb stairs, dress and wash himself, and cut his own toe-nails.[8] The incapacity scale was devised by Peter Townsend.[9]

Methods of writing reports on social research can no more be discussed in the abstract than can methods of research design. In the present case the author believes that failure to include a substantial body of material about the interviews might result in misleading the reader. This method enables the careful reader both to see the precise wording of the question and the often muddled and confusing results that emerge. The interview reports also help to illustrate some of the special problems involved in interviewing old people. Moreover, in conveying something of the flavour and atmosphere of the interview, these reports should impress upon the reader the tentative nature of the findings.[10]

---

[8] See Appendix 2. The score is based on question 17 in the follow-up schedule.

[9] The incapacity scale was adopted direct from the national survey. This in turn was a shortened version of that developed by Peter Townsend and reported in his *The Last Refuge* (1962), pp. 464–76.

[10] The practice of including in the text of a research report substantial amounts of material about a small number of individuals is, of course, far from new in sociology. Examples include William I. Thomas and Florian Znaniecki, *The Polish Peasant in Europe and America* (Dover Publications, 1918–20); W. Lloyd Warner and Paul S. Lunt, *The Social Life of a Modern Community* (Yale University Press, New Haven, 1941); David Reisman, *Faces in the Crowd* (Yale University Press, New Haven, 1952).

Summary

I. FORMS OF BEING ALONE

Living alone (Chapter 2). The proportion of people aged 65 and over who live alone is increasing and is now over 20 per cent. Old women, the widowed of both sexes, those over 75, and the childless are most likely to live alone. There is no difference between the social classes. Wide variations exist between localities, with city centre areas and London having the highest proportions of their old people living alone. Many old people prefer to live alone, especially if they can see their children regularly. Underlying factors in old people living alone probably include changes in the size of family, the supply of housing and of work for women, and social policy itself.

Social isolation (Chapter 3) is closely connected with living alone, but not all old people who live alone are socially isolated. Those in paid employment are unlikely to be isolated. Social isolation does not vary with social class, physical incapacity or residential mobility. The incidence of isolation varies between urban areas but the rural pattern is similar to the general urban pattern. There is little connection between isolation and social participation with friends, neighbours, or in clubs.

Loneliness (Chapter 4) is connected with social isolation but the 'often lonely' are a smaller group. The physically incapacitated, childless widows, and widows with children whom they don't see frequently all have a high chance of being lonely. When old people feel lonely for a particular person, it is usually a dead person. The worst times are night and the winter.

Anomie (Chapter 5). Anomia is connected with low social class and lack of social participation. The anomic tend to be old men rather than women, but there is no positive connection with childlessness, widowhood, or the single state. Retirement may be a key factor.

2. GROUPS AT RISK

The single (Chapter 6) are more likely than other old people to live alone and to be socially isolated, but not to be lonely.

Summary

Single old women tend to have been domestic servants, teachers or factory hands. They quote a variety of reasons for having remained single, and most would have liked children of their own. The single have tended to live in a world of other single (or widowed) people.

The recently widowed (Chapter 7) are especially likely to feel lonely and to live alone – although the majority also see children regularly. The shock of the death tends to be followed by a period of anxiety about future plans; they think a lot about their dead spouse but do not feel guilty. Widowhood poses special problems for old people who lack work and dependent children.

The housebound (Chapter 8) are especially predisposed to loneliness. The housebound tend to be women, aged over 75 and suffering from arthritis. The majority live with either spouse or children, who also look after them – the social services play a much smaller role. A minority of the housebound live alone and are socially isolated.

3. PRIVATE PURSUITS AND PUBLIC PROVISION

Use of time (Chapter 9). The most common activities of isolated old people are cooking, housework, shopping, listening to the radio, reading newspapers, seeing relatives and watching television. The great majority of this activity takes place in the isolated old person's own home. Activities such as gardening give great pleasure to some (and pain to others) but are much less widespread than consuming the offerings of the mass media.

Money (Chapter 10). Few isolated old people have other than State contributory pensions; nearly half receive National Assistance and the great majority have incomes not much above the National Assistance rates. Poverty and social isolation are found mainly among the same groups – single and widowed women, those over 70, and the retired.

Social services (Chapter 11) have a fairly low coverage among the groups involved in this study. For the socially isolated the family doctor has the highest spread, followed by clubs and home helps. Other services, such as home nursing, meals-on-

Discussion

wheels, and voluntary visiting have only a very marginal impact. A good deal of criticism of the social services – including specially built housing – is expressed by the old people concerned.

4. DISCUSSION

Personality (Chapter 12) is an important variable in adjustment to ageing; 'successful' adjustment inevitably involves value judgements. Important recent studies of the role of personality in retirement and of 'disengagement' in old age may paint too optimistic a picture because they tend to concentrate on the majority of old people and ignore the isolated minority.

Social theory (Chapter 13) has not yet dealt adequately with old age. There is little evidence of automatic respect for old people in primitive or peasant societies; groups such as childless women seem always to have lacked social recognition. Many of the most respected and powerful people in contemporary society are old. Social theory has concentrated on the conjugal family's basic function of child-rearing and ignored the looser and wider family with its other secondary functions such as looking after its older members.

Social policy (Chapter 14). The old-age pension allows old people the choice of living independently. To make this independence more positive, better financial provision is necessary, unmet medical needs require attention, domiciliary services for old people and other social services must be radically expanded and overhauled.

Part I

FORMS OF BEING ALONE

Each of us is alone, from womb to grave. In another sense none of us is completely alone; even in solitary confinement a man has some contact with his fellows and remains a highly social animal. There are as many ways of being alone as there are people to have the experience. It is one of the great subjects of literature and art.

Any definitions adopted will be very rough and any method used to measure degrees of aloneness will inevitably be a blunt instrument. The interviews included in the text of this book are a reminder – if any is needed – of the complexity of human individuals.

Four different forms of aloneness are defined and examined – living alone, social isolation, loneliness, and anomie.

Living alone

The simplest of these categories is living alone. (A person who lives in the same house as others but does not share housekeeping and at least one main meal a day is defined as living alone.) The significance of living alone is obvious for old people – most of whom do not go out to paid employment. With the exception of a few marginal cases, this is a category which can easily be recognized both by the old person and the outside observer. Living alone is also the only one of the four forms of aloneness to appear in the national Census.

Social isolation

In using the concept of 'social isolation' sociologists have adopted two main emphases. Firstly there is social isolation

Forms of Being Alone

from the wider society. Paul Halmos writes: 'Certainly, ours is a desocialized society in which social isolation is widespread. . . . In a primitive community the daily contact with each and all was in harmony with the general rhythm of life, with a recurrent cycle of daily activities.'[1] Participation in community activities has been measured, by F. Stuart Chapin.[2] This meaning of social isolation – isolation from the broader society – has been used not only of individuals but also of family units. Harriet Wilson writes of problem families of two adults and six or seven children huddled together in a kitchen and a limited number of beds, which are extremely 'socially isolated' – in the sense of being cut off from contact with wider social values.[3]

The second main usage of social isolation is in terms of the individual's isolation, not from the wider society but from his primary groups of family and work. Retirement from work removes men, in particular, from a major source of social intercourse and may precipitate social isolation. If the old person has few relatives or sees little of them, social isolation becomes more probable. Talcott Parsons uses the term in this sense when he talks of 'extreme loneliness and social isolation' which may force an old person to adopt the otherwise 'unnatural' mode (according to Parsons) of living with a married child.[4] Erwin Stengel writes:

> The inevitable social and psychological isolation of old age is accentuated by the tendency of the family in our society to break up into its smallest units . . . The higher risk of suicide in *urban communities* has been attributed to the greater risk of social isolation and the anonymous life of the big cities, compared with the closely-knit village community . . .[5]

Two studies of old people have adopted a usage which relies primarily on the second type, social isolation from primary groups. Marjorie Fiske Lowenthal defined as isolated only

[1] Paul Halmos, *Solitude and Privacy* (1951), pp. 19, 89.
[2] F. Stuart Chapin, *Experimental Designs in Sociological Research* (New York: Harper), 1955 edition, pp. 275–8.
[3] Harriet Wilson, *Delinquency and Child Neglect* (Allen and Unwin, 1962).
[4] Talcott Parsons, *Essays in Sociological Theory* (1964 edition), p. 195. Parsons's argument as distinct from his usage of the term is discussed below in Chapter 14.
[5] Erwin Stengel, *Suicide and Attempted Suicide* (1964), pp. 23–5. Not everyone is convinced that the correlations found are anything more than between social isolation (or living alone) and the social processes by which suicides are reported (or kept secret by relatives or doctors with obvious motives for so doing).

18

Forms of Being Alone

people who had had no contact with a friend or relative during the previous three years; most of these were unmarried men who were not currently working and who had previously worked as itinerant labourers and the like.[6] A similar but less extreme definition of social isolation adopted by Peter Townsend builds up a score of 'social contacts' per week and because it thus emphasizes frequent or daily social intercourse in effect becomes mainly (but not entirely) a measure of the old people's isolation from family and work.[7]

The present study relies upon a somewhat modified form of the Townsend approach. The social participation definition is not used here primarily because social participation, in such organizations as clubs and church groups, plays a large part only in the lives of a small minority of old people in Britain. But almost all old people have some social contacts and the Townsend scoring system seems to the present writer to come closer to the central day-to-day social intercourse of most old people.

Social isolation thus defined is an observer's category, but the individual is placed in it only after a fairly comprehensive list of questions about the old person's social intercourse, especially during the previous week.

Loneliness

'For a crowd is not company, and faces but a gallery of pictures, and talk but a tinkling cymbal, where there is no love,' wrote Francis Bacon in his essay *Of Friendship* (1592).

Some recent writers, while continuing to distinguish between physically being with people and yet still *feeling* alone, have regarded loneliness as being less completely negative. Thomas Wolfe wrote of loneliness as 'the central and inevitable fact of human existence'.[8] A similar theme has been presented by novelists like Celine in *Voyage au bout de la nuit* and Sartre in *La Nausée*; Clark Moustakas has written an interesting book from this position called simply *Loneliness*.

[6] Marjorie Fiske Lowenthal, 'Social Isolation and Mental Illness in Old Age', *American Sociological Review* (Feb. 1964), pp. 54–70.
[7] Peter Townsend, *The Family Life of Old People* (1957), pp. 166–72.
[8] Thomas Wolfe, *The Hills Beyond* (New York: Harper, 1941), p. 186.

Forms of Being Alone

Maurice Halbwachs in *Les Causes du Suicide* (1930) distinguishes between isolation and the feeling of 'being suddenly alone'. David Reisman makes the contrast strikingly in the title of *The Lonely Crowd* (1950), although he seldom specifically mentions loneliness in his book.

Following J. H. Sheldon in the *Social Medicine of Old Age* (1948), a number of investigators have used the concept of loneliness in studies of old age in various parts of Britain. Peter Townsend used it in a study of old people in institutions.[9] Information on loneliness in old age is also available from studies in Italy,[10] Holland,[11] and elsewhere; all of these studies have stressed the connection between widowhood and loneliness.

The fact of loneliness being not merely a term in general popular use but a word with strong emotional overtones inevitably produces its complications. The investigator may think that some old people are denying feeling lonely out of pride or for other reasons; however, since loneliness is not an observer category but one into which the old person places himself, nothing can be done about this. In practice the definition has to be accepted that an old person is lonely only if he says he feels lonely, and not otherwise. Complications can arise when an old person tells her children that she is lonely but tells the social scientist that she is not lonely.[12] Such contradictions remind us once again of the complexity of aloneness; moreover, the concept of loneliness has the advantage of being familiar to the informant who can thus be asked further questions about it.

Anomie

Anomic individuals are alone in the sense of feeling cut off from the broad social values of society. Robert Merton refers to anomie as a state of 'normlessness' which results when there is a lack of congruence between such cultural goals as the pursuit of economic success and the 'acceptable modes of

[9] Peter Townsend, *The Last Refuge* (1962), p. 350.
[10] Angelo Pagani, 'Social Isolation in Destitution' in C. Tibbitts and W. Donahue (eds.), *Social and Psychological Aspects of Aging* (1962).
[11] R. J. Van Zonneveld, *The Health of the Aged* (1961) and Joep M. Munnichs, 'Loneliness, Isolation and Social Relations in old Age', in P. From Hansen (ed.), *Age With a Future* (1964), pp. 484–91.
[12] Peter Townsend, *The Family Life of Old People* (1957), p. 172.

Forms of Being Alone

reaching out for these goals'.[13] De Grazia refers to 'A painful uneasiness or anxiety, a feeling of separation from the group or of isolation from group standards, and a feeling of pointlessness or that no certain goals exist.'[14] Leo Srole talks of 'social malintegration'.[15] Meier and Bell think that anomia might be described as despair, hopelessness, discouragement, personal disorganization, demoralization or disheartenment.[16]

The concept of anomie has had a somewhat chequered career. Durkheim writing in 1897 used the term to describe one type of suicide.[17] Robert Merton in his influential article 'Social Structure and Anomie' was interested in the consequences of anomie for the behaviour of 'persons variously situated in the social structure'; Merton's lead has been followed in numerous studies of social aspiration[18] and social deviance.[19] Leo Srole first used his anomia-scale in a study concerned with authoritanianism and prejudice; and more recently De Grazia's inclination to give anomie a social psychology emphasis has received more support.[20]

Anomie seems a useful concept to use in the present study because a previous investigation has found socially isolated old men (who belong to, and identify with, the working class) to be extremely prone to anomia.[21]

Unlike loneliness, the concept of anomie has been used in a large number of studies of age-groups other than the old in the United States.

[13] Robert Merton, 'Social Structure and Anomie' in *Social Theory and Social Structure* (1957 edition).
[14] Sebastian De Grazia, *The Political Community* (Chicago University Press, 1948), p. 5.
[15] Leo Srole, 'Social Integration and Certain Corollaries', *American Sociological Review* (Dec. 1956), pp. 709–16.
[16] Dorothy L. Meier and Wendell Bell, 'Anomia and Differential Access to the Achievement of Life Goals', *American Sociological Review* (April 1959), pp. 189–202.
[17] Emile Durkheim, *Suicide* (1952 edition), pp. 250–8.
[18] Reported in Ephraim Mizruchi, *Success and Opportunity* (1964).
[19] Reported in Marshall B. Clinard (ed.), *Anomie and Deviant Behavior* (1965).
[20] E.g. Herbert McClosky and John H. Schaar, 'Psychological Dimensions of Anomy', *American Sociological Review*, Vol. 30, No. 1 (Feb. 1965), pp. 14–40.
[21] Dorothy L. Meier and Wendell Bell, 'Anomia and Differential Access to the Achievement of Life Goals', *American Sociological Review* (April 1959), pp. 196–7.

Forms of Being Alone

Interview Reports

Of the four old people with whom the following interview reports deal, only the first – Mr. Thomas – comes into all four of the categories of aloneness; he lives alone, is often lonely, gets the maximum score for high anomia and he is extremely socially isolated with only three social contacts in the last week. Miss Pritchard lives alone, and Mrs. Marshall is often lonely, but neither is alone in any of the other three ways. Mr. Meade falls into two of the four categories – he is often lonely and socially isolated.

Two interviews illustrate the difference between living alone and social isolation. Like a number of other old people Miss Pritchard lives alone but has sufficient contacts outside to prevent her being socially isolated. Mr. Meade, on the other hand is more unusual; he is socially isolated despite living with someone – his wife.

The social contact scores in these interviews cover nearly the complete range of the whole sample. Mr. Thomas has only three, but Mrs. Marshall has ninety-three social contacts in the previous week; Mrs. Marshall's score has been perhaps somewhat artificially inflated by many brief visits from grandchildren and great grandchildren; but quite apart from these contacts, her contacts with her sister, her neighbours, and her daughter and son-in-law would carry her into the high social contact group (41 +).

Mrs. Marshall also illustrates the point that an old person, despite living with her sister and having a high level of social contact, can still say she is 'often lonely' – in her case this is apparently due to her husband's recent death, her bronchitis and other health complaints and possibly the bad housing conditions in which she lives. In contrast Miss Pritchard lives alone but is 'never lonely'.

Only one of the four gets a high score for anomia – namely Mr. Thomas, who greatly misses his former job as factory foreman. On the other hand Miss Pritchard, who is content to have retired from teaching, gets the minimum possible score and is non-anomic.

INTERVIEWS

Mr. Thomas   *Oldham*
Aged 80   Lives alone
Widowed (20 years)   Extremely isolated (3)
Retired foreman   Often lonely
Moderate incapacity (4)   Highly anomic (5)

He is a bald old man with a small fringe of grey hair, who does not look his eighty years, although he talks slowly and tends to repeat himself. His recent memory is poor and he is extremely pessimistic. His home is in a very bad state; the Victorian grate is filthy yet with a fire burning in it. A coat of dust covers the furniture. His sitting-room is lit by one dim unshaded bulb in the ceiling. Both legs of his trousers have tears in the thighs. The only clean things in the sitting-room are the curtains – recently supplied by his daughter; she lives across the street but Mr. Thomas says he has to 'be careful' in his relations with her and his son. His house on the outside looks dirty and unwashed. He lives on a main street about a mile from the centre of Oldham.

Mr. Thomas was born in Blackburn, but came to Oldham in 1918. He has lived in Oldham ever since. He worked in the cotton industry, only giving up work altogether four years ago when aged 76. This was part-time work, about 10 to 15 hours a week – and somewhat irregular. He had to stop because they discovered his real age. His work was the great thing in his life. He occasionally sees people he worked with and they offer him a pint of beer. For most of his working life he had an overlooker's job. He shows me a book in which he kept the names of all the people who worked under him – there are about a hundred names, mostly women. In 1895 he began work in the cotton industry at the age of 11 – he worked half-time and went to school half-time; he made 1s. 3d. a week for 27 hours' work.

23

Forms of Being Alone

He left school completely at the age of 13. He worked till he was 17 and then went into the army for three years. He went back to cotton and back to the army again for the First World War. He bought some shares in a cotton company, but it went broke in 1920 – 'call them preference shares. What's the good of preference shares when the company's in liquidation?' He keeps returning to his job, the present high wages in the cotton industry and the number of people who worked under him. He thinks the cotten industry will never be the same again until they get some of the old men back to work.

Mr. Thomas can get out of doors, but he can only walk slowly and has to stop frequently. He stands at the top of the street quite often. He has difficulty with climbing stairs, and at present is sleeping on the ground floor – he has a bed in the front room. He admits he is short winded. He has no difficulty getting about the ground floor but 'they'd soon put me in the cemetery if I were to abuse myself'. Cutting his toe-nails takes him a long time; when cutting them he is afraid of having a dizzy bout.

He does the light housework and as much of the heavy cleaning as he can, but he knows it is not done very well. He used to have a home help but does no longer. He pays to have the outside of the windows cleaned – although they look dirty to me. He cooks, but badly. He does the shopping. About four shillings worth of washing goes to the laundry once a fortnight, but he says his things don't get very dirty. (The clothes he is wearing look extremely dirty.) He does not want to go into a Home, although people sometimes tell him that he ought to.

He visits the doctor about once a month and his kidneys are his major complaint; his urine is discoloured – he has had trouble with it ever since the First World War. He has slight rheumatism and dizzy spells, due to 'nerves'. He had a heart attack ten years ago and was in hospital. He has indigestion for which he gets prescriptions. He used to have a chiropodist until last year, he went every month and it cost six shillings; but now he can't afford it any more. He has been in hospital once in the last five years – to have a prostate operation. Before the operation he was in bed at home. He says if he were ill his daughter from across the road would come in to look after him.

He does not want meals-on-wheels; it might be nice but the

24

food might get wasted. He gets up at about ten o'clock in the morning, because he takes a long time getting to sleep. His main meal of the day is breakfast eaten in the middle of the morning and consisting of bacon, fried egg and tea. He doesn't have a midday meal but has a meal at about 4.30, usually cold meat and bread and butter. His one hot meal a day, breakfast, is always fried – he knows he shouldn't fry things because of his indigestion. He owns a cookery book but has no patience to learn to cook at his age. If he went out to eat it would cost too much.

He has no home help but would like one. He did have a help for some time but then she stopped coming; he needs someone to do the heavier cleaning jobs. After he gave up working at 76, he had the same home help coming for about two years. She did heavy cleaning, and some cooking and washing. He says she was very good. But suddenly she stopped coming. He was promised another but she never came. A few months ago a young lady came and asked him about it, but nothing happened. He says 'What's the good?' He thinks they are short of labour because the factories are paying so much money for women to work on the evening shift.

With his glasses he can see quite well, and he has only slight difficulty with hearing. He thinks services in Oldham for older people are all right. 'But you must go. I could get a home help if I went. But I haven't the patience. I'm too idle to go. You must catch 'em unawares, and then it depends how they're feeling.' He thinks the Government ought to increase the pension for people over the age of 75. 'Old chaps can't live long. Why can't they live in comfort? Those Cabinet Ministers ought to live on an empty belly.' The children's allowances are wonderful but 'they only think about the young'.

Mr. Thomas has three children, all still alive. One daughter lives in Cornwall and he has not seen her since last year. The eldest daughter, aged 53, lives across the street. She is married, and has one child aged 17 who is a secretary. The daughter herself goes out to work all day. Mr. Thomas says he can go there any evening or at week-ends; but in fact he only goes about once a week. Apart from making the new curtains in his home, his daughter evidently hasn't done much else because the place is so filthy. However, he talks about her having been in a few weeks ago and says that when she does something the atmosphere is quite different and he feels like doing some cleaning himself. His other child is a son who is also married and lives on the other side of Oldham. The son comes down to see him every Saturday morning; his son is a joiner and has two children. Mr. Thomas says his children would shop for him if he let them, but they would spend too much of his money. He says he has to be 'careful' when he is with them and he has to get on with the in-laws. He has political arguments with his son, who is Labour, while he himself is Conservative.

Mr. Thomas was one of a family of five children, but the other four are now all dead. Two of them lived in America and two lived in Blackburn so he never saw much of them from middle age onwards. The only other relative he sees is one of his grandchildren – the daughter of his daughter. He sees very little of the neighbours. (When he is out at my first call, I ask one of the neighbours where he is and am told that Mr. Thomas goes out to work, which he has not done for four years.) He mentions talking to friends and acquaintances but this mainly seems to be snatched conversations at the street corner.

Time often passes slowly. It passes slowly in the day and also at night because he can't get to sleep, often not until two in the morning. He has no pleasures except the radio. He says 'when you get old if you're not prepared to suffer, you'll die. It's easy to die.' He watches television about one night a week at his daughter's across the street. He wouldn't mind a television of his own, but the licence fee is too expensive and the plays on television remind you of your own sufferings. He does a little cooking every morning. He does nothing to the garden and says it 'wants titivating up'. He reads the Oldham evening paper occasionally but not regularly. He used to read books but he can't find any good books any more. He smokes a certain amount, rolling his own cigarettes.

He used to belong to a working men's club, but hasn't been to it for about ten years now. 'Everything's so expensive. It's ridiculous. Beer's 8d. a glass – I've had it at 1d.' He thinks old people's clubs are definitely a good idea. He doesn't go because 'wherever you go you need the money, I think you'll agree. I'd be made welcome; people would buy me drinks. How would you feel about that if you couldn't buy them back?' I tell him there are clubs near by for older people where they drink tea and it is very cheap; he insists that there are no clubs of that kind in Oldham, all the clubs serve alcohol. 'Pocket won't stand it. The Government should open their hearts.' He does not go to church. He did not go on a holiday last year, and he spent Christmas Day alone.

He used to be a good letter writer – he is proud of his literary ability. But he has given up writing letters to people now. He does not use the telephone. He is Conservative in politics – the Conservatives have the money and are therefore better able to run the country; if the Labour Party got in they would have the money against them and they would not be able to govern. At the 1959 election he was asked by the Conservatives to write letters and he wrote a lot of letters for them – he thinks he should have been paid for it. Although a Conservative at general elections, he votes Labour at local elections because he likes one of the Labour councillors.

He rents the house at 24s. 6d. a week. It has three bedrooms, two ground-floor rooms, one of which is his sitting-room and the other his bedroom. There is a small kitchen/scullery and the toilet is outside in the yard, but when he goes to relieve himself during the interview he uses the basin in the scullery. He says he is glad when the week-ends are over, it's nearer to Thursday and pension day. He finds the house inconvenient in some ways: 'it gets on my nerves. If more people came in it would be better. I've enjoyed your company this evening (to me). In a public-house they talk you to death.' The house is too big for him and in the three bedrooms upstairs there is nothing except two pieces of furniture. But he does not want to move at present. He thinks the idea of flats for older people is good, but he thinks you take a big chance 'when you go to live against a stranger'.

He is often lonely. He is more lonely than when younger – 'you could get out amongst them when you were younger'. He is most lonely during the daytime but also at night as well. 'It's a terrible thing is loneliness.' The winter is worse because in the summer he can get out better. He does not feel lonely for anyone in particular, but getting out to work would make all the difference. The other thing he wants is more money. Then he could have a cleaner in and he would probably do more himself as well. He would also spend more money on food. If his wife was still alive he would not feel as lonely. But he would not consider getting remarried – he had too many dealings with women in the cotton mills. He thinks older people do get lonely and one cause is their bad eyesight – although his eyesight is good. Going to a club would not help him with his loneliness – 'they get chatting, all their troubles. You can't get a word in edgeways. They won't listen. What pleasure would that be?' He dislikes waiting in a shop while some old woman 'keeps twittering away', and sometimes he tells them to hurry up. He has just 'lost my pleasure', which is the football pools – it being May and the football season having just stopped. He puts on 2s. 6d. a week during the season.

His wife died twenty years ago. Afterwards he got drunk several times, 'my wallet was all right then'. He describes somewhat incoherently several encounters with women. He also hints darkly that he had many opportunities with women in the factories in the past.

He thinks National Assistance is very good but he does not get any himself. He gets the ordinary £3 7s. 6d. pension – since he first stopped work at sixty-five. He also gets a pension from his employers of £4 15s. a month. This gives him a total income of about £4 10s. a week. He spends 24s. 6d. on rent, 22s. a week on fuel and 5s. a week on gas and electricity. He says he spends only about £1 a week on food. He saved up some money a year or two ago and bought a new hat and overcoat.

His father outlived his mother by about thirty years. The father was blind and lived with him and his wife for a while – but then he went into an Old People's Home. His life has been 'a hard one, very hard'. Asked about his happiest times, he cannot remember any. He does not think there were any in his life. 'I've always been on the worry. I'm still on the worry.' His unhappiest time was during the First World War, especially the Battle of Mons. He was invalided home to Britain and says he was suffering from undernourishment. He also had a flesh wound in his thigh. Once again he says what he really needs is some more money.

Interviews

Mrs. Marshall　　　　　　　　　　　　　　*Northampton*
Aged 74　　　　　　　　　　　　Lives with widowed sister
Recent widow (6 months)　　　　High social contact (93)
　of a lorry driver　　　　　　　Often lonely
High incapacity (7)　　　　　　　Intermediate anomia (3)
Housebound (3 years)

A small woman with a bun of black hair and a sad grey face, she is still suffering from the shock of her husband's death. She lives with her widowed sister, three years older than herself. The sister is very bent when standing; she only looks me in the eyes when I am sitting down. They spend the day in the back room of their gas-lit house, and do the cooking there also. The walls are covered with black smears, the windows and the floor are also dirty, and there is a strong smell of filth and decay. They keep the fire burning all the time. The house is rickety, damp, and due soon for demolition; it is in one of the poorest streets in Northampton, close to several shoe factories and near the central market-square.

Mrs. Marshall and her husband were both born in London and moved to Northampton in 1942. He worked most of his life as a lorry driver. He retired only shortly before he died, six months ago. She herself has not been out to work since she was married, aged 22. Before marriage she worked in the East End of London in a linen drapers; she left school at 14 and started work for 2s. 6d. a week. She cannot climb stairs, and sleeps in the front ground-floor room. She can move about on the level fairly well, and gets to the door to let me in. She sometimes finds it painful getting in and out of bed. She can wash herself and also puts a dressing on her leg twice a day. She can dress herself and with a 'struggle' can cut her own toe-nails.

She does only the lighter domestic tasks, making her bed, and doing some washing up, but she is unable to stand for more than a few minutes. The heavier cleaning is done by their daughters. Mrs. Marshall can cook – she has the gas cooker going immediately behind her chair, all the time she talks to me. The pension is collected from the Post Office by one of her granddaughters. The sister she lives with does the shopping and takes the washing to the launderette; the daughter mangles the washing but apparently it is not ironed. Mrs. Marshall does not have her hair cut, but lets it grow long and has it in a bun.

She has not walked down the street for three years. She gets out only about every other month when one of her granddaughters orders a taxi, which takes Mrs. Marshall up to the housing estate where the granddaughter lives. Her immobility is due to the trouble with her leg, which comes from varicose veins in the first instance – but now involves an open wound which has to be dressed frequently; at first when this trouble began thirty years ago the doctor thought her leg would have to be amputated. She also has severe bronchitis – and her sister says this bronchitis is 'very frightening' in the winter. She sometimes goes to bed at six in the evening, to rest her leg. She gets out into the back garden to the only toilet, which is several yards away down the yard; in summer Mrs. Marshall sits on the front door-step on the edge of the street pavement. What she misses most is the fresh air. She is not keen on the idea of being driven out, even if this could be arranged more often, and says she prefers to stop inside. After her husband died the minister who conducted the funeral service sent a Red Cross woman round to see her – and this woman asked if she would like a wheel-chair; but Mrs. Marshall says it was too late.

She is visited about once a month by her doctor – 'he's a lovely doctor, I wouldn't change him'. She has no other contact with the health service; she herself does the dressing on her leg twice a day; but she pays for a number of medicines and for liniment. She has not been in hospital recently although she had a lengthy operation on her leg twelve years ago. However, she is regularly ill in bed with bronchitis, averaging about three weeks each winter. She coughs and chokes very badly in the winter but has been told by her doctor that it is better to stay up. When she is ill her daughter comes to cook the meals – apparently they are not cooked by her sister, although the two sisters eat at the same table every day and appear to be on good terms with each other.

Mrs. Marshall has a hot meal at midday, consisting mainly of vegetables. She has a boiled egg or fish for tea, and at about eight o'clock in the evening before bed she has coffee made with milk. Her sister eats separately, partly because she has meat and heavier puddings.

The house is extremely dirty; Mrs. Marshall says her daughter cleans it free, and she is against home helps because one of her sisters who died recently had a home help who was lazy.

She is not wearing glasses, and when she looks at her rent book, she holds it within three inches of her eyes. At first she insists she can see without glasses, but then admits she ought to have spectacles; the last time she went to an oculist he told her she ought to have an operation on her eyes. She refused because her sister had a cataract operation but lost the sight of one eye. Mrs. Marshall's hearing is very good.

She has only once been given anything by the town of Northampton; that was last Christmas when a lady came to talk to her and then a parcel of food arrived from the Mayor, consisting of small items of food and 30s. – she believes this was given to people who had been housebound for three months or longer. She is strongly against children's allowances and in favour of increased old age pensions. 'They should put a bit more on the old age, and let 'em have a bit more firing.'

She has had four children, one a boy who died in infancy. Only one of the children lives in Northampton, a married daughter aged 49, with four children, and four grandchildren. Mrs. Marshall sees this daughter about each other day, and the daughter's husband calls in briefly from work most days. At some points she says this daughter is kind to her, but at other times she implies that the daughter neglects her.

The other two children both live in London, where they were born. She last saw her son at his father's funeral six months ago. The younger daughter she has seen twice since the funeral six months ago. Mrs. Marshall has a total of three living children, eleven grandchildren, and eleven great grandchildren. She says that they often call in to see her. Last Saturday fourteen of her offsp ing were in the house at the same time. She also receives a large number of visits during the week, some of which are rather brief. She has been to stay with her London daughter for one week since her husband died, but she thinks the daughter could have done more. She complains two or three times that this youngest daughter has been neglecting her.

Mrs. Marshall is herself the youngest of thirteen children.

Forms of Being Alone

The first eleven are all dead. The only one still living is the sister with whom she lives. This sister was widowed in 1940, and came to live with her soon after they both moved to Northampton in 1942. For nineteen years her sister lived with Mrs. and Mrs. Marshall. The sister has three children all living in Northampton, of whom Mrs. Marshall also sees a certain amount.

Mrs. Marshall has a large number of nephews and nieces – one of her brothers had fourteen children and many grandchildren, but she is not in touch with any of them. Some of them are in Australia and Canada.

Every day she sees a neighbour, who is present briefly during the interview; she lives next door, is a Northampton woman, eight years older than Mrs. Marshall but much more active.

Last year went very quickly. Her main pleasures are 'messing about and doing me bits of cooking'. She does not like television and they have not got a set. There is a radio in her bedroom, but she only listens to it at night. She does some cooking every day. She claims to read the local evening paper, paperback books, 'murder and love stories', and women's magazines when given them by her neighbour. (However, reading appears to cause her extreme difficulty.)

The only thing to which she has ever belonged was a Mothers' Union in the East End of London, and she went there for many years – but not within the last twenty. She thinks the idea of old people's clubs is quite good. 'It would pass half an hour.' Her sister is registered as partially sighted and belongs to a blind club with which she is pleased.

They have lived in the present house since they came to Northampton twenty-one years ago. It is rented, at 10s. 6d. a week. It has two bedrooms, one of which is not used, and two rooms on the ground floor – one is in the front room where Mrs. Marshall sleeps, and the back room is a kitchen-cum-sitting-room. The sole basin is in this room and has only cold water. There is no bath and only a non-flush toilet at the end of the yard: 'You've got to go up the yard, and then down again to fetch the water. And we put three bottles of disinfectant a week down the toilet.' The most inconvenient thing about the house is the damp; in the front room where Mrs. Marshall sleeps there are damp patches. 'When it's wet the walls is soaking.

32

Interviews

Last winter when there was the snow, it was like a bucket of water thrown on the wall. But the landlord won't do anything because the house is coming down.' There is a loud noise of water running when the tap is turned on in the next-door house. Mrs. Marshall would like to move to another house, but she is not on the Council list and she prefers the older terrace type of houses. When I ask about small Council flats Mrs. Marshall and her sister are both enthusiastic – 'we want a place that's dry', but are worried about the higher rent. Mrs. Marshall has been corresponding with the landlord of the house through a solicitor. She shows me a letter from the solicitor; the address on the crisp white sheet of paper is St. James's Place, London, S.W.1.

Mrs. Marshall is worried about the neighbourhood. 'Teddy boys' often knock on the windows of the house late at night, and when she used to open her window on the street a policeman told her to close it; he said he could not be responsible if the window were left open. Both sisters are worried about people swearing outside in the street. The house is particularly damp in winter. There is no electricity, the lighting is gas. In the sitting-room Mrs. Marshall has a coal fire, and also a gas cooker (which may contribute to the thick smelly atmosphere); the window is closed and there is a packet of detergent placed on the bottom part of the window suggesting it is kept permanently shut. Mrs. Marshall has no heating in her bedroom. It would be impossible to light a fire, because in order to keep her bed away from the damp walls it is in front of the fireplace. Nor does she have a hot-water bottle in her bed, because she thinks they are unhealthy.

Mr. Marshall died six months ago with heart trouble. He was ill in bed at home for six weeks, and before that he had felt very cold and they had had the fire burning all summer. He was only in hospital two weeks before he died. He knew he was dying. 'He walked out of this house a dying man, he said he'd never come back.' Only the children came to the funeral, no relatives of Mr. Marshall – they are all dead. She thinks it has affected her health. But of course she was housebound before he died. She says, rather tremulously, that she did everything for him she could. 'I miss him, I know that. Fifty years isn't a day.' He used to sit in the chair beside the fire,

33

Forms of Being Alone

where her sister is now. She thinks widowhood is probably worse for older people, because young ones can go out to work and may get married again. She spent all the insurance money on the funeral and on buying 'a bit of black' to dress herself in.

Mrs. Marshall is often lonely. She thinks it is due to being housebound and missing her husband. 'I miss him more than ever. He always used to be in, except when he went to the football. And he used to run errands.' She thinks the only thing to do about loneliness is to 'take hold of a book' or put the radio on. Young people can liven themselves up but old people have a lonely life. She thinks going to a club would not help a lot because she is not used to mixing. Her sister is sometimes out in the day visiting her children. But Mrs. Marshall says: 'I don't take no notice, if I've got a fire and a bit of grub.'

She thinks national assistance ought to be more than the 16s. she gets a week – 7s. 6d. is recommended by her doctor for extra nourishment. She also gets back about 7s. a week for medical prescriptions. She thinks the national assistance people are quite good, and they know her case well. She gets a pension of £3 10s. 6d. because her husband worked past 65; they never had any savings. The worst expense is coal and she complains about the price of food. She receives no money from her family; 'I don't ask the family for anything, I'd sooner starve.'

Mrs. Marshall lost her father when she was twenty-one and her mother whom she nursed when she was nineteen. She has had a good life, and her happiest time was when her little ones were around her. The unhappiest was when her husband died recently. She also lost one of her sisters aged 79 in the last year. Mrs. Marshall talks to her sister about how long they are going to live. The sister says for her part she intends to live to a hundred because 'when you're dead you're dead for a long time'; but Mrs. Marshall mumbles that she doesn't care when she dies – 'you don't when you've lost your husband'. The only thing she needs is more help with the 'firing' because they have the fire burning right through the summer now. The thing that ought to be done for older people is to give them more money.

34

Interviews

Miss Pritchard   *South Norfolk*
Aged 72   Lives alone
Single   Intermediate social contact
Retired teacher   (35)
No incapacity (o)   Never lonely
                           Non-anomic (o)

She has a rather heavy face, long dark-grey hair tied in a bun, and a formidable appearance. With this goes an extremely friendly and warm manner. Her home is neatly kept but the floor is littered with the current *Times Literary Supplement*, *Times*, last Sunday's *Observer*, etc. She lives alone in a solid two-bedroomed cottage on the edge of a small village, about ten miles from Norwich.

She retired seven years ago from teaching English at an adult education college in London. During term she was thirty hours a week in the building, and had essays to read at the week-end. At 17 she won a scholarship to London University and she read English. She used to have a private reading circle to which she invited particularly bright students. She lived in a flat in Bloomsbury which until the 1957 Rent Act cost her only £120 a year rent.

She misses nothing at all from work – which is 'battles long ago'. She felt very exhausted after she retired and used the lump sum of one year's pay for a three months' voyage on a cargo ship around Italy. She also made two trips to South Africa and then wrote a book on African history; she is disappointed not to be able to get it published. Miss Pritchard was earning £750 a year when she retired in 1956 – four-fifths of the rate paid to men. If she were still working she might be making as much as £2,000 a year.

For a time Miss Pritchard lived in a house where she was given a free flat in return for cooking meals at week-ends for the lady who owned the house; but it was unsatisfactory because she was the 'mental superior and social equal' of her employer. A year ago she got this cottage – having no connection with Norfolk previously – and since living here she has

35

Forms of Being Alone

spent much of her time decorating the house and gardening. She still has literary ambitions and is thinking of writing children's books. She corresponds regularly with her students, two of whom have paid her lengthy visits during the last year.

Asked about getting upstairs she says she cannot run upstairs any more – Edith Evans said the same recently. If she has any aches from gardening for three hours a day, she does some exercises and the pain is gone the next day. She collects her pension in Norwich because there is no post office in the village; there aren't any shops or a policeman or a laundry. She takes her heavy washing to a launderette in Norwich. A bus goes from the village twice a day, but she does not mind walking to the next village two miles away to catch a more frequent bus.

Miss Pritchard has seen her doctor about six times during the past year because she has had some nasal inflammation. She went twice to see a specialist, and says that he told her not to pick her nose. She told him to stop being so insulting. She has little faith in doctors. Her general practitioner told her she has had arthritis for years in her knees, but she says this is absolute nonsense because she has never felt anything in her knees. She does not go to a chiropodist, although a friend took her to one about two years ago; he only did what she can do as easily herself by scraping her feet with a razor blade.

She has not been in hospital in recent years nor has she been ill at home. Retirement is, she thinks, very good for her. She expects to live to be a hundred, so she has 'another thirty years to live'. Asked what will happen if she is ill she says the last time she had a pain in her back from digging in the garden she told her neighbour about it; the neighbour would look in if she were not about the next day. She also intends to have a telephone soon.

Miss Pritchard has one big meal each day at six o'clock – consisting of meat, vegetables and dessert. She is fairly hungry by the evening. She makes jam which she gives away at the Women's Institute. She is proud of growing all her own vegetables. Most meals are eaten alone.

If she were ill she would probably have a home help rather than go into hospital, which she hates. Miss Pritchard has glasses for reading. But she says that all her senses are very good.

36

Interviews

She thinks the Norfolk Council is good and if she were ever in need of anything she would certainly go straight to them. She knows several social workers. Asked about children's allowances she says it is difficult for a single person to express an opinion. She thinks some married old people are resentful because they did not have allowances for their children but she also thinks that some people spend children's allowances for the wrong purpose. The pension ought to be bigger; all of her old age State pension is spent on food and things for the house.

Miss Pritchard was the eldest of four children. The others were brothers and are all dead. However, she was never close to her brothers after she left home at the age of eighteen, and they all went into the forces – she was already a pacifist. She is temperamentally against any kind of quarrelling and as a result is rather easily bullied. Her brothers' children are alive but she hardly knows them, because she had so little to do with their parents. She has no contact at all with any relatives. She thinks most people lead lonely lives.

Miss Pritchard is on good terms with a number of people in the village, in which she has only been living just over a year. She says it depends upon your attitude; she is friendly to people so they are friendly to her. She quotes Dr. Johnson – 'A man to have friends must show himself friendly.' A woman she knows in the village sometimes has her house damaged by hooligans, but when Miss Pritchard sees a group of local boys she invites them into her house and they have worked in her garden several times. She has got to know people in the village through inviting small children aged 6 to 10 into her house and giving them biscuits and telling them stories about her travels. Miss Pritchard says the bus is the great social centre and she always talks to people on the bus going into Norwich. She has now reached the stage where people come and sit next to her on the bus and start talking to her. She is particularly interested in small children and says they have a very 'different mentality' – to which she is not accustomed, having spent most of her time with young people between 16 and their early twenties. One little girl in the village is very intelligent and is interested in words. The girl is surprised that Miss Pritchard uses long words and talks in a different way and one day she said, 'you talk so grown-up'.

37

Forms of Being Alone

Time never passes slowly and she wishes she did not have to waste time on sleep. She goes to bed at about 9.30 p.m. and gets up early in the morning. She sleeps badly and sometimes she wakes about 4 a.m. and makes herself a cup of tea. She reads herself to sleep with poetry. She finds it particularly difficult to sleep if she has been talking to somebody in the evening. She is against television but listens to the radio a good deal. She is interested in serious music and thinks the Third programme has greatly deteriorated. At present (October) she spends three hours digging each morning and she shows me the garden, which is quite large and well cultivated. When she moved into the cottage she redecorated it; previously she went to a carpentry class, because she thought she had not been using her hands enough. She reads a lot, her daily paper being *The Times*. She disagrees with *The Times* politically, and is strongly against the Conservative Government. She takes an active interest in cooking, and reads a lot of poetry. At present she is reading a Henry James novel. There is a photograph of Virginia Woolf on one of the bookshelves. She also makes all of her own clothes. She is critical of the Press and thinks it is not society which is corrupt but the popular newspapers.

She belongs to the Women's Institute and goes to a Quaker meeting once a month. She does not belong to an old people's club: 'I don't think of myself as an old person.' She is always flattered when she is told how young she looks. Only ten years ago a man of 35 wanted to marry her. She says her mind is as active as ever; she is learning German from the radio and still keeps up her Greek grammar. She meets various people at her Quaker and Women's Institute meetings.

She has not been away on holiday this year, partly because living in the cottage is so new to her. She would like to go on another boat trip to Africa. She does a lot of writing of letters. 'I take letter-writing seriously. It's the only way there is to keep in touch with your friends and I keep a record of when each last wrote to me.'

The house is a hundred years old and she rents it on a short lease, at 25s. a week. There are two bedrooms, a third bedroom having been turned into a bathroom. The toilet is inside. She is very pleased with the house and can hardly believe her own good fortune. It is not too big to keep clean and having a spare bedroom is nice.

There are many compensations for being single and few disadvantages. Several of her married friends envy her. She likes children but never wanted to have her own. 'I could never have had more than fifteen children of my own, but I have had many more vicarious children.' She thinks a woman can quite easily remain perfectly normal when she is single, whereas the majority of men who stay bachelors become 'queer'. She chose to be single and thinks that this attracted men to her. (She refers to several men during the interview.) She was very much in love in her middle twenties with a man who 'hung about for years'; but she is glad she did not marry him. She does not respect men much – the evidence of their weakness is their dependence on women. However, she has plenty of men friends. A friend who got married recently says she has more status as a married woman, even in her own family, but Miss Pritchard told her it was absolute nonsense. She does not think position in the family has much to do with being single and she left home anyhow when she was seventeen. Several times she repeats that many married women are very frustrated. She admits that she also was frustrated from a career point of view; there is no real equality for women even in professional jobs.

She gets the £3 7s. 6d. contributory pension and a pension from her job which gives her a total income of about £9 a week after tax. She has only a very small amount of savings and has to be 'careful' with her expenses.

When she was 17 her father died; he was unemployed a good deal and her childhood was a tremendous struggle. She left home at 17 and went to live in a bed-sitting-room in London, to work and finally to go to university. She says her mother did not like her and preferred the sons. Her mother married again – a man fifteen years younger than herself who had previously wanted to marry Miss Pritchard. A friend has told her that she ought to write a novel about it. Her mother incorrectly imagined that Miss Pritchard was resentful, but consequently she saw little of her mother. She has had a very happy life, but she wishes she had risked trying to be a professional writer. Publishers aren't interested in manuscripts from old people, because they want a whole succession of books. The

happiest time in her life has been recently. 'Retirement has
given me a big satisfaction. Not having to work for money and
being my own mistress.' She has always been happy apart
from the frustrations of teaching – the rapid turnover of
students, the long hours, and the unequal position of women.
She repeats she is going to live to be a hundred. She thinks
about death quite often, but it does not worry her at all.

INTERVIEW NUMBER 4

Mr. Meade	*Harrow*
Aged 73	Lives with wife
Married	Socially isolated (8)
Retired small shopkeeper	Often lonely
Moderate incapacity (4)	Intermediate anomia (3)

He is a small, sad-faced man, very uncertain of himself. He is
wearing one of his old business suits with a waistcoat, and
apologizes because he has just removed his collar and tie. His
wife, he says, has betrayed him. His flat above a shop is
approached by a steep flight of fire-escape stairs. The sitting-
room is sparsely furnished, but neat and tidy. There are photographs of his wife's friends and relatives, several of them looking
rather important in their best clothes. Mr. Meade mumbles a
good deal and changes track in mid-sentence. He is confused
about his own age and his wife's age and he forgets simple words
like 'refrigerator' – he calls it 'that white thing'. He continually
complains of his almost useless left leg. Several times he says
he is waiting to die.

He owned a small confectionery and tobacconist shop in
north London, and retired eight years ago at the age of 65.
At first he says he gave up because 'I went broke', due to 'my
rotten wife'. Then he says he did not go bankrupt, and he
managed to sell the business. After he retired, he and his wife
moved to their present flat. When he came to Harrow he wanted
to get work and went to the Employment Exchange. He says
he tried so hard to get work that he nearly drove them mad
at the Employment Exchange; but nobody wants to employ a
man of 65.

'My rotten wife. I hate my wife. My wife is a bitch,' he says,

40

and complains that she went to Australia for two months leaving him to run the shop and get his own meals. He also claims she received £1,000 from somebody who died recently. His wife was married previously, and when he married her he did not realize that her school-age daughter was against her re-marriage. He is very antagonistic to her daughter.

His wife is aged 64 and she works three days a week as a shop assistant; she also spends much of the rest of the week with her daughter who is married and lives not far away. He says his wife never does anything for him, will not even make him a cup of tea, comes in late in the evening and does not talk to him. 'I haven't talked to her for a week.' His wife spends some nights away and he doesn't care where she is. But she keeps the flat clean and he refuses to have anything to do with domestic duties. They had a serious dispute soon after he retired and they have had another major row a few weeks ago.

Despite a very weak left leg, Mr. Meade goes out every day to buy milk and bread – because they will not deliver up the stairs – and he usually walks at midday to a café several hundred yards away. He has considerable difficulty with stairs; the stairs inside the flat he can climb only by sitting and going up backwards one stair at a time. He also has some trouble in getting out of his chair, because his left leg will not support his weight and several times recently he has become giddy and fallen. Getting out of the bath is also difficult, which annoys him because his great pleasure is having a bath every day. When he bends down to cut his toe-nails the blood pressure makes him dizzy – but his wife will not help him. In the bath he sits with his back to the taps, so he can always pull the plug out to save himself from drowning.

He can do light housework, but 'I wouldn't touch it if the dust was an inch thick. My wife does all that. She's a blasted idiot, a beast, the wickedest woman in the world.' He makes cups of tea for himself and does a little cooking, mainly boiling eggs. He takes his heavy washing and shirts to the laundry. His wife doesn't change the sheets on his bed more often than once a month.

He saw his doctor about six times in the last year. His major trouble is his left leg, which he drags behind him when he

Forms of Being Alone

walks around the room. The doctor has said the 'nerves' in his leg are to blame – he was wounded in the legs in the First World War. He also has high blood pressure, and thus is unable to have a necessary operation on his throat. He has pills for his blood pressure.

He has been in hospital twice in the last five years, but is rather vague why he was there. He refers to a growth on his groin and also to blood pressure. He has not been ill in bed at home during the last five years – he hates staying in bed. He says his bad memory is due to his wife's ill-treatment. If he were ill upstairs his wife wouldn't know, he claims, because she gets up in the morning before him to go to work, and often comes in to bed after him. They have separate bedrooms, and she avoids talking to him; he says he could lie dead in his bed for several days and she wouldn't even know.

He gets up at about 9.30 a.m. and has breakfast of tea and cereals. He makes a great effort to remember the name of the cereals, but cannot. At midday when he normally goes out to eat, he has to stop several times for breath. He normally has minced meat or stew and cannot afford a sweet. Today he was not feeling well and so he stayed at home and had two boiled eggs – he knows no other way of cooking them. For tea he has tea and biscuits and at night he has just tea again. He can't fry anything and says his wife hasn't cooked anything for him for a long time; she won't even make him cups of tea. He shows me a cupboard where she keeps her separate things for breakfast. He eats all his meals alone.

They have no domestic help, and his wife keeps the flat in its present clean and well-dusted state. His attitude is again hostile – 'I've got nothing to do with housework.' He wears glasses, has not had his eyes tested for eight years and says he couldn't afford to. When he reads something out to me he uses two pairs of glasses – wearing one and holding the other pair near the paper. He has slight difficulty with hearing, but can hear ordinary conversation. His false teeth are inadequate and he cannot chew meat properly.

He knows nothing about social services for older people in the vicinity. However, he thinks I am connected with a leaflet his wife has given him about the local old people's welfare committee. Despite this pamphlet he says he doesn't know anything about the services. When I read out from the leaflet the addresses of places where he can get cheap midday meals, he says he couldn't possibly go that far. He thinks the old age pension is only enough for 'starvation'.

Mr. Meade sees nothing of any relatives – apart from the strained relationship with his wife. He seldom sees her daughter or three grandchildren. His step-daughter came to the front door one day when his wife was in; he opened the door and when he saw her he walked away without saying anything. He describes his step-daughter as 'a bitch like her mother'. Mr. Meade himself is one of a family of eight children. The other seven are all dead; he used to see some of them when he had his shop and they were still alive. Now he sees nothing of his nephews and nieces. He only has two neighbours and he sees nothing of them. His wife has 'taken away all my friends and chased them off'. He says that if somebody came to the front door to see him, she would open the door and whisper something to make the person go away – and then she would not tell him about it afterwards.

Time never goes slowly. He has no pleasures, but he would have some if he were able to go out. Most of the time he sits in an arm-chair with his 'dead' leg on a hard chair. After he comes in from lunch he stays in the sitting-room all the time. In the afternoon he reads the *Daily Express*; he watches television, usually from 5 to 10 p.m. each evening. He makes cups of tea and smokes about ten cigarettes a day. He reads nothing apart from the newspaper. He watches sport all of Saturday on television and on Sunday he reads the *News of the World* and watches religious programmes.

He has never belonged to any clubs. He knows nothing about old people's clubs. He does not go to church, but he 'respects' the Church of England. He has had no holiday for twenty-six years – he holds this against his wife and says it would be financially quite impossible now.

He seldom writes or receives letters. There is a telephone but – 'I don't use it. If anybody rings it won't be for me, it'll be for her.'

The flat has two bedrooms upstairs, and downstairs a sitting-room, kitchen and bathroom and lavatory. They have television and a refrigerator, but no radio. Despite the stairs he does not want to move, especially since the flat and its heating is provided free by a relative of his wife.

Mr. Meade is often lonely. 'You don't speak to a soul all day long.' He forgets things, but – 'if somebody came to talk to me, I'd soon remember and it would all come back to me'. He is lonely 'from the blessed minute I get up in the morning and I say, "Come on, God Almighty, take me away".' There is no time when he is least lonely; then he says when he has the television on he is not lonely. Even when he looks out of the back window he can't see anyone – just an expanse of roof, buildings and chimneys. 'If the Almighty takes me, it doesn't do any harm.' His seventy-fourth birthday is due in three days and after that he will be happy to die. His loneliness is no different in summer or winter. There is no particular person for whom he is lonely. He would like someone to visit him. Going out to work would greatly reduce his loneliness. If his leg was all right he would be happy to do 'any little job' for £5 a week and then 'it would all come back'. The main trouble is being by himself all the time. The only thing he can do about his loneliness is to watch television and the week-end is best – because of the sport and religious services. Asked whether people generally become more lonely as they get older, he says 'I never mix with old people. Maybe. But if he's got a proper wife and a proper family behind him they'd do all they could to keep him lively.'

He knows nothing about national assistance except that some people get a few extra shillings. He thinks he probably would not be entitled to it because they would take his wife's money into account – he says she has lots of money – she earns it and also she gets left £1,000 by one person and £1,000 by another. His total income is the £3 7s. 6d pension – 'it's very, very bad'. He had some savings when he stopped work, but he claims he gave it all to his wife for housekeeping. He discovered indirectly that his wife was getting money from a rich relative. He claims he gets none of this money. It is difficult to pin him down on how much he spends, but he says he never spends more than four shillings on his midday meal. He also buys bread and butter and tea and eggs and cereals – a total of about £2 a week for all food. He smokes ten cigarettes a day. This would leave him under one pound a week for all other expenses. He complains particularly about clothes – and says he has not had any new clothes since he retired. He is wearing pin-stripe trousers and a black jacket; this suit is rather shabby, but his white shirt looks in good order. He says his suits are so old that he doesn't even want to be seen wearing them under an overcoat.

Both his parents died when he was a young man. He describes at length being shelled in the First World War and wounded in the legs. He recalls being in hospital – he was unconscious for ten days – the pain of being on the train and going over on the hospital ship; a nurse offered him some chocolates and cigarettes when he arrived in Southampton – and he remembers the conversation very clearly. His sharp memory of suffering in 1917 contrasts with his failure to remember simple things in the present. He says he has had a terrible life. But the present state of severe conflict with his wife is comparatively recent. When they were married his wife did not tell him she was incapable of having any further children. Asked about unhappy times he says 'It's all unhappy' – but then he says that it has become more unhappy since he retired and moved to Harrow. He repeats that he is going to be 74 in a few days. Then he will be ready to die.

Chapter Two

LIVING ALONE

I. MORE OLD PEOPLE ARE LIVING ALONE

Since 1951 there has been a sharp increase, not only in the total number, but in the proportion of old people who live alone. In 1951 13·4 per cent of people of *pensionable age* in Britain lived alone; ten years later in 1961 this proportion had increased by over two-fifths to 19·5 per cent.[1] Before going on to discuss why this increase has taken place, let us consider which old people live alone.

Although a substantial minority live alone, a big majority – 78 per cent of *old people* in private households – live with other people.[2] Most of them live with either their spouse, or a child, or both. Table 2.1 shows that 32·8 per cent of old people live only with their spouse, while 32 per cent live in a household containing at least one child.

The four-area survey shows that of those old people who do not live alone, over two-thirds live with only one other person – the most common being a spouse or an unmarried daughter. (The four-area survey produces a somewhat higher figure, 28·1 per cent of old people living alone)[3].

There is no reason to regard Britain as unusual in the pro-

---

[1] These figures must be treated with caution because of some differences in the way the information is reported for the 1951 and the 1961 Censuses. The 1951 figure is approximate because the proportion of women aged 60–64 living alone is only an estimate. The 1961 figure is based on a sample of counties including about half the pensionable population of Britain. See Registrar-General's *Housing Report* for 1951, p. 133, and County Tables of 1961 Census.

[2] The difference between 22·2 per cent of those aged 65 and over living alone in the national sample in 1962 and 19·5 per cent of people of pensionable age (men 65+, women 60+) in the 1961 Census is partly accounted for by less women aged 60–64 being widowed and living alone.

[3] All tables in this book, and also figures not referring to tables are from the four-area survey unless another source is quoted. Figures from the national survey will be shown thus: '22·2 per cent (national).'

portion of its elderly population which lives alone. The national surveys conducted in 1962 showed 27·7 per cent of old people in Denmark to be living alone and 21·5 per cent in the United States. The great majority of old people who are not living alone in Denmark and the United States were living with their spouse or with a child. Thus the basic household composition of old people in Britain appears broadly similar to that in other developed countries – including a country like Denmark which contains a strong rural element.

2. LIVING ALONE: SEX, MARITAL STATUS, AGE

Women make up four-fifths of all old people who live alone, and old men only one-fifth. This preponderance of women is partly because they outnumber the men among the elderly, but mainly because 29·7 per cent of all old women live alone against 10·9 per cent of old men (Table 2.1).

Women are more likely to live alone, primarily because elderly widows are so much commoner than widowers. When the elderly population is divided up by marital status (as in Table 2.1) the difference between men and women becomes much smaller. The pattern of household composition is virtually identical between married men and women. According to the definition of 'married' used in the national survey all married people live with their spouses – the separated and divorced are included with the 'widowed'. The same proportion – just over two-thirds – of married old men and women live with their spouses and nobody else.[4]

Among the widowed also there is not much difference between the household types of old men and old women. The most obvious difference is between the married and the widowed group – the proportion who live alone jumps from nil to 43·1 per cent for both sexes. The proportion of the widowed who live alone amounts to about two-thirds of the proportion of the married who live with their spouse only.

Just over a fifth of the married share their household with an unmarried child (in addition to their spouse); the proportion is the same among the widowed. This seems to be because

---

[4] This despite the fact that the spouses of people over 65 – especially the wives of men over 65 – are often under 65 and thus not included in the survey.

47

TABLE 2.1 BRITAIN: HOUSEHOLD COMPOSITION OF OLD PEOPLE BY MARITAL STATUS AND SEX

	Married			Single			Widowed			All old people		
	Male	Female	Both sexes	Male	Female	Both sexes	Male	Female	Both sexes	Male	Female	Both sexes
	%	%	%	%	%	%	%	%	%	%	%	%
Living alone	—	—	—	25·5	46·5	42·7	38·3	44·6	43·1	10·9	29·7	22·2
With spouse only	67·5	68·0	67·8	—	—	—	—	—	—	47·1	23·2	32·8
Married daughter	4·1	3·7	4·0	—	—	—	18·4	16·6	17·0	7·6	9·8	8·9
Married son	0·6	0·8	0·7	—	—	—	9·0	5·6	6·4	2·7	3·1	3·0
Unmarried child	22·5	21·2	22·0	4·3	1·9	2·3	20·7	23·5	22·8	20·8	19·7	20·1
Sibling	1·7	2·4	2·0	46·8	36·6	38·5	4·7	4·0	4·2	4·6	8·1	6·7
Grandchildren	1·3	1·4	1·3	—	—	—	—	0·9	0·7	0·9	0·9	0·9
Other relatives	0·9	1·2	1·0	4·3	5·6	5·4	2·7	1·3	1·7	1·7	1·9	1·8
Non-relatives	1·4	1·4	1·4	19·1	9·4	11·1	6·3	3·5	4·2	3·7	3·6	3·6
Total	100	100	100	100	100	100	100	100	100	100	100	100
Number	701	510	1,211	47	213	260	256	773	1,029	1,004	1,496	2,500

Source : National survey.

48

Living Alone : Sex, Marital Status, Age

unmarried children tend to live with their elderly parents, when both parents are still alive, and when one parent dies the unmarried child continues to live with the widowed parent. However, there is a sharp contrast between the proportions of married and of widowed old people who live with *married* children. Only 4·7 per cent of married old people of both sexes live with married children; but 23·4 per cent of widowed old people live with married children. While it is uncommon for elderly married couples to share a household with their own married children, it is not unusual for a widowed old person to move in to live with a married child – especially a married *daughter*.

The single, of course, are in a different position since they lack both categories of kin with whom old people are most likely to live – the single have neither spouse nor children. (A few single people do have children, of course, and some of them live with these illegitimate children, as Table 2.1 shows.)

Two-fifths of single old people live with their siblings – in contrast to the widowed who are much less likely to live with their brothers or sisters. The high propensity of the single to live with their siblings is sufficiently strong to make the single no more likely to live alone than are the widowed. Among both the widowed and the single just over two-fifths live alone.

The proportion of the widowed increases in the higher age-groups among both men and women. Among those aged 85 years and older there are ten widows to each married woman. Since living alone is closely connected with the widowed state, the proportion of old people living alone must be expected to rise in the higher age-groups. The following proportions of old people of both sexes live alone:

16·4 per cent of those aged 65–9
21·9 per cent of those aged 70–4
29·9 per cent of those aged 75–9
25·3 per cent of those aged 80 + (national)

However, although the proportion of those aged 75–9 who live alone is nearly double the proportion of those ten years younger there is a drop after the age of 80. This is interesting in view of the continuing increase in the incidence of widowhood among those aged 80 and over (Table 2.2).

In the highest age-group both widowed men and women are

49

Living Alone

Male	65–69 %	70–74 %	75–79 %	80–84 %	85+ %	All 65+ %
Single	7·3	7·6	7·9	7·7	7·3	7·6
Married	81·1	73·3	62·4	48·7	33·7	70·3
Widowed	11·1	18·7	29·4	43·5	58·8	21·9
Divorced	0·4	0·3	0·2	0·1	0·1	0·3
Total	100	100	100	100	100	100
Number	818,924	599,580	389,134	204,621	90,164	
Female						
Single	15·1	15·4	15·5	16·0	17·2	15·6
Married	49·3	36·6	25·0	15·2	7·1	34·3
Widowed	34·8	47·4	59·2	68·6	75·6	49·8
Divorced	0·6	0·4	0·2	0·1	0·1	0·4
Total	100	100	100	100	100	100
Number	1,159,854	942,092	679,798	400,510	211,810	

Source : Registrar General, 1961 Census.

less likely to live alone and more likely to live with children, especially *married* children; of the widowed aged 65–9 only 14·2 per cent live with married children, against 30·2 per cent of those aged 80+ (national). Those in the oldest age groups are increasingly frail and are less able to live alone; they are also much more likely to enter institutions.

Of every ten old people who live alone eight are women – six widows and two spinsters; the other two are widowers[5] (national).

3. CHILDREN

No married old people – according to the definition used here – live alone. But the widowed as a group mainly either live alone or with children. Table 2.3 shows that of old women

[5] Single men are only 2·2 per cent of the total living alone group.

Children

without living children 44·1 per cent live alone – and well over half of childless *widows* live alone. (The proportion of childless men who live alone is much lower, mainly because most old men still have their wives alive.)

While 35·6 per cent of childless old people live alone only half this proportion of old people with living children do so. Why do this still substantial proportion of 18 per cent live by themselves despite having children? One important factor is the sex of the children. Old women who only have sons are substantially more likely to be living alone than are those with daughters. This may be partly due to old women finding it more difficult to live in a household with their sons' wives, but comparatively easy with their own daughters; indeed three times as many elderly widowed women live with their married daughters as with married sons (Table 2.1). Yet this is only part of the explanation since although 16·6 per cent of elderly widowed women live with married daughters, 23·5 per cent live with unmarried children, mainly single or widowed daughters.

It is hardly surprising perhaps that more widows live with their daughters than with their sons. More striking is the evidence on the number of children and the propensity to live alone. There is no significant difference in living alone between those with only one living child and those with two, three or more children alive. Presumably this is due to stronger ties of mutual affection or a stronger sense of obligation on the part of only children.

Another possible explanation is that some widowed elderly people with several children, despite being invited, intentionally refrain from going to live with one particular child – in order to retain an equal relationship with the other children. It certainly must not be assumed that all old people who live alone despite having children are being rejected by them. Many old people undoubtedly prefer to live alone and to exchange visits with their children. Of those who had children and yet lived alone 52·9 per cent had seen a child on the day of interview or the previous day and 80·2 per cent (national) had seen at least one child during the previous week. This phenomenon has been reported in previous British research and also in studies of old people in West Germany, the United States and

51

TABLE 2.3 BRITAIN: LIVING ALONE AND HAVING CHILDREN ALIVE

Old person having children as follows	Male %	Proportion living alone Female %		Both sexes %	
No living children	18·8	44·1		35·6	
One child – son	10·5 } 9·1	37·3 } 27·0		25·8 } 19·3	
One child – daughter	7·9	18·2		13·7	
More than one child, at least one daughter	8·9 } 9·0	21·6 } 23·7		16·3 } 17·6	
More than one child, no daughter	10·0	36·9		26·5	
Total	10·9	29·7		22·2	
Number living alone	110	444		554	
Sample number	1,004	1,496		2,500	

Source: National Survey.

elsewhere. Viennese sociologists have commented on old people's preference for 'Intimacy at a distance.'[6]

4. SOCIAL CLASS

Are middle class or working class old people more likely to live alone? The four-area evidence, using Registrar-General's occupational social class,[7] shows 27·6 per cent of old people in the non-manual classes living alone and 28·7 per cent in the manual working class. Thus no significant social class difference emerges.

There are, of course, a whole range of factors which might be expected to make for a different proportion. The higher social classes might be less likely to live alone because of the better survival rate of spouses, and because their children would have more house space in which to accommodate them. On the other hand the higher social classes with better financial resources are more able to buy domestic assistance and to keep in touch with children outside the household by means of telephone and cars.

On the present evidence pictures of the working class as either callously neglecting all its elderly parents or cosily integrating them all into three generation households are equally without foundation.[8]

5. LOCAL VARIATIONS

The lack of any social class factor in the proportion of old people living alone is further confirmed by Table 2.4, which shows similar proportions living alone in working-class Dagenham and middle-class Orpington; the same point is strikingly made in central London where working-class areas like Bermondsey and Bethnal Green have as high a proportion living alone as do affluent Chelsea and Westminster.

[6] Leopold Rosenmayr and Eva Köckeis, 'Propositions for a Sociological Theory of Aging and the Family', *International Social Science Journal*, No. 3 (1963), pp. 418-19.

[7] The old people were classified on occupation for 'most of life'. Married and widowed women were classified by husband's occupation.

[8] The national survey also indicates no significant social class difference in living alone.

Living Alone

The older industrial regions of the north come very close to the general figure for England and Wales. Rural areas are somewhat below and the old London County Council area is rather above. But the biggest extremes are within the London region. The highest proportion of people of pensionable age who live alone is in inner London; this falls in the larger L.C.C. area and the lowest figure, about 12 per cent, is found in the suburbs around London. Farther out in the Home Counties the proportion begins to rise again (the figures for the rural districts of Kent and Essex are 15 per cent and 16·1 per cent) and continues rising farther from London (e.g. Brighton, 19·4 per cent).

TABLE 2.4 VARIATIONS IN THE PROPORTION OF PEOPLE OF PENSIONABLE AGE (WOMEN 60 +, MEN 65 +) LIVING ALONE, 1961

Approximate percentage living alone	*Type of district*	*Examples*
12	London suburbs	Dagenham, 12·9% Hendon, 12·9% Orpington, 12·6% Wembley, 11·6%
16	Rural areas	Combined rural districts of: Cumberland, 15·4% East Riding, 16·1% Essex, 16·1% Leicester, 16·7% Norfolk, 16·5%
20	Old industrial regions	Lancashire, 19·6% West Riding, Yorkshire, 21·4%
22	Ten largest cities	Edinburgh, 21·5% Leeds, 22·8% Manchester, 20·6% Nottingham, 22·2%
25	London (L.C.C.)	London, 24·9%
30	Inner London	Bermondsey, 29·5% Bethnal Green, 29·8% Chelsea, 31·9% Holborn, 29·6% Westminster, 29·0%

Source: Registrar-General, 1961 Census (County Tables)

Do Old People Want to Live Alone?

This London conurbation pattern appears to be repeated elsewhere; for instance areas near the centre of cities, like Salford and the Gorbals, have a higher proportion living alone than Manchester and Glasgow. In the Manchester conurbation area the proportion living alone falls from Salford, to Manchester to suburban Cheshire. All of this suggests that the age of the district (and its housing) is an important variable in the proportion of old people who live alone.

6. DO OLD PEOPLE WANT TO LIVE ALONE?

What do these old people say about living alone? The overwhelming majority say they prefer it. Of those living alone only 9·4 per cent said they would rather live with others; 2 per cent gave no answer, and the rest – nine out of ten – said they preferred to live alone (national). Of course this is a very bald question about a complex reality. Much depends on who there is available to live with, the terms and arrangements. Some old people certainly claim to be satisfied with living alone out of pride and unwillingness to admit their unhappiness. Nevertheless the old people most likely to live alone are those without spouse or children alive, and for many there is no person alive with whom they are likely ever to share a home. Taken in this sense, the answer of nine out of ten that they prefer to live alone may not greatly overstate the old people's feelings; but it does not mean they would not have liked a spouse or child to live with.

Old people living with married children appear to accept their position nearly as overwhelmingly. 83·9 per cent (national) of those living with married children say they prefer it to living alone; 11·3 per cent say they would prefer to live alone. Nearly half as many again – 4·8 per cent of all those living with married children – gave no answer. The fairly large 'no answer' category may reflect a fairly widespread ambivalence on this subject. However, no correlation emerged between being dissatisfied at living with married children and any of the obvious variables such as degree of incapacity, social class, or whether the old people had only daughters or only sons. Here again, the old people are probably not always saying what they really think. Married children or children-in-law, present during the

55

interview, probably inhibited some old people from saying they would prefer to live alone. Of course, wanting to live alone rather than with married children again depends upon the available possibilities. For many there are strong economic reasons for not living alone. Old people with severe incapacity who say they would prefer to live alone may be expressing dissatisfaction more with their incapacity than with the married children.

Such findings may lead one to suspect that whatever the proportions living alone or living with children, the majority of old people would say they prefer the *status quo*. Old people not infrequently say they cannot face the prospect of moving home and belongings. An old person who is contemplating moving to stay with a child tends to be worried about a number of things – loss of independence, fear of the consequences if living together disturbs amicable relations with the child, loss of the familiar neighbourhood, concern about furniture, the actual physical strain of moving, and the cost in money. Many old people still do move to live with children, but these moves are often precipitated by a crisis – especially widowhood or severe ill-health – which leaves the old person living alone in a vulnerable state, and ready to accept whatever is suggested by her children.

When talking about living alone, old people repeatedly stress their independence. Old women often proudly refer to having their own door-key, their own hearth, their own kitchen or other symbols of domestic autonomy. The popular preference, given reasonable health, is to maintain regular contact with children, siblings, or others – without imposing upon them, or becoming too dependent on them. Other things being equal, many (or even most) widowed or single old people prefer to live alone, while maintaining close ties with relatives outside the household. However, other things often are not equal; many old people share a house with a child or sibling and appear to feel no loss of independence; the choice is often between living with a daughter or not seeing her at all; ill-health and incapacity often intervene; shopping, cleaning and other help vary greatly for individuals from time to time and from place to place.

7. IMPORTANCE FOR SOCIAL POLICY

From the point of view of physical frailty and incapacity to perform simple domestic tasks, old people who live alone do not differ significantly from those who live with others. Among men, 26·6 per cent of those living alone were moderately or severely incapacitated, and for women the proportion was 34·6 per cent (national). However, incapacity is a more serious problem for those living alone – they, unlike other old people, have nobody else in the house to do some or all of the domestic work.

Of old people living alone 9·4 per cent have home helps provided by the local welfare authority, compared with only 2·8 per cent of those who live with others (national). Moreover, a somewhat higher proportion receive non-welfare domestic help – from relatives, neighbours or friends. But the proportion of those with an unmet need for domestic help is also higher; 7·5 per cent of old people living alone are not receiving welfare help but say they want it.

Old people were asked whether they had sole use of a kitchen, sole use of a fixed bath, and sole use of an inside toilet. Only 40·1 per cent of those living alone had all three of these facilities, against 56·4 per cent for all old people; 13·9 per cent of those living alone had none of the three facilities against only 6·1 per cent of all old people (national). A basic reason for those living alone being worse off is, of course, the low economic resources of old people in general. An elderly widow sharing a home with a married daughter will usually be in a more modernized home than if she lived in a household by herself with only her own income.

Any discussion of income is complicated by the income of married couples being taken as one unit, while the two people receive less than twice the pension (and national assistance) received by one person; but single and widowed women – among whom those living alone are heavily concentrated – constitute 'the problem group' in terms of low financial resources. Those who live alone are twice as likely as old people in general to have incomes below the national assistance scales, yet not to be receiving national assistance. One in every six of those who lived alone came into this category.[9]

[9] Peter Townsend and Dorothy Wedderburn, *The Aged in the Welfare State* (1965).

Living Alone

Old people who keep house alone do not receive any allowance for the replacement of 'durable' consumer goods – and they are much less likely to live in households containing these than are old people in general. A radio is the only durable consumer product which those who live alone are as likely to have in the household as are all old people. Those who live alone are only half as likely to have a television set in the house as are old people who live with others – and even less likely to have a washing-machine, refrigerator or car (national).

The living alone group are also highly relevant in the provision of institutional care for old people. The institutional survey shows that 38·3 per cent of old people in institutions had previously been living alone – against 22 per cent of the elderly population at large. This is particularly striking with Old People's Homes – 48·7 per cent of residents in this type of institution had previously been living alone.[10]

Old people living alone are thus of special importance to the providers of domiciliary services, in the field of housing and domestic facilities, in the provision of retirement pensions and other financial support, and in plans of institutional care. Moreover, long-term planning in these areas must take into account the long-term trend for an increasing proportion of the elderly population to live alone.

8. UNDERLYING TRENDS IN LIVING ALONE

Why has the proportion of old people living alone increased? Although there is no very reliable evidence on the proportions living alone at the turn of the century, Seebohm Rowntree in his *Poverty: A Study of Town Life* (1901) reported on membership of all the houses in four streets in York. Of thirty-one people aged 60 or over three were living alone. Such a small number of people from a survey in only one local area obviously must not be taken too seriously.[11] Nevertheless the York evidence is interesting; 23 per cent of the old people in 1900

[10] Peter Townsend in *The Last Refuge* (1962) found that of those in Old People's Homes who were admitted from private households, 48 per cent had been living alone.
[11] Especially since Rowntree's evidence on relationships within the household is not always clear. Sometimes he does not give the age of the wife, only the householder. At least one of his entries appears to be internally inconsistent.

Underlying Trends in Living Alone

TABLE 2.5 HOUSEHOLD COMPOSITION OF OLD PEOPLE
IN BRITAIN 1900 AND 1962

	People aged 65 and over in Britain, 1962	People aged 60 and over in York, 1900
	%	%
Living alone	22·2	10
With spouse only	32·8	19
Married child	11·9	10
Unmarried child	20·1	26
Sibling	6·7	–
Grandchildren	0·9	13
Other relatives	1·8	–
Non-relatives	3·6	23
Total	100	100
Number	2,500	31

Sources : National Survey.
Seebohm Rowntree (1901), pp. 16–25

lived in households with non-relatives – a much higher figure than for 1962. There is no indication here of a simple progressive decline of family life.

The basic demographic picture of old age has, of course, changed radically during this century. In 1901 people aged 65 and over made up 4·7 per cent of the population, and this had more than doubled to 11·9 per cent by 1961. A possible explanation for the increased proportion living alone might be that there had been a decrease in the proportion of married old people. However, on the contrary, the proportion of married people among the elderly actually increased between 1921 and 1961 – from 60·1 per cent to 70·3 per cent of old men and from 32·6 per cent to 34·3 per cent of old women.[12]

The increasing proportion of old people in the population has, of course, been accompanied by a shortening of the generations and a decrease in the average number of children in a family. This has meant that less old people have available a child with whom they could conveniently share a household – in particular an unmarried child. The decrease in the size of family has made less common the earlier practice of women with

[12] Registrar General's figures for England and Wales, 1961 Census.

59

Living Alone

a large number of children handing over one or two of them to be brought up by a grandparent; Table 2.5 suggests a decrease between 1900 and 1962 in the proportion of households in which old people live with grandchildren (but not children). The better survival rates of people in middle age has also meant that parents are less likely to die before grandparents.

The decrease in the size of families since 1900 has, of course, also been accompanied by a decrease in the number of people making up an average household. Of Rowntree's old people in 1900, three-fifths lived in households of three or more persons, against only one-fifth of old people living in households of this size in the four-area survey in 1963–4. An increase in the number of old people living alone can thus be seen as only part of a general reduction in household size. Rowntree's old people in 1900 were on average sharing one toilet between about ten people living in three households; the households were mostly paying between two and four shillings a week in rent.

The supply and quality of housing will inevitably affect the proportion of old people living alone – both as it impinges on the old people themselves and on their children. Most old people living alone today have been living in the same home for some time – four-fifths have been at the same address for at least six years and 57 per cent for twenty-one years or more (national). Rent-control in many cases obviously provides a strong economic disincentive to move. This fairly long period of tenure indicates that old people now living alone have usually lived in the same home previously with their spouse, children or other relatives. The type of housing in which this is least likely to have happened is obviously the most recently built housing; hence the low proportion of old people living alone in suburban areas (where new housing is common) and the high proportion in areas with much old housing.

The housing situation as it affects younger people is also relevant to old people living alone – in view of the preference of many old people to live alone, but near to their married children. Availability of housing for young married couples, of course, varies markedly between areas and probably is a factor in local differences in old people living alone.

By the end of 1962 no less than 300,000 'single bedroom dwellings suitable for elderly people' had been built by local

Underlying Trends in Living Alone

authorities in England and Wales. This number equals over a quarter of all old people living alone. Of course, not all of these dwellings actually go to people aged 65 and over, while some go to elderly married couples. Many of the dwellings go to single and widowed old people who were living alone previously – often in much larger houses. Nevertheless it seems likely that these dwellings have had at least some impact in raising the proportion of old people living alone.

Such 'special' housing is only one sort of local authority action designed to assist those old people who desire to continue living alone. Domiciliary services such as subsidized home helps, meals-on-wheels and home nurses are others. These services vary considerably between local authority areas – and may play a part (probably small) in local variations in the proportions of the people living alone.

Another type of relevant local authority action is the provision of institutional care, which also varies greatly in quality and quantity between areas. Moreover, it is not only the actual supply of beds but also how the old people themselves – and their children – perceive the various kinds of institutional care, which is important. In 1900 the major institutional alternative was the workhouse, which was of course intended to carry a social stigma. Some kinds of institutional care, especially the psychiatric hospitals and the ex-workhouse Old People's Homes still carry the stigma. However, more enlightened social policies may in the long run alter this.

An expansion of domiciliary services may eventually weaken the motivation of children in providing nursing, shopping and cleaning services for old people – although this would be most difficult to measure; it is, however, a possible factor which obviously cannot be ruled out.

The availability of work for younger women is another relevant factor. An old person may only be able to live alone because she is looked after by her married daughter – who in turn is thus unable to go out to paid work in the local factory. Daughters may be more willing to help their elderly parents in this way in areas where work for women is not available. But the connection here is by no means clear.

The availability of work for the old people themselves may have a bigger impact on the proportion of old people in an

Living Alone

area who live alone. For instance areas like Oldham with a long tradition of work for women may have attracted in the past single or childless women – the groups most likely to live alone in old age.

In the long run the level and nature of public economic provision for old age plays a vital part in the proportion of old people who live alone. A retired person who lacks a private income cannot continue to live on her own without some kind of financial support. State contributory retirement pensions obviously provide such support. In 1900 these pensions did not exist. The only widespread form of public provision – poor law relief – carried a marked social stigma. Some old people did manage to live alone with this support; Rowntree comments on one such old widow in 1900: 'Has very little to live upon, as all three sons have married and left her on Parish relief.' However, the nature of relief probably forced some old people to live with their married children. Other old people took in lodgers to provide financial support. This mainly accounts for the 23 per cent of old people in York in 1900 who shared their household with non-relatives (Table 2.5). Rowntree comments on one widow who shared with a lodger: 'Disreputable old woman, ill, ought to be in workhouse. . . . House is very dirty, probably used as house of ill-fame.' [13] This is an extreme example but it may help to guard against the danger of thinking of the recent increase in living alone as being necessarily socially undesirable.

Old people are most likely to live alone in areas where living alone is common among all age-groups. Out of 157 towns in Britain the ten towns with the highest proportion of one person households (mainly in S.E. England) had a combined figure of 23·3 per cent of people of pensionable age living alone against only 12·9 per cent in the ten towns with the lowest proportion of one person households (places like Dagenham, Scunthorpe and Huyton). A high proportion of small dwellings (one to three rooms) and a high proportion of dwellings without basic domestic amenities is also associated with a high proportion of old people living alone. This seems to suggest that the *supply* of housing, both as it affects old people and their children, is a crucial factor.

The ten towns with the highest proportion of women in the

[13] B. Seebohm Rowntree, *Poverty: A Study of Town Life* (1901), p. 17.

Underlying Trends in Living Alone

labour force had 24·5 per cent of their people of pensionable age living alone (against 18·4 per cent for the ten towns with the lowest proportion).[14]

It seems clear that the proportion of old people living alone in any locality is connected with a number of broad socio-economic variables of which the quality and supply of housing is probably the most important. Unfortunately although Census data is available on the proportions of old people living alone in local areas there is no such data on the proportions who are childless. The national survey indicates that only 18·8 per cent of old people in Wales are childless against 32·2 per cent in the North-West. Such figures must be treated with some caution but they do indicate that there are probably substantial local variations in the proportions of childless old people.

A childless old person has about twice the chance of an old person with children of living alone. All the indications are that this variable of childlessness – and marital status – is more important than any of the broad socio-economic variables reported in the national census.

[14] Based on C. A. Moser and Wolf Scott, *British Towns* (London: Oliver and Boyd, 1961), and Registrar General's 1961 Census, County Tables.

Chapter Three

SOCIAL ISOLATION

1. MEASURING SOCIAL ISOLATION

Having decided to concentrate on social isolation in the sense of isolation from primary groups at work and in the family, how does one proceed? Perhaps the most basic methodological question is whether to use the usual sociological digging tool, the interview. The diary is another possibility. But although there is much to be said for the diary in collecting information on a matter like household expenditure, a diary of daily activities has serious disadvantages. Some investigators have experienced refusal rates of 80 per cent or higher for activity diaries.[1] Even apart from this, diaries are unsatisfactory since the diary itself would constitute a major activity. The method, like direct observation, would in this case too greatly distort the very social activity under investigation.

Interviews seem the best method. What is the interview intended to discover? Most of the screening interview in the four-area study was aimed at discovering whether the old person was socially isolated – only one question each was devoted to living alone, loneliness and anomia.[2] Each old person was given a 'social contact score', in effect placed along a continuum between extreme social isolation at one end and high social contact at the other. A deliberate decision was taken to go for sensitivity to social isolation, if necessary at the expense of making the system of measurement less sensitive at the high contact end of the continuum.

In practice another basic decision must be taken on roughly how big the isolated group will be. Lowenthal adopted a very extreme definition – people only being isolated if they had had no contact with a friend or relative during the last three

[1] Nelson N. Foote, 'Methods for Study of Meaning in Use of Time', in Robert W. Kleemeier (ed.), *Aging and Leisure* (1961), p. 164.
[2] Appendix 2.

64

years.[3] In the present study a less extreme definition of the socially isolated was used. In particular it was intended to select a group which would be comparable with, but a little smaller in extent, than the living alone group.[4]

After this a number of decisions must be taken on the time span to be used, the unit of measurement, and the duration, frequency, quality and depth of the social intercourse (or lack of it) under investigation.

A modified version of the system used by Peter Townsend in Bethnal Green was adopted. (Details of the modifications are explained in Appendix 3.) This system concentrates on the *week* previous to the interview – with some emphasis on the previous month as well – and is justified by the general impression from all the social research on the subject, that most old people do have a well-defined weekly routine. The unit of measurement used is the 'social contact': 'By "contact" . . . is meant a meeting with another person, usually pre-arranged or customary at home or outside, which involves more than a casual exchange of greetings between, say, two neighbours in the street.'[5] The minimum duration for a contact is about ten minutes.[6] Social meetings longer than this do not score extra social contacts; however, since eating one of the two main meals of the day in company scores one 'contact', an old woman who, for instance, spent all day with her daughter would normally score three contacts for this.

As to frequency of social intercourse, emphasis is placed on daily or near daily frequency. An old person who lives alone but spends each day with a child (including meals) scores twenty-one contacts for this alone – just enough to raise her out of the 'socially isolated' category.

The 'social contact' system largely avoids the difficult questions of the emotional depth or quality of social intercourse. Undoubtedly it is possible to have a high level of social contact with someone, and for the relationship still to be empty of

[3] Marjorie Fiske Lowenthal, 'Social Isolation and Mental Illness in Old Age', *American Sociological Review* (Feb. 1964), pp. 54–70.
[4] The scoring system was so arranged as to produce a somewhat larger group than that reported by Peter Townsend in Bethnal Green.
[5] Peter Townsend, *The Family Life of Old People* (1957), p. 167.
[6] In the four-area study this rule of thumb was adopted for the screening interviews.

Social Isolation

emotion, or even full of antagonism. But this chapter does not deal with emotional relationships, although the emotional content of relationships between old people and, say, their children are undoubtedly both important and interesting. This is a chapter about social isolation or non-isolation.

Nor is it claimed that the modified version of the Townsend system used in this study is by any means the only possible one – even accepting the same definition of social isolation and admitting that any scoring system must be crude and arbitrary. However, before reporting the findings it may be worth looking at one other system of scoring social isolation.

Bernard Kutner for his *Five Hundred Over Sixty* study in New York used this approach:

> Social isolation was determined by the use of an index of isolation, based on items dealing with the degree of human contact with friends or relatives. The lower the index score the higher the degree of social isolation. (1) Seeing children at least once a month, (2) seeing other relatives at least once a month, (3) having very close friends living, (4) having personal friends, (5) having made new friends.

Those old people who scored only 1 or 2 were designated as socially isolated; 60 per cent of the men, 53 per cent of the women and 56 per cent of both sexes came out as isolated by these criteria. 65 per cent of those lived alone and 50 per cent of those who lived with others were isolated.[7]

Kutner's system designates the majority of all old people, and half of those who share households, as isolated. He uses one fixed time-span and an unfixed one, and for two questions he uses 'seeing' people, while for the others he relies on 'having' friends. The system relies primarily on *breadth*, using no frequency less than a month's duration. Perhaps the most serious weakness of Kutner's system is its vagueness; another difficulty is that a man aged 66 despite working full-time, living with his wife and seeing several children frequently, because he had no friends alive scores only 1 or 2 points and is 'socially isolated'.[8]

---

[7] Bernard Kutner *et al.*, *Five Hundred Over Sixty* (1956), pp. 110–11.

[8] On the system used in the present study such a man would score something like this: living with wife – 7; eating all meals in company – 14; seeing four children and children-in-law each three times a week – 12; working forty hours a week and talking 'often' to fellow workers – 18. Total 51; the man would thus be in the high social contact group.

Measuring Social Isolation

On the other hand, a person who lives alone, sees a child and grandchild once a month and has friends alive – perhaps thousands of miles away – may yet get the maximum non-isolated score for what Kutner calls 'a broad range of inter-personal relations'.[9] In fairness to Kutner's pioneering study, however, it must be emphasized that social isolation was not his major focus of interest.

Where the cut-off point is placed along the continuum be-tween the socially most isolated and those with the highest social contact score is inevitably arbitrary. The present study in four areas of England produced scores varying from 0 to over 100. It was decided to place the cut-off point between 20 and 21 contacts a week. The number of old people in Table 3.1 with scores from 21 to 25 is more than three times the number with scores from 16 to 20. To a considerable extent this dividing line is between those who live alone and those who live with others. But the sharp rise from 11 per cent of the sample who have between 11 and 20 contacts to 28 per cent of the sample who have from 21 to 30 contacts, is partly due to some old people who live alone still having enough social contacts to carry them over the cut-off point; the 21 to 25 contacts band also contains some old people who live with and eat all meals with one other person – thus scoring 21 contacts – but have few other social contacts.

The cut-off point could be placed lower down, say, at 15, 10 or 5 contacts, thus producing a lower percentage of isolated people in the elderly population. Some attention is paid later in this chapter (Section 8) to a more extreme group of isolated elderly – those who score not more than 5 contacts a week and make up only 4 per cent of the total sample of elderly people.

2. SOCIAL ISOLATION AND LIVING ALONE

Table 3.2 shows the correlation in the four-area sample between living alone and social isolation. Of those who live alone, 64 per cent of men and 69 per cent of old women are categorized

---

[9] In the present study such an old person would score, e.g. lives alone – 0; eats all meals alone – 0; saw one child last month – ½; saw grandchild once last week – 1; saw one friend last week – 1; no paid work – 0. Total 2½; the old person would thus be 'extremely socially isolated'.

67

Social Isolation

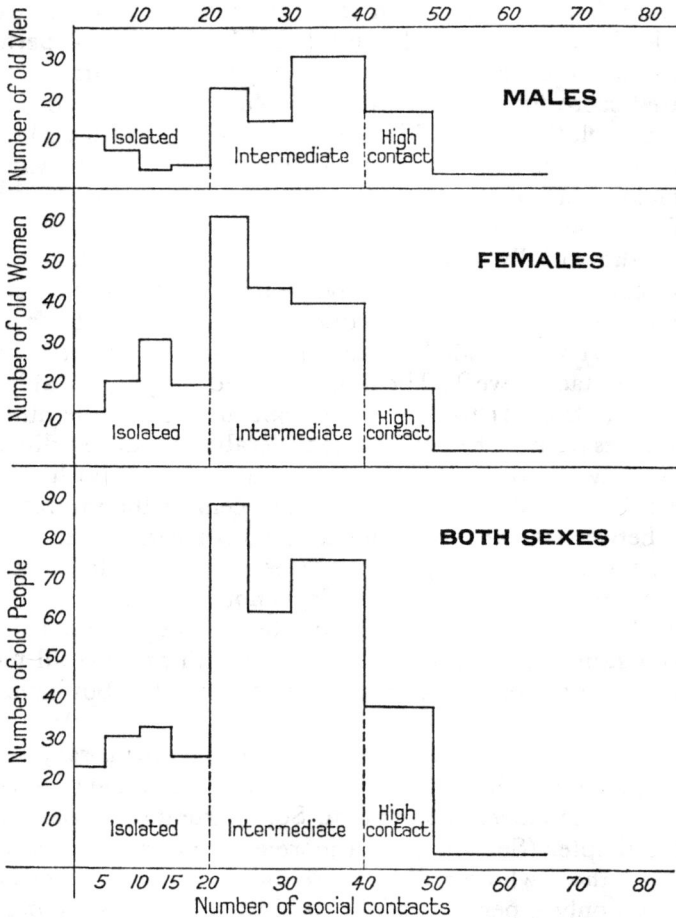

TABLE 3.1 SOCIAL ISOLATION AND SOCIAL CONTACTS BY SEX

as socially isolated. However, of all old people who live alone 32 per cent are not socially isolated. 6 per cent of those living alone have a high level of social contact (41 contacts a week or more), against 26 per cent of the total sample of old people, who have high social contact.

The main distinction, from the point of view of household composition and social isolation, is between living alone and not living alone. There is no significant difference in the likeli-

68

Social Isolation and Living Alone

TABLE 3.2 SOCIAL ISOLATION AND LIVING ALONE

	Alone	2-person household	3-person + household	All	
Males					
0–10 contacts	(49)	1	(0)	10 ⎫	
11–20	(15)	2	(2)	5 ⎭	15
21–30	(15)	27	(5)	20	
31–40	(8)	37	(20)	28	
41–50	(5)	18	(27)	18	
51+	(8)	15	(46)	20	
Total	100	100	100	100	
Number	39	130	41	210	
Females					
0–10 contacts	29	1	0	10 ⎫	
11–20	40	1	0	14 ⎭	24
21–30	20	50	18	32	
31–40	8	30	39	25	
41–50	4	8	22	10	
51+	0	8	22	9	
Total	100	100	100	100	
Number	112	142	74	328	
Both sexes					
0–10 contacts	34 ⎫	1 ⎫	0 ⎫	10 ⎫	
11–20	34 ⎭ 68	2 ⎭ 3	1 ⎭ 1	11 ⎭ 21	
21–30	19	40	13	28	
31–40	8	33	32	26	
41–50	4	13	24	13	
51+	2	11	30	13	
Total	100	100	100	100	
Number	151	272	115	538	

hood of an old person being socially isolated whether living in a household of two, three, four or more people. There is only one case of an old person living in a household of four or more people who is socially isolated. This is unlikely to happen – two-thirds of all old people in households of this size have a high level of social contact. If the old person sees each of three other household members each day during the previous week, this scores 21 contacts, and if the old person has all meals in company this scores another 14 contacts – making 35 contacts from these sources alone. The one old person who lived in a large household but was nevertheless 'socially isolated' was a widower, aged 78. He lived in a public-house with his son, daughter-in-law and two grandchildren. The old man spent all his time in an upstairs room and had his meals there alone. The screening interviewer reported: 'Daughter-in-law very difficult. Hates the old man.' When the present writer called for a second interview, the daughter-in-law complained that the old man suffered from 'senile decay', and should be in an Old People's Home – but the doctor refused to arrange it. The old man, in his upper room, talked quite coherently. He said: 'Under the circumstances, I'd rather not answer any more questions. I'm rather a special case.' This interview thus became a refusal at the second stage.

Although only 68 per cent of all people who live alone are socially isolated the correlation the other way round is much stronger; 92 per cent of all old people who are isolated are living alone.

3. SOCIAL ISOLATION AND HAVING RELATIVES ALIVE

Of old people who have no spouse, no children and no brothers or sisters alive, two-thirds are isolated and none have high social contact; on the other hand, of old people who have a spouse and at least one living child and one living sibling only 1 per cent are socially isolated and 44 per cent have high social contact levels (Table 3.3).

Only 2 per cent of married old people are isolated against 37 per cent of the non-married. Among the latter of those who have one child but no siblings alive only 20 per cent are isolated – as against those who have a living sibling but no living child,

TABLE 3.3 SOCIAL ISOLATION AND HAVING SIBLINGS OR CHILDREN ALIVE

BOTH SEXES

	At least 1 child and 1 sibling alive	At least 1 child but no siblings alive	At least 1 sibling but no children alive	No children or siblings alive	All
Married					
(0–20) Isolated	1	3	(0)	(6)	2
(21–40) Intermediate	55	60	(87)	(88)	64
(41+) High contact	44	37	(13)	(6)	35
Total	100	100	100	100	100
Number	123	67	38	17	245
Non-married					
(0–20) Isolated	31	20	46	(67)	37
(21–40) Intermediate	45	50	46	(33)	45
(41+) High contact	24	30	7	(0)	18
Total	100	100	100	100	100
Number	117	64	82	30	293

of whom 46 per cent are isolated. These percentages are based on small numbers and some discrepancies appear. But a general impression emerges that the most important category of relatives from the point of view of social isolation is the spouse, followed by children, with the availability of living siblings being of less importance.

Less old men than women are without spouses, and 15 per cent of all men are isolated against 24 per cent of all old women; moreover, 38 per cent of old men have high social contact against only 19 per cent of old women (Table 3.4). Out of 111 cases of isolated old people, only 27 per cent are men and 73 per cent are women.

Widowed old people make up over two-thirds of the isolated group. About a quarter are single and 4 per cent are married. There are several reasons why an old person can be socially isolated, despite being married. One old woman was temporarily, at least, living in extreme isolation while her husband was in hospital. In the other cases either the spouse was out at work all day or there was some conflict between the couple and they did not eat all of their meals together. An old woman whose husband is at work in the day may score only 9 contacts for meals (7 evening, but only 2 midday meals) and 7 for living with him, making a total of 16. If she has only one or two other contacts during the week, she will be socially isolated.

Table 3.3 shows that apart from being without a spouse, being childless is what most predisposes an old person to isolation; Table 3.4 shows that 52 per cent of the single are isolated against only 32 per cent of the widowed. This is another respect in which the incidence of isolation is sharply different from the incidence of living alone. The proportions of single and widowed living alone are almost identical (Table 2.1); but some widowed old people who live alone are not isolated, because of social contacts with their children, children-in-law and grandchildren – sources of social intercourse not available to the single.

4. CHILDREN

Having at least one child alive makes an old person less likely to be isolated (Table 3.5). Of childless old people 35 per cent

TABLE 3.4 SOCIAL ISOLATION BY SEX AND MARITAL STATUS

Social contacts	Male				Female				Both sexes			
	Married	Single	Widowed	All	Married	Single	Widowed	All	Married	Single	Widowed	All
0–10	1	(58)	21	10	1	(20)	13	10	1	28	15	10
11–20	1	(0)	16	5	1	(30)	18	14	1	24	17	11
21–30	22	(17)	16	20	35	(26)	32	32	28	24	29	28
31–40	34	(17)	15	28	38	(20)	18	25	36	19	17	26
41–50	18	(8)	18	18	10	(0)	12	10	15	2	14	13
51+	23	(0)	13	20	15	(4)	6	9	20	3	8	13
Total	100	100	100	100	100	100	100	100	100	100	100	100
Number	143	12	55	210	102	46	180	328	245	58	235	538

are isolated, against only 18 per cent of those with one living child. The major contrast is between having no children and having one child. Among men the number of children alive between one and four or more makes no difference to isolation. Among women there is some trend for fewer of those with more children to be isolated.

At the high contact end of the scale the picture is somewhat different. Seventeen per cent of the childless men still have high social contact – mainly due to some men having a lot of contacts at work – while the proportion of childless women with high contact is negligible. An old person of either sex is much more likely to have high social contact if he has several children than if he has only one. Of old people with one living child 18 per cent have high social contact, but for those with three or more children this rises to half the whole group.

Only 7 per cent of those with living children have had no contact at all with the children or children-in-law in the last month (Table 3.6). For those with only one living child the median score is about 5 contacts during the previous week with the child or the child's spouse. (Since Table 3.6 includes contacts with children and children-in-law the maximum contact with children for an old person with only one living child is 14.) Of those with only one child 19 per cent in fact have 10 contacts or more – which is up to or near the maximum.

The proportion having 10 or more contacts a week with children rises from 19 per cent of those with one child, to 37 per cent, 62 per cent and finally to 65 per cent of those with four children or more alive. The proportion of those with 20 or more contacts a week with children also rises sharply – from 4 per cent of those with two children (this score is not possible with only one child), to 24 per cent and 30 per cent of those with four or more children; this alone is enough social contact to carry these old people out of the socially isolated category.

The literature on the family indicates that most older parents see more of their daughters than their sons. One would thus expect less old people with only daughters alive to be isolated than those with only sons. However, for old people of both sexes there is no difference in propensity to isolation between those only with sons and those who only have daughters (Table 3.7). The explanation is that although old people do

TABLE 3.5 SOCIAL ISOLATION AND NUMBER OF CHILDREN ALIVE

Male	*Nil*	*One*	Two	Three	*Four +*	*All men*
			Number of Children Alive			
(0–20) Isolated	26	11	6	(11)	(15)	14
(21–40) Intermediate	57	65	42	(37)	(24)	49
(41+) High contact	17	24	52	(53)	(61)	37
Total	100	100	100	100	100	100
Number	54	54	50	19	33	210

Female	*Nil*	*One*	Two	Three	*Four +*	*All women*
			Number of Children Alive			
(0–20) Isolated	40	22	15	(19)	(8)	25
(21–40) Intermediate	58	64	64	(29)	(53)	57
(41+) High contact	2	13	20	(52)	(39)	18
Total	100	100	100	100	100	100
Number	113	76	59	31	49	328

Both Sexes	*Nil*	*One*	Two	Three	*Four +*	*All*
			Number of Children Alive			
(0–20) Isolated	35	18	11	16	11	21
(21–40) Intermediate	57	65	54	32	41	26
(41+) High contact	7	18	35	52	48	54
Total	100	100	100	100	100	100
Number	167	130	109	50	82	538

Social Isolation

TABLE 3.6 SOCIAL CONTACTS WITH LIVING CHILDREN

Number of contacts with children and children-in law*	Old people of both sexes with living children – Number of children				
	One	Two	Three	Four	All
No contact last month	10	9	2	1	7
Contact last month but not last week	8	3	0	2	4
1– 2 Contacts last week	24	17	14	7	17
3– 4 ,, ,, ,,	5	5	6	11	8
5– 9 ,, ,, ,,	33	28	16	13	25
10–19 ,, ,, ,,	19	33	38	35	29
20–29 ,, ,, ,,	0	4	20	21	8
30+ ,, ,, ,,	0	0	4	9	2
Total	100	100	100	100	100
Number	130	109	50	82	371

*The child-in-law is only included in this table if the child is also still alive.

see less of sons than daughters, they see more of daughters-in-law than they do of sons-in-law.

Despite the importance of contacts with children in the scores of the great majority of old people who have any living children, a minority of old people are still isolated despite having children. Eleven per cent of old people who have four or more living children are isolated (Table 3.5). The children of some of these old people live as far away as Australia, but others have children living near by.

5. PAID EMPLOYMENT

Old people in full-time work are unlikely to be isolated. The numbers involved (Table 3.8) are very small but only 6 per cent of those in full-time work are isolated among both sexes, against 22 per cent of those who do no paid work. Four-fifths of those in full-time work have a high level of social contact – most of them are married men with children.

The proportion of those in part-time work (under 30 hours a week) is the same as for the whole sample. Thus the group who do part-time work would be markedly more isolated than the sample as a whole, were it not for their work – and the social contacts it produces. The numbers are again too small for a

TABLE 3.7 SOCIAL ISOLATION AND SEX OF LIVING CHILDREN

	Old Men having:				Old Women having:				Old People having:			
	only sons alive	only daugh- ters	sons and daugh- ters	no child- ren	only sons alive	only daugh- ters	sons and daugh- ters	no child- ren	only sons alive	only daugh- ters	sons and daugh- ters	no child- ren
0–20 Isolated	(5)	(15)	10	26	22	16	14	40	15	15	13	36
21–40 Intermediate	(47)	(60)	35	57	64	69	47	57	57	64	42	57
41+ High contact	(47)	(25)	55	17	15	16	38	3	38	20	45	7
Total	100	100	100	100	100	100	100	100	100	100	100	100
Number	38	47	71	54	55	57	104	112	93	104	175	166

77

Social Isolation

firm conclusion, but there is some indication that for some single and widowed old people paid work serves to mitigate severe social isolation.

6. SOCIAL CLASS, INCAPACITY AND RESIDENTIAL MOBILITY

The pattern of social isolation by class follows quite closely that for living alone.[10] Twenty-one per cent both of those in non-manual and manual occupational classes are isolated – and thus there is no evidence of any social class factor in social isolation.

Incapacity might play a part in social isolation, since, of course, severe incapacity must restrict an old person's ability to visit other people and score up social contacts. However, in the four-area sample only 21 per cent of the isolated old people were moderately or severely incapacitated, which is little different from the figure of 24 per cent of all old people with this degree of incapacity (national). Even though incapacity prevents some old people from going to visit others, nevertheless there are factors working in the opposite direction – the incapacitated have somewhat more social contact within their own homes.

Old people's major social relationships tend to have long histories – with the possible exception of relationships with neighbours. Thus old people who have recently moved house or moved to an unfamiliar district might find themselves in a state of social isolation. This may be true of some old people who, for instance, move to a seaside town and then lose their spouse. But the vast majority of old people do not move to sea-side towns. In fact 30 per cent of the socially isolated have been at their present address for thirty-one years or more, 50 per cent for twenty-one years or more, and 61 per cent for at least eleven years; the figures for all old people for the same periods are 27 per cent, 53 per cent and 66 per cent (national) – a very similar pattern. As to length of residence in the same *local area*, in the four-area sample 63 per cent of the isolated elderly reported having lived in the same locality for thirty-one years or more compared with 55 per cent of all old people (national).

[10] See above, p. 53.

TABLE 3.8 SOCIAL ISOLATION AND PAID EMPLOYMENT

	Male				Female				Both Sexes			
	No work	*Part time*	*Full time*	*All*	*No work*	*Part time*	*Full time*	*All*	*No work*	*Part time*	*Full time*	*All*
0–20 Isolated	16	(14)	(3)	14	24	(32)	(14)	25	22	(21)	(6)	21
21–40 Intermediate	59	(34)	(7)	49	58	(48)	(43)	57	58	(40)	(14)	54
41+ High contact	24	(52)	(90)	37	18	(21)	(43)	18	20	(40)	(81)	26
Total	100	100	100	100	100	100	100	100	100	100	100	100
Number	152	29	29	210	302	19	7	328	454	48	36	538

Social Isolation

Thus there is no sign of short duration or residence in the area being a general contributing factor in social isolation.

The negative findings of this section do not preclude the future possibility of more sophisticated correlations being discovered between social isolation and these variables. But there is no evidence here to support such simple hypotheses as that manual or non-manual classes are the more disposed to isolation, or that the isolated are transient residents in the areas where they live.

Nor is there any evidence of a rural–urban difference. The proportions of socially isolated among old people in the four areas are: Harrow 24 per cent, Oldham 23 per cent, South Norfolk also 23 per cent, and Northampton 15 per cent. The rural area, South Norfolk, has the same level of isolation as the urban areas of Oldham and Harrow. The area with the lowest level of isolation is Northampton, another urban area.

7. SOCIAL ISOLATION AND SOCIAL PARTICIPATION

Old people who had no social contact with friends during the previous weeks are not more likely to be isolated than other old people (Table 3.9). The same holds for those who have had no contact with neighbours in the previous week and also those who have not attended a club in the previous month.

In the case of each activity the percentage of those with no participation who are isolated – 19 per cent for friends, 17 per cent for neighbours, and 20 per cent for clubs – is just below the 21 per cent level of the sample at large. Since each of these activities scores contact points, this is all the more striking. For instance, old people who have had 3 or more contacts with neighbours in the previous week are nevertheless more likely to be isolated than those reporting no neighbour contact; indeed had it not been for these 3 or more contacts, a still larger proportion of the group would have been isolated. This evidence suggests that isolation encourages old people to see more of their neighbours.

Clearly, a social isolation scale which relies mainly on contacts with primary groups such as spouse, children, or household members, other relatives and workmates is indeed measuring something radically different from a social participation scale

TABLE 3.9 SOCIAL ISOLATION AND SOCIAL PARTICIPATION: BOTH SEXES

	Friends			Neighbours			Clubs		All old people
	No contacts last week	*1 or 2 contacts last week*	*3 or more contacts last week*	*No contacts last week*	*1 or 2 contacts last week*	*3 or more contacts last week*	*No attendance last month*	*At least one attendance last month*	
Isolated	19	27	14	17	24	23	20	22	21
Intermediate	54	54	49	57	59	45	57	46	54
High contact	25	18	37	25	17	32	23	33	26
Total	100	100	100	100	100	100	100	100	100
Number	290	146	106	251	121	166	400	138	538

which relies to a considerable extent on contacts with friends
or taking part in clubs and communal activities.

Table 3.9, then, indicates firstly that the way in which social
isolation is measured is of the greatest importance in deciding
which old people are categorized as isolated. Second, it shows
that old people who have contacts with friends and neighbours
and who participate in clubs – despite having their contact
scores raised thereby – are still at least as likely to be socially
isolated as other old people.

The information on social participation is also interesting in
view of the low level of activity by the sample at large. Those
who had as many as 3 contacts with a friend (or friends) in
the previous week constitute only 21 per cent of old men and
19 per cent of old women; over half of men and women had no
contacts with a friend in the week. Slightly more had contacts
with neighbours. A third of the women and a quarter of the
men had had at least 3 contacts with neighbours in the week;
but nearly half of all old men and women had had no neighbour contacts in the week. Only 26 per cent of old men and
women had been to any kind of club in the past *month*.[11]

In view of the high proportion of old people who have lived
in their present home for a long time, it is perhaps not surprising that some have a fairly high rate of social interaction with
neighbours. But the restricted level of social participation by
most old people is illustrated by the low level of interaction with
friends and participation in clubs.

8. EXTREME ISOLATION

The 'extremely isolated' are old people who report 5 contacts
or less during the previous week. There are only twenty-four
of them – about a fifth of the full socially isolated group. Some
of these old people have only 1 or 2 contacts a week. The median
score for the whole group of extremely isolated old people is
less than 3 contacts a week. They are a minority of a minority
group, but still 4·5 per cent of all the old people in the four-area
sample.

The extremely isolated are like the whole socially isolated
group, but more so. With the exception of one married woman

[11] Clubs are discussed further below, pp. 218–23, and 286–88.

whose husband was in hospital, all of the extremely isolated live alone and none of them are married. Two-thirds are widowed. Three-fifths have no living children. Most of them lack the close kin with whom other old people have the majority of their social contacts. They also lack another important source of social contacts, namely work; only one of the twenty-four extreme isolates works at all, and he only for a few hours a week. The extremely isolated are also older, not only than the median for all old people, but also than the broader group of the socially isolated. Among those aged 75 and over extreme isolates are twice as common as among those who are younger.

Social class which did not emerge as significant in social isolation in general, similarly is not a factor in extreme isolation. Old people in the white-collar social class are no more and no less likely to be extremely isolated than are old people of the manual working class. Among the extremely isolated are the widow of a company director and retired agricultural labourers.

A smaller proportion of the extreme isolates had been to a club in the last month (only two out of twenty-four), and fewer had a contact with a friend in the last week (only five out of twenty-four). But the extreme isolates did not differ in the proportion having had a contact with a neighbour in the last week – a third had done so.

In one important respect the extremely isolated group does differ from the larger socially isolated group. Although women are more likely to be isolated, a higher proportion of old men than of old women are extremely isolated. Bearing in mind the small total numbers – eleven extremely isolated men and thirteen women – it remains interesting to note that while a third of the isolated men are extremely isolated, only a sixth of the isolated women are. Thus although old women have a bigger chance of being socially isolated, when an old man is socially isolated he is more likely than an old woman to be *extremely* isolated.

Social isolation is fairly evenly spread among the four areas, but extreme isolation is heavier in South Norfolk. The rural area has about a quarter of all the old people in the four-area sample but nearly half of the extreme isolates – eleven out of the total twenty-four. Five of the eleven extreme isolates have either

83

been farm labourers or smallholders or are widows of men from those occupations. Of all the single or widowed agricultural labourers and smallholders in the Norfolk sample, over half are extreme isolates; of the other single and widowed old people in the Norfolk sample, only one-tenth are extreme isolates. The numbers are very small and one cannot firmly conclude that agricultural labourers and smallholders or their widows are especially destined for extreme isolation; nevertheless the evidence points away from any comfortable conclusions about the true sociability of the rural life.

Even though the extremely isolated group differs in some respects from the socially isolated at large there is not much resemblance to the kind of 'community isolates' described by Lowenthal in San Francisco.[12] The San Francisco isolates differ sharply from these extreme isolates in four areas of England – two-fifths come from San Francisco's Skid Row, they are overwhelmingly of low social class and most are single men (only a sixth of the English extreme isolates were single men); in particular the San Francisco isolates differ in having mainly had itinerant occupations and been extremely isolated all their lives. Three-quarters of the English extreme isolates are widowed and the other main contributing factor to their isolation appears to be a lack of living children.

9. CONCLUSION

Lowering the cut-off point to only 5 contacts a week produces a group of extreme isolates who differ in some respects from the larger group of socially isolated and this raises again the question of where the cut-off point should be placed. The broad similarity of the larger and smaller groups, however, underlines the common factor of a scoring system which emphasizes household members and repeated or daily contacts with kin in particular, but also with neighbours and friends; apart from the matter of size between the two groups – the extreme isolates who are 4·5 per cent of all old people and the socially isolated making up 21 per cent – the difference is mainly one of degree, principally the degree to which the old people lack other household members, and close kin with whom to interact. There is no

[12] See above, pp. 64–65.

Conclusion

correlation between social isolation, as scored under this system, and social interaction with friends and neighbours and in clubs; the really radical difference is not between sliding the cut-off point up or down the social contact scale but between the sorts of social contact or social participation which are measured.

There are, no doubt, good grounds for being interested in and scoring such matters as whether old people make new friends or participate in clubs. However, the evidence suggests that only a minority of old people engage in regular social participation of this kind. But for the majority of old people contact with household members and close kin takes up a large part of their time and is a major focus of interest. It is isolation, in the sense of lack of much social contact of the latter kind to which the present chapter has been devoted.

Chapter Four

LONELINESS

I. THE LONELY

The old people were asked during the screening interview whether they felt 'often', 'sometimes' or 'never' lonely. This wording followed directly a question in the larger national survey.

Table 4.1 distinguishes between loneliness and social isolation. Only a quarter of isolated old men and women were 'often lonely'. There is a smaller total number of 'often lonely' than isolated old people and a more marked correlation is evident the other way round. Of only forty-five 'often lonely' old people three-fifths are socially isolated. While only 14 per cent of all old people with high social contact are often or sometimes lonely, this increases to 65 per cent of the socially isolated. Thus even though the majority of the isolated are not also 'often lonely', a marked correlation emerges between the two separate phenomena of isolation and self-ascribed loneliness.

Of all old people only 6·7 per cent are often lonely but when the 'sometimes' lonely are added the total comes to 28 per cent of all old men and women. Being often lonely is nearly twice as common among old women as among old men. When the 'sometimes' lonely group is added, women still greatly predominate (national);[1] loneliness thus broadly follows both living alone and social isolation.

[1] The national and four-area surveys compare as follows:

	National	Four-area
Proportion of old people being often lonely	6·7%	8·6%
Proportion of old women being often lonely	8·4	10
Proportion of old men being often lonely	4·6	6
Proportion of often lonely who are women	72	71
Proportion of old women being often or sometimes lonely	34	40
Proportion of old men being often or sometimes lonely	19·4	24

86

TABLE 4.1 LONELINESS AND SOCIAL ISOLATION

	Males				Female				Both Sexes			
	Isolated	*Inter-mediate*	*High contact*	*All male*	*Isolated*	*Inter-mediate*	*High contact*	*All females*	*Isolated*	*Inter-mediate*	*High contact*	*All*
Often lonely	(17)	6	3	6	27	5	2	10	25	5	2	8·6
Sometimes lonely	(34)	19	11	18	42	29	14	30	40	26	12	25·2
Never lonely	(48)	74	87	75	31	66	85	60	35	69	86	66·1
Total	100	100	100	100	100	100	100	100	100	100	100	100
Number	29	98	75	202	81	184	59	324	110	282	134	526*

* No answer—12

87

Loneliness

Old people who live alone are also much more likely than those who live with others to be lonely (Table 4.2). Both among old men and old women those who live alone are about four times more likely to be 'often lonely' than are those who live with others. Over half of both old men and women who live alone are often or sometimes lonely.

The incidence of loneliness increases with age among old people of both sexes. This is so also among married old people; between the age-group 65–9 and those aged 80+ the proportion of married men who are often or sometimes lonely increases from 11 per cent to 30 per cent and among married women from 23 per cent to 35 per cent (national).

But the increase with age is also associated with the increasing proportion of widowed old people in the older age-groups. The sometimes or often lonely are 14 per cent of the married old men but 33 per cent of the widowed; among women they are 22 per cent of the married and 43 per cent of the widowed (Table 4.3). For both sexes the incidence of loneliness among the single is between the figure for the married and the widowed. But among old men the single are closer to the widowed (based on a small total number), whereas among single women the incidence of loneliness is closer to that for married women.

Loneliness increases also with another age-related factor, namely incapacity. Those who are often or sometimes lonely make up 13 per cent of men and 25 per cent of old women with no incapacity; these figures jump to 43 per cent of men and 52 per cent of women suffering from severe incapacity (Table 4.4). Since the degree of incapacity is not a significant factor either in living alone or social isolation here is a firm indication that 'loneliness' does not merely reflect an old person's frequency of social interaction. Loneliness also reflects a negative reaction to physical incapacity; even though such incapacity probably does alter the quality of social relationships, it seems clear that some old people say they are lonely as a way of expressing general unhappiness and dissatisfaction with their health and physical mobility.

A striking finding about old people's loneliness and children is that married people who have no children are not more likely to be lonely than are old people in general. The married but childless old person is only as likely to be lonely as the

TABLE 4.2 LONELINESS AND HOUSEHOLD COMPOSITION

	Male					*Female*				
	Living alone	*Spouse only*	*With child(ren)*	*With others*	*All male*	*Living alone*	*Spouse only*	*With child(ren)*	*With others*	*All Female*
Often lonely	18	3	4	4	4·6	16	4	5	4	8·4
Sometimes lonely	35	12	13	15	14·8	39	19	22	17	25·6
Never lonely	48	85	84	82	80·5	45	77	73	78	66·1
Total	100	100	100	100	100	100	100	100	100	100
Number	107	472	315	103	997	442	344	486	213	1,485

Source : National Survey.

TABLE 4.3 LONELINESS AND MARITAL STATUS

	Male				*Female*			
	Married	*Single*	*Widowed*	*All males*	*Married*	*Single*	*Widowed*	*All females*
Often lonely	3	(11)	9	4·6	4	4	12	8·4
Sometimes lonely	11	(17)	24	14·8	18	24	31	25·6
Never lonely	86	(72)	67	80·5	77	72	57	66·1
Total	100	100	100	100	100	100	100	100
Number	699	46	252	997	514	211	760	1,485

Source : National survey.

TABLE 4.4 LONELINESS AND INCAPACITY

	Male				Female				All old people Both sexes
	No incapacity	*Slight incapacity*	*Moderate incapacity*	*Severe incapacity*	*No incapacity*	*Slight incapacity*	*Moderate incapacity*	*Severe incapacity*	
Often lonely	3	5	7	18	5	6	12	19	6·7
Sometimes lonely	10	21	28	25	20	30	30	33	21·2
Never lonely	87	73	64	56	74	64	56	48	71·4
Total	100	100	100	100	100	100	100	100	100
Number	639	219	72	55	708	361	172	221	2,500

Source: National survey.

The Lonely

married person who has seen a child very recently; the married but childless old person is less likely to feel lonely than is the married old person who has children but has not seen one very recently (Table 4.5).

This can be explained in terms of deprivation. Married people of both sexes who have children, but have not seen one recently, appear to feel *deprived* and have a high propensity to feeling lonely. Another indication of the importance of deprivation as a factor in loneliness is that while the married old person is less likely to feel lonely than are the widowed (Table 4.3), old people who have never been married are less likely to feel lonely than are married people who have been deprived of their spouse by death.

TABLE 4.5 LONELINESS, MARITAL STATUS AND CHILDREN

| | Percentage often or sometimes lonely | | | |
| | Married | Widowed | Married | Widowed |
	Male		Female	
Has children and seen at least one yesterday or today	13%	26%	20%	38%
Has children but not seen one yesterday or today	16%	40%	28%	55%
Has no children	12%	49%	20%	49%
All old people	14%	33%	22%	43%

Sample Size – 2,500.   *Source :* National Survey.

Although childless married old people are no more likely to be lonely than are married people who have seen a child recently, the situation is different with the widowed. Widowed childless old people are markedly more likely to be lonely than are the widowed who have seen a child recently. Widowhood seems to involve more total deprivation for the childless than it does for those widows who still have frequent contact with children.

91

Loneliness

The most lonely group in terms of these two factors of marital status and contact with children are those widowed women who are deprived not only of their spouses but also of recent contact with children (despite having living children). In this group of doubly deprived women, 55 per cent claim to be lonely (Table 4.5). For a childless married woman her husband normally seems to occupy most of the social horizon and is the main bastion against loneliness; when the husband dies the loss is felt severely. But when a woman with children loses her husband the children act as some compensation – so long as she is in regular contact with them.

There is no correlation between self-ascribed loneliness and social class (national). The lonely tend to be women rather than men; the propensity to feel lonely increases with age, and with two age-related factors – widowhood and physical incapacity. Especially likely to be lonely are widows without children, and widows with living children who are not in frequent contact with them.

2. ATTITUDES TO LONELINESS

The four-area sample found only 45 'often lonely' out of 538 old people. An attempt was made to re-interview all of these and 38 longer interviews of the 'often lonely' were conducted by the author. When questioned further about their loneliness the old people gave much the same sort of explanations as those above. Asked whether they felt lonely for someone in particular, two-thirds of those who answered mentioned a specific dead person, most usually a dead spouse.

About a quarter said they were not lonely for anyone in particular. Only one-tenth of those who replied felt lonely for a living person. One of these was lonely for a husband who was in hospital and not expected to live much longer; one woman was lonely for a woman friend who had moved away to the seaside; one widowed woman was lonely for her daughter. But since nine out of ten are not lonely for any living persons there is a general impression of finality.

Asked directly about the main cause of their loneliness, the most common answer is widowhood. No relatives other than spouses were mentioned at all; half of all those who gave an answer attributed it to widowhood, while others mentioned being alone, living alone, seldom going out, being housebound, being ill, or being blind.

The lonely attribute being lonely at least partly to increasing age. Nine in ten of those who answered think they are more lonely now than when they were younger. Moreover, the majority think that all old people get more lonely with increasing age.

3. WHEN DO THEY FEEL LONELY?

The majority felt most lonely at night or in the evening. Widows said they had been used to welcoming their husbands home from work at night. Others missed the people and traffic passing on the street outside.

'She is most lonely at seven in the evening, and she sometimes has a cry and goes to bed.' *Spinster, Norfolk.*

Others said that they stayed up late, reluctant to go to bed alone. Those who found the morning the worst time specifically mentioned getting up alone in an empty home:

'The worst time of the day is the early morning and especially getting up in an empty house and making his own breakfast. He can't sleep now after 4 a.m., and in the summer he gets up at 5, and is already sitting on the doorstep by 6 a.m., smoking his pipe.' *Widower, aged 76.*

The only two of the often lonely group who mentioned specific days of the week both said that Sunday was the worst day for loneliness:

'Sunday is the worst time, especially Sunday evening. Usually she does not talk to anyone all that day.' *Widow, aged 75, Northampton.*

'She says that the worst time is on Sunday because everything is quiet and there is no housework or shopping to do.' *Widow, aged 73, Northampton.*

Those who live with others tend to feel most lonely at different times from those who live alone. Those living with people who go out to work find the day or the afternoon the most lonely time.

There is more general agreement as to which is the worst time of the year for loneliness; those who answered this question

Loneliness

were overwhelmingly of the opinion that the winter is the worst time.

'In winter she locks the doors at 5 p.m. and does not go to bed until 10.30 p.m.' *Widow, aged 66, South Norfolk.*

'The winter is the worst time for loneliness and in the summer, when it is light, she can see people out of the window – although they cannot see her.' *Widow, aged 81, Harrow.*

But at least as important as the short days, the cold, and the impossibility of getting outside the home on winter evenings, seems to be a feeling that in summer one is more aware of life going on near by – whereas in winter the bad weather and the early approach of darkness cut one off from the sight and sound of other people, alone behind closed doors and drawn curtains.

4. WHAT CAN BE DONE ABOUT THE OFTEN LONELY?

Since the often lonely tend to quote their widowhood as the main predisposing factor, and since most are already over 70 years of age, perhaps it is not surprising that nearly half of all those who answered the question think there is nothing they can do to alleviate their loneliness. However, over half thought there was something that they could do. The most popular suggestion was to go outside for a walk or to the shops; after this came the solutions of going to visit someone, or staying at home with television, radio or reading matter.

'To make herself less lonely, she can go out. She doesn't usually go to anybody's house, but sometimes she goes into town and walks around the market and sees people – she likes to chat or pass a word or two with people she knew when she worked there.' *Spinster, aged 69, Oldham.*

She says that six weeks after her husband died 'I couldn't stand sitting here'. She went out, walked along the street, and saw a middle-aged woman sitting on a seat; this woman followed, came up to her, and said that she was lonely. The other woman had been living with a friend who had just died. Mrs. L. said 'You will be lonely' but she didn't tell the other woman that she herself had just buried her husband. *Widow, aged 67, Oldham.*

'When she gets very lonely the best she can do is look at television; also she takes the dog out into the back yard and then goes to bed at 9.30 p.m., taking the dog with her.' *Widow, aged 71, Oldham.*

The often lonely were specifically asked whether they thought going out to work would make any difference. Of those who answered, half thought that it would. However, the question was obviously hypothetical, most of the old people being aware that work was not a practical possibility; because of the fairly high age of this group, most were well beyond normal retiring ages, and few were fit enough for full-time work.

Only three people in the sample were doing any sort of work and only one was working as much as half-time. Of the other two, one was a gardener who still did a few hours a week. The second was a man who attended a local authority workshop for old people. Since the often lonely group are mainly women, some of them have not done paid work for many years. Nevertheless, only one in ten of those who answered said definitely work would make no difference. Four-fifths thought work either would or might affect loneliness. The old people regard the absence of work – even if work is not a practical possibility – as a factor in their being often lonely.

A somewhat similar pattern of response is shown towards clubs. Only a tenth had been to any kind of club during the previous week. But those who thought a club either would or might make a difference to loneliness were about four-fifths of all who answered. Some of the people who expressed these positive, or tentative, attitudes towards clubs nevertheless said clubs did not appeal to them personally.

Do these answers about paid work and clubs indicate that the old people think more social contact is the answer to the problems of loneliness? After all, these lonely old people may prefer to be alone; their loneliness is usually due to the death of their marriage partner or some other close relative, and, since this cannot be reversed, they might prefer to be left alone. Being with other people might make them feel even more lonely. The often lonely group were asked: 'Are you more lonely when by yourself or with other people?' Five-sixths of those who answered said they were more lonely when by themselves. Some of the old people found the question difficult to understand – the idea of being lonely when with other people seemed absurd. But several said they were most lonely when they returned to their own homes after leaving relatives or other people.

'Asked whether she is lonely when by herself or with other people, she at first says, "I'm not with anybody." When prompted about her daughters, with whom she spends about two days a week, she says, "I feel it, after being with them all day."' *Widow, aged 81, Harrow.*

'She is not lonely when with other people, but when she comes back from her sister's – whom she sees once a week – she does feel lonely.' *Widow, aged 71, Oldham.*

The two old people who said they were more lonely when with other people – at least sometimes – were reminded of their widowhood:

'Her friends are mainly married, and when they discuss their anniversaries, or say how long they have been married – then she feels most lonely.' *Widow, aged 68, Harrow.*

In general, however, the often lonely think their loneliness would be relieved by more human company.

5. OFTEN LONELY DESPITE SOCIAL CONTACT

Not all of the 'often lonely' group are widowed, live alone and have low levels of social contact. Indeed 27 per cent of the often lonely are married (national). The most obvious reason for a married person to feel often lonely is the absence of the marriage partner. One married woman was living alone in a state of social isolation because her husband had been for several years in a mental hospital, from which he was not expected to emerge alive. A married woman was often lonely because her husband was at work all day, and her mother-in-law – to whom she was devoted, and who had lived in the house – had recently died. In a third case a man saw very little of his wife, who spent much of her time with a daughter by another marriage.[2]

Another married old woman claims to be often lonely apparently because of dissatisfaction with her second husband:

She missed her mother, who died of cancer twenty years ago. She nursed her mother for three years and says it was horrible –

[2] Reported in Interview 4.

Often Lonely Despite Social Contact

'her motion came out of her side'. She talks a lot about her first husband, who was killed in the First World War – 'They wanted cannon fodder, so he went.' She was only married to him for two years; 'he was more of a gentleman' – a clerk at the public library. She would be better off if he were still alive. Her second husband is a skilled manual worker – she describes him as a 'rough and ready sort'. She has tried to make him less so, but has not succeeded. *Married woman, aged 67, South Norfolk.*

In another home there are hints of domestic conflict between a retired clerical worker, his wife, and their two single daughters:

> He used to spend most of his evenings in the local pub, and he misses male company in this all-female household. He introduces me to his wife in a strangely awkward and aggressive way. Of his two daughters he says, 'They tell me I'm out of date and an old fool. I say when I'm gone and the undertaker has carried me out, they won't need to bother any more. That shuts them up.' *Married man, aged 73, Harrow.*

In this case and another where a married man complained of frequent loneliness, the wives were in poor health and several years older than the men. All of these four men were dissatisfied about their retirement. One man, despite having severe rheumatism, was extremely eager to get any kind of light work, such as being a watchman or sweeping up. The three other married, but often lonely, men seized every possible opportunity to get the conversation back to the subject of their work.

Five other people each lived in households with one person – two had lodgers, two lived with children, and one with a sister. None of them are categorized as socially isolated. The only thing all have in common is that they have all been widowed – four widows and one widower. Four of the five say specifically that they are lonely for their dead spouses.

Another, at first sight, paradoxical group are those who see their children very frequently and still describe themselves as often lonely. A third of the often lonely group have seen a child or child-in-law once a day over the week previous to the interview. The explanation for their still being lonely appears to lie primarily in the familiar fact of widowhood.

Chapter Five

ANOMIE

I. MEASURING ANOMIA

As in other empirical studies of anomie the Srole scale was used. The scale has five components:

1. The individual's sense that community leaders are detached from and indifferent to his needs.
2. The individual's perception of the social order as essentially fickle and unpredictable, i.e. orderless.
3. The individual's view beyond abdication of future life goals that he and people like him are retrogressing from the goals they have already reached.
4. The deflation or loss of internalized social norms and values, reflected in extreme form in the individual's sense of the meaningless of life itself.
5. The individual's perception that his framework of immediate personal relationships, the very rock of his social existence, was no longer predictive or supportive.[1]

For each component there is a statement with which the interviewer asks the respondent to agree or disagree.[2] Only an unequivocal 'agree' scores a point. Anomia[3] scores thus range from 0 (the extreme non-anomic score) to 5 (the highest anomic score).

There is need for some caution in using the Srole scale with old people in Britain, since although the scale has been used in

---

[1] Leo Srole, 'Social Integration and Certain Corollaries', *American Sociological Review* (Dec. 1956), pp. 712–13.

[2] Appendix 2. Screening questionnaire. Q. 23.

[3] Anomia is a condition of individuals, Anomie a condition of social systems. Robert Merton, 'Anomie, Anomia, and Social Interaction', in Marshal B. Clinard (ed.), *Anomie and Deviant Behavior* (1964), pp. 225–30.

Measuring Anomia

numerous empirical studies, they have almost all been in the United States,[4] and seldom concerned with old people.[5]

Wendell Bell reporting his San Francisco research, in which anomia increased with age, commented that old people's high anomia scores might result from a tendency to compare the present and future with an idealized picture of the past. As Bell points out, four of the five items on the Srole scale take a gloomy view of the present and future.[6]

However, there is no certainty that this does happen. Many old people have a far from idealized picture of the past. But the problem to which Bell refers is one example of a more general problem involved in classifying old people. Take, for instance, another variable relevant to anomia – social class. Most social class categorizations depend upon occupation – as does the Registrar-General's one used in the present study. But of course the majority of old people have retired; some widows have to be classified on the occupation of a husband who died years ago. There is no easy way around this problem.

2. ANOMIA AMONG OLD PEOPLE

Meier and Bell's strongest correlation was between anomia and social class, followed by social participation, with age only third.[7] Nevertheless although the age correlation was not very strong, the obvious hypothesis for a group of old people was that anomia would continue to increase with increasing age.

However, as Table 5.1 shows, on the contrary there was a trend for anomia to *fall* with increasing age. The over-80's have the lowest proportion of the highly anomic. But, the trend is not significant and is not supported by the trend for the non-anomic.

What about social class? Table 5.2 shows high anomia concentrated among the lower social classes. The highest level of

[4] In pilot interviews 'the average man' seemed to make old people think of a younger man earning 'an average wage'. It was decided to use 'ordinary person' instead.

[5] A full summary of empirical and theoretical studies appears in Marshal B. Clinard (ed.), *Anomie and Deviant Behavior* (1964).

[6] Wendell Bell, 'Anomie, Social Isolation and the Class Structure', *Sociometry* (June 1957), p. 112.

[7] Dorothy L. Meier and Wendell Bell, 'Anomia and Differential Access to the Achievement of Life Goals', *American Sociological Review* (April 1959), pp. 189–202.

Anomie

TABLE 5.1 ANOMIA AND AGE

Both sexes	age 65–9	age 70–4	age 75–9	age 80+	all old people
(4–5) Anomic	20	21	17	14	19
(2–3) Intermediate	42	41	43	52	43
(0–1) Non-anomic	38	38	40	34	38
Total	100	100	100	100	100
Number	175	166	83	87	511

Note: No replies from 16 males and 11 females – in this and following tables on Anomia.

anomia is found in the lowest social class; and the lowest level is in the non-manual part of class three. The combined figure for all the non-manual social class is 13 per cent who are anomic, against 22 per cent anomic among the manual classes. The trend is strongly in the same direction at the non-anomic end of the table; 50 per cent of the non-manual classes are non-anomic against only 32 per cent of all in the manual classes. This finding is consistent with that of Wendell Bell in San Francisco,[8] and in line with other studies of anomia. Perhaps the most interesting point is the sharp difference between the non-manual and the manual sections of social class three. Across this divide the proportion of the anomic rises from 6 per cent to 23 per cent; the fact of the rise being even sharper among men – 6 per cent to 32 per cent – suggests that the key factor may be their work, or retirement from work. The skilled manual worker may feel a particularly strong loss of status in

TABLE 5.2 ANOMIA AND SOCIAL CLASS

Both sexes	Classes One– Two	Class Three non-manual	Class Three manual	Class Four	Class Five	All old people
(4–5) Anomic	15	(6)	23	21	(24)	19
(2–3) Intermediate	38	(35)	38	55	(53)	43
(0–1) Non-anomic	47	(58)	39	24	(24)	38
Total	100	100	100	100	100	100
Number	126	48	177	123	34	508

retirement, whereas a clerical worker, whose status has not been so closely tied up with physical prowess or dexterity, may be more contented in retirement. Another possible explanation is that clerical workers are more likely than manual workers to receive occupational pensions.

The connection between old people's anomia and factors such as social isolation, social participation and loneliness is shown in Table 5.3. The anomic make up 22 per cent of the socially isolated and 15 per cent of those with high social contact. There is a similar narrow difference between seeing and not seeing neighbours in the previous week. Somewhat stronger correlations emerge between attending a club or going to a religious service in the previous month. Twenty-eight per cent of the 'often lonely' are anomic against only 16 per cent of the 'never lonely' – but this correlation with anomia is much weaker than the correlation found between loneliness and some other factors. Thus anomia among old people is only very weakly related to the other types of aloneness.

3. SEX, MARITAL STATUS, AND WORK

On the basis of the existing literature on anomia, hypotheses in the four-area survey included: 'The most anomic groups are the widowed, the single and the childless' and 'widowers are more anomic than widows.' These hypotheses were not substantiated.

Table 5.4 shows that married old people of both sexes have about the same distribution of anomia as the whole sample; 19 per cent of widowed old men and women are anomic – the same percentage as the whole sample. Within the widowed group recent widows are more anomic, but this is not so for men. While the widowed emerge as equally anomic with the married, the evidence for the single points in the opposite direction from the hypothesis. Again the numbers are small, but only 11 per cent of the single of both sexes are anomic, against 19 per cent for the whole sample. Ephraim Mizruchi found with his sample of adults in New York State that the single were more anomic;[9] but this is not necessarily as inconsistent as first appears. The single are without spouses and

[9] Ephraim H. Mizruchi, *Success and Opportunity* (1964), p. 101.

TABLE 5·3 ANOMIA AND SOCIAL ISOLATION, SOCIAL PARTICIPATION, LONELINESS BOTH SEXES

	Social Isolation			Loneliness			All old people
	Socially Isolated	Intermediate	High social contact	Often lonely	Sometimes lonely	Never lonely	
(4–5) Anomic	22	19	15	(28)	22	16	19
(2–3) Intermediate	44	43	43	(49)	47	41	43
(0–1) Non-anomic	34	37	42	(23)	31	42	38
Total	100	100	100	100	100	100	100
Number	109	270	132	43	127	341	511

	Social Participation							
	Neighbours		Friends		Clubs		Religious Service	
	Seen at least one last week	None last week	Seen at least one last week	None last week	Been at least once last month	No visits last month	Been at least once last month	No visits last month
(4–5) Anomic	16	22	18	20	12	21	11	21
(2–3) Intermediate	42	45	39	48	36	46	43	44
(0–1) Non-anomic	42	33	44	32	51	33	46	35
Total	100	100	100	100	100	100	100	100
Number	279	232	245	266	136	375	109	402

children all their lives and old age may prove – by comparison with earlier life experience – to be easier for single people to accept; for the married or the widowed old age means children moving away from the home, the loss or potential loss of the spouse, and so on.

The widowed and childless were expected to be the most anomic group. On the contrary, however, those who are

TABLE 5.4 ANOMIA AND MARITAL STATUS

Male

	Married	Single	Recently widowed	Long-term widowed	All
(4–5) Anomic	24	(33)	(16)	(39)	26
(2–3) Intermediate	41	(42)	(42)	(32)	40
(0–1) Non-anomic	35	(25)	(42)	(29)	34
Total	100	100	100	100	100
Number	135	12	19	28	194

Female

	Married	Single	Recently widowed	Long-term widowed	All
(4–5) Anomic	15	(4)	(30)	12	14
(2–3) Intermediate	40	(49)	(41)	50	46
(0–1) Non-anomic	44	(47)	(30)	37	40
Total	100	100	100	100	100
Number	99	45	37	136	317

Both Sexes

	Married	Single	Recently widowed	Long-term widowed	All
(4–5) Anomic	21	11	25	17	19
(2–3) Intermediate	41	47	41	47	43
(0–1) Non-anomic	39	42	34	36	38
Total	100	100	100	100	100
Number	234	57	56	164	511

TABLE 5.5 ANOMIA, MARITAL STATUS AND CHILDLESSNESS

Both Sexes	Married		Widowed		All old people including single
	Childless	At least one child	Childless	At least one child	
(4–5) Anomic	21	21	13	21	19
(2–3) Intermediate	49	39	48	45	43
(0–1) Non-anomic	30	40	38	35	38
Total	100	100	100	100	100
Number	53	177	52	168	511

Sex, Marital Status, and Work

without children and spouse are less likely to be anomic than the widowed with a living child, or the married whether childless or not (Table 5.5). One possible explanation is that those who have never had children do not miss them, but the finding remains perplexing.

Perhaps the most interesting finding on anomia from the four-area survey is that old men are more anomic than old women. Table 5.4 shows 14 per cent of women to be anomic, but 26 per cent of men; two-thirds of the anomic men are married. This is especially important since a markedly lower proportion of men than women, live alone, are socially isolated, report feeling lonely, are single, widowed, or severely incapacitated.

The evidence for anomia and social class (Table 5.2) and the sharp difference between anomia immediately on either side of the division between manual and non-manual workers, especially for men, indicated that anomia might be affected by varying experiences of work and retirement from work. If this were so a difference might be expected in anomia for those still at work and those retired.[10] In Table 5.6, however, this expected correlation does not emerge. The same proportion of men who are retired and of men still working are anomic. However, this does not necessarily mean that work and retirement and the other changes connected with retirement – such as loss of earnings, status, and physical activity – are not behind the markedly different anomia rates of old men and old women.

TABLE 5.6 ANOMIA AND RETIREMENT: OLD MEN ONLY

	No paid work	Part-time work	Full time (30 hrs + a week) work	All
(4–5) Anomic	26	(32)	(19)	26
(2–3) Intermediate	41	(32)	(38)	40
(0–1) Non-anomic	32	(36)	(42)	34
Total	100	100	100	100
Number	140	28	26	194

[10] 'Social Structure and Anomie: Continuities' in Robert Merton, *Social Theory and Social Structure* (1957 edition) p. 188.

105

Anomie

Men aged 65 and over who are still working are in the minority and are faced by the impending possibility of retirement. The majority of men still working after 65 are not doing the same kind of work they did for most of their lives – many have already suffered a loss in status and earnings.[11] The figures in Table 5.6 are very small, but there is a sharp difference between anomia among those in part-time and those in full-time work. Those in part-time work are more anomic, and this may be because these men – part way between full-time work and retirement – are most directly exposed to the changes and losses retirement involves for men.

4. ANOMIA BY AREAS

Harrow is the least anomic area followed by Northampton, South Norfolk and Oldham (Table 5.7). Harrow has the lowest proportion of anomic old people at 15 per cent and Oldham the highest at 26 per cent. Harrow has the highest proportion of non-anomic old people at 49 per cent against Oldham, the lowest, with 30 per cent. This is in line with the social class correlation reported in the literature and in Table 5.2. Of the areas, Harrow does rate highest on social class and Oldham lowest.[12]

TABLE 5.7 ANOMIA BY AREAS: – BOTH SEXES

	Harrow	Northampton	Oldham	South Norfolk	All
(4–5) Anomic	15	17	26	18	19
(2–3) Intermediate	36	46	43	47	43
(0–1) Non-anomic	49	37	30	35	38
Total	100	100	100	100	100
Number	111	165	102	133	511

There is no reason to expect any difference between rural and urban areas as such, if social class is the main factor. South Norfolk might be expected to fall between a heavily white-

[11] Fifty-nine per cent of old men who are still working did some other kind of work most of their lives (national).
[12] See Appendix 1.

Anomia By Areas

collar area like Harrow and a heavily working-class area like Oldham, which is what happens. In South Norfolk 18 per cent of the old people are anomic against 19 per cent for the whole sample. Ephraim Mizruchi reported from his New York State study that anomia was not merely a big-city phenomenon.[18] The findings of the present study are also consistent with the evidence already cited that the position of old people in a rural area is not radically different from urban areas.

5. THE RELEVANCE OF ANOMIA AMONG OLD PEOPLE

In general the evidence of this study supports the kind of findings of most research on anomia. The anomic tend to belong to the lower social class and to have a low participation in social and religious activities. On the other hand, although there is some correlation with loneliness, anomia among old people shows no evidence of being connected with widowhood or lack of living children.

Nevertheless two tentative conclusions are of some interest. Firstly although no significant correlation emerges between anomia and social isolation there is a connection with social participation; the anomic may be no more socially isolated than other old people, but they participate less in social activities. The anomic feel alone in the sense of being cut-off from the larger society.

Secondly high anomia is probably connected among men with retirement. Further study of this is required, including information about anomia among men before the age of retirement. Other research indicates that during and before retirement men tend to experience a crisis which makes them feel alone and cut off from their main means of relating themselves to the larger society. The sharp increase in anomia between the white-collar and skilled manual class points in this direction, as does the high level of anomia among part-time workers. The trend of anomia to fall, rather than rise, with increasing age is consistent here – old men may feel less alone as they become adjusted to retirement. The evidence on anomia is thus a reminder of the importance of retirement.

[18] Ephraim H. Mizruchi, 'Social Structure and Anomie in a Small City', *American Sociological Review* (Oct. 1960), pp. 645–54.

Anomie

The accompanying table summarizes some of the main findings about aloneness:

	Living alone	Social Isolation	Loneliness	Anomia
Female sex	+	+	+	−
Widowhood	+	+	+	o
Single	+	+	o	−
Childlessness	+	+	o	−
Age 70+	+	+	+	o
Physical incapacity	o	o	+	o
Retired	+	+	+	o
Manual social Class	o	o	o	+
Low social participation	o	o	o	+
Rural residence	o	o	o	o

+ = positive correlation
o = no correlation
− = negative correlation

The lack of uniformity clearly indicates differences between the categories. Living alone and social isolation are quite closely connected, and both have some common correlations with loneliness; anomia differs the most from the other three categories.

Correlations with three types of aloneness are shown for female sex, widowhood, age 70+ and the retired. There is no correlation with three types of aloneness for manual social class, low social participation and physical incapacity. Only one line on the table is completely consistent – there is no connection between any of the four kinds of aloneness and rural residence. Thus the firmest conclusion is that the popular idea of old people being more alone in urban centres than in rural areas is without foundation.

Part II

GROUPS AT RISK

Part I concluded with a summary which indicates certain groups of old people who are likely to be alone. Part II deals with three of these groups – namely the single, the recently widowed, and the housebound. Other possible groups – such as the childless, the retired, the very elderly and those living on the lowest incomes – are not dealt with below partly because a good deal of social research has already been conducted about them.[1]

The single have a high propensity to live alone and be socially isolated. (In contrast the single as a group are less anomic than other old people.)

The recently widowed are important because widowhood predisposes old people not only to living alone and social isolation but also to loneliness; the smaller group of the recently widowed are even more prone to loneliness. Recent widows are more anomic than other widows.

The housebound are of significance because physical incapacity is strongly associated with loneliness.

These three groups of old people are of approximately equal size – in each case containing about one in ten of all old people.

Women greatly outnumber men in all three groups. Elderly spinsters outnumber elderly bachelors by more than three to one. Old women widowed within the last five years outnumber recent widowers by two to one. Among the housebound the women outnumber the old men by about four to one.

Members of all these groups are much more likely to enter *institutions* than are old people in general. Primarily because they have a much higher propensity to be alone the single make up 36 per cent of all those in Old People's Homes; in Psychiatric

[1] See Bibliography.

III

Groups at Risk

Hospitals 42 per cent of the elderly patients arc single (institutional survey).

Widowhood is often a precipitating factor in an old person entering an institution and this gives an added significance to the recently widowed group. Finally of all old people in institutions about half are bedfast or housebound; this is much higher than the figure for private households. Nevertheless the institutional population is relatively small, and of all bedfast and housebound old people in the population only one is in an institution for every three in private households. Thus inevitably the much higher proportion of the housebound who are in private households are of great importance for institutional policy.

Interview Reports

The three following individuals each belong to one of the groups at risk with which Part II deals. Miss Hughes is single; Mrs. Merton is recently widowed; Mrs. Leach is housebound.

Miss Hughes lives alone and is socially isolated; this is in contrast to Miss Pritchard (Interview 3) who also lives alone but is not isolated. However, like Miss Pritchard and many other spinsters, Miss Hughes is 'never lonely' and is non-anomic. Half of all Miss Hughes's social contacts come from a subsidized lunch club she attends five days a week.

Mrs. Merton's husband died a month before the interview, and she is very much under the impact of his death, although she claims to be only 'sometimes' lonely. Her husband's death has not merely been a great shock in itself on a number of levels, but has also shattered her daily routine – because for several years she has been looking after and nursing him. Like another recently widowed woman, Mrs. Marshall (Interview 2), she seems unable to talk for two or three minutes without returning to the subject of her husband.

Mrs. Leach, although having been housebound for four years, says she is never lonely and she does not come into any of the other alone categories. Her comparatively contented state appears to be partly due to the attentiveness of her husband and also to the recent slight improvement in her arthritis. Unlike another housebound old woman, Mrs. Marshall (Interview 2), who receives monthly doctor's visits, Mrs. Leach

Interviews

despite being crippled and housebound with arthritis has not seen her doctor for four years.

INTERVIEW NUMBER 5

Miss Hughes   *Harrow*
Aged 73   Lives alone
Single   Socially isolated (10)
Retired dressmaking   Never lonely
  machinist   Non-anomic (o)
No incapacity (o)

She is a very thin woman, who although quite physically attractive for 73, is still dressed in pyjamas at 10.30 a.m. and remains so until after noon. She has a first-floor bed-sitting-room and a kitchen. The interview in February takes place in the kitchen which is unheated. She has lived for twenty years in the Harrow area, in her present home for only six months, moving with the people who were her previous landlords for three years.

Miss Hughes spent all her working life in the dress business. She used to live in the East End, and she worked for many years at a firm in the City as a machinist. She retired eight years ago because of poor health at the age of 64, when she was working about thirty hours a week; she was glad to stop. She has one good friend from work whom she still sees.

She has slight trouble only in climbing the stairs – due to arthritis in her feet. She does the housework and her own cooking. She collects her pension and does her shopping, but sends her heavy washing to the laundry.

Miss Hughes suffers from a rheumatic skin complaint and from arthritis. She has to use three different kinds of ointment and spends eight shillings a week on them and polythene for dressings; she also pays fares on the Underground to a hospital in central London. Last year she has visited her doctor about ten times and she has been to the hospital six times as an out-patient. In five years she has been in hospital three times for her rheumatic skin complaint, on each occasion for about eight weeks; during the same period she has not been ill in bed at

113

home at all. If she were ill the people downstairs, her landlords, probably would help her but she would not like to ask them – 'I'm afraid I'm an independent sort of person.' Her doctor has told her to rest, so she gets up late and goes to bed early.

For breakfast she has tea, bread and marmalade and in the afternoon just a cup of tea; at 6.30 p.m. she has coffee and a cheese sandwich and an apple. She goes to the local assembly rooms for a subsidized midday meal five days a week; the last meal consisted of soup, fish pie, swedes and potatoes, and black-currant pie. This cost 1s. 2d. and there is tea for an extra 1d. The service is provided for pensioners by the Council and it is very near to where Miss Hughes lives. She says the largest numbers go on Tuesday and Thursday, because on these days two old people's clubs meet there after the midday meal. On these popular days about fifty pensioners go and on the other three days about thirty. She was reluctant to go to the assembly rooms at first, but 'I made myself go. It's the first time that's difficult.' Miss Hughes has no assistance with catering apart from the five meals at the assembly rooms, which are the only meals she eats in company.

She knows little about the home help service. One old couple she knew who had it complained that the home helps were unpunctual and irregular. Miss Hughes wears glasses, had her eyes tested one year ago, and can see well. Her hearing is all right. She thinks the local provision for old people is very good, and that Government old age pensions are good compared with the old days. 'You can be independent today. I can remember the workhouse.' She approves of children's allowances but thinks widows require more.

She was fifth in a family of six children. Her three eldest sisters all died in infancy. The youngest sister died when giving birth to her own third child. Miss Hughes has one living sibling, a brother. He lives about twenty miles away in Essex, is widowed and has four children; she sees him about twice a year. In addition she had one stepsister who died fairly recently in her seventies. She has a nephew who lives only a few miles away, and she sees this nephew when he comes to see his father, Miss Hughes's brother – twice a year. About once a week she sees the young couple who live downstairs; she has known them for three years, having previously been their controlled tenant in the house where she last lived – and she trusts them implicitly. She sees two other neighbours in the street during the summer. She also has two friends whom she used to see a good deal, but now she only sees them each two or three times a month.

Time never goes slowly, because her day is quite short. Her main pleasures are reading, her budgerigar and watching TV. She spends more time on reading than anything else – she reads novels, mainly historical or romantic, lent to her by her two friends. She does not visit the local public library which is a 3d. bus ride away. She reads the *Evening News* but no morning paper and she also has *Woman's Own*. Her second pleasure, which she says is television, suffers from her set only receiving one channel rather badly. She listens to the radio every day, especially in the morning and Woman's Hour in the afternoon. She knits a lot, and smokes twenty cigarettes a week. She goes out little apart from going to her meals and the local shops; she thinks people in the East End are more friendly than those in Harrow.

She has never belonged to any clubs until four years ago when she joined an old people's club. She says the club enables her to meet people and sometimes there is a concert or an outing. She does not play cards, which is one of the main activities. There are usually sixty to seventy people, mainly women. She gets to know people at the club including one person who used to be a next-door neighbour. The club meets once a fortnight from 2 to 4 p.m. on Fridays. She is 'actually not too keen on these places' and she would not want to go more often. She first went to the club four years ago because 'one of the helpers lived down the street and asked me to go'.

She does not go to church and has not been on a holiday during the last year. She writes about two letters a week mainly to her brother and her two friends.

Miss Hughes pays 22s. 6d. a week rent for her largish bed-sitting-room and her tiny kitchen; she has the use of the bathroom, sharing it and the toilet (on her own floor) with the landlord downstairs. She does not find this inconvenient—having lived in rooms often before. Her present home is satisfactory, and she does not want to move, but she thinks special housing for old people is 'lovely'. Before moving to her present place she applied for a bungalow, but says the council wouldn't accept her name on the list because she was a controlled tenant. She would prefer a bungalow but wouldn't mind a flat. She was keen to get a bungalow because in the house where she previously lived 'it was a worry. There were people moving in and out all the time; they kept trying to make me go because I was a controlled tenant. A builder offered me £200 to go.' She thinks more should be done for older people who want to live on their own in convenient accommodation.

She does not know whether being single makes much difference in illness. She likes the independence of being single but she would have preferred her own children. When her sister died in childbirth she helped to bring up the three children; her brother-in-law and children moved in with Miss Hughes and her mother.

She is sorry she never got married. Her fiancé was killed in the beginning of the First World War in 1914 when she was herself aged 23; she could have married other men but somehow she didn't want to. One man who wanted to marry her was her brother-in-law, but he was too ill (from the First World War) and he drank too much. Once she had to stop work and look after him and his three children when they were all ill together. Later the brother-in-law married another woman and the children were taken away, which she found a great loss. Asked whether her parents had anything to do with her being single she at first says no. But her father died when she herself was one year old and she thinks that looking after her mother may have had something to do with it. Her brother, the only other surviving child of her mother, could not help because he had a big family of his own. About her fiancé, she says the marriage might not have worked, because he might not have liked her looking after her mother.

She thinks national assistance is very good, but some people don't like asking for it because they think it's charity. She was receiving 6s. 6d. a week from the National Assistance Board; but three years ago when her step-sister died, Miss Hughes was left some money, and she immediately sent the book back to the national assistance and has received nothing from them since. She now has under £100 of savings left. She wonders whether she could get the national assistance to pay for her prescription charges. She is receiving £4 0s. 6d. contributory pension, because she worked to the age of 64. Out of this she is paying 22s. 6d. in rent and 8s. a week in prescription charges – leaving only £2 10s. for other expenses. The gas fire is expensive; she normally sits in the kitchen during the daytime with a small paraffin heater, to avoid having the gas fire on during the daytime. (She is not aware that she is currently entitled to national assistance.)

She was one year old when her father died and 48 when she lost her mother. At the age of 30 she became solely responsible for her mother, who was ill for many years; and there was also the brother-in-law and the three small children. Miss Hughes says of her life that 'for a good many years it was grim, but now it's much easier and I'm better off.' She was seldom sure how much she was going to earn in those days when she was supporting her relatives. Of a children's club in Stepney she says: 'It was the displays for the children. When I used to see them marching along looking so smart – it was the happiest thing in my life.' The unhappiest event was the death of her step-sister three years ago. The step-sister had a weak heart and a blood clot formed on her leg. The doctors wanted to amputate but waited for several weeks. Because of her heart condition they could not give her enough drugs. After the amputation she was in agony for three weeks and every time Miss Hughes went to the hospital her step-sister screamed without cease. She thinks it is wrong to allow anyone to live in so much pain. 'I didn't want to go to the hospital. Each night I was coming home alone after it, and nobody to talk to.' Calm during most of the interview, Miss Hughes shivers violently as she talks about her step-sister's death.

Groups at Risk

Mrs. Merton
Aged 82
Recent widow (1 month)
of a clog-maker
Low incapacity (1)

Oldham
Lives with single daughter
Intermediate social contact
(22)
Sometimes lonely
Intermediate anomia (2)

She is of medium height, fairly thin with grey hair neatly clasped in a hair-net. She has a scar on one cheek. She thinks she is young for her age but she looks at least 82 to me. She has lost weight since her husband died five weeks ago and the skin is loose around her neck. She is tearful when she opens the door but not thereafter. She continually talks about her husband right through the interview, although she becomes more emotional when discussing the death of her son about eighteen years ago. She lives in a quiet street near a main road. The house (c. 1890) is in fairly good shape. The front sitting-room has been decorated with real and artificial flowers by her daughter since Mr. Merton died. At the end of the interview Mrs. Merton is reluctant for me to go.

She was born about ten miles away, and came to Oldham when she was twenty. Her husband was a clog-maker. After they married, he moved around from place to place and she followed him to three different towns getting jobs in the cotton-mills. They came to live in her present house when in their early thirties. He continued to work as a clog-maker until he was 73, and then he retired; he died when he was aged 81, being one year younger than her. She herself went out to work most of her life, the last work she did was helping in a bakehouse. When she retired at 63 she missed the company – her husband was still working.

She first went out to work in 1892, the year they ceased taking 'part-timers' at the age of 10 and advanced the beginning to 11; but she worked from the age of 10, half-time for 2s. 6d. a week. She began full time at the age of 13. She first worked in the ring spinning because it paid 3d. a week more than the weaving job she wanted to do, and her mother was anxious for her to

118

earn the extra 3d. Her father was a coal miner, making 18s. a week. She had no time off for a honeymoon. She had her son after twelve months of marriage; one month after his birth she returned to work, leaving her mother to nurse the baby. She came to her mother's to fetch the baby at 1 p.m. each Saturday when they stopped work and took him back again on Sunday night to her mother's. Her youth and early adulthood were very hard – she refers to 'the bad old days'. She had arthritis even at the age of 10, and she hated getting up at 5.30 a.m. to start work at 6.30, and then going to school in the afternoons. All the time in the cotton industry she worked in the ring-room, except during the First World War when the factories made munitions.

She can get out of doors but has gone out very little recently – first she was nursing her husband, particularly for the six weeks before he died, and since then she has not felt like going out; but she went out yesterday and collected her pension. She can get upstairs, although at night sometimes she feels very tired climbing the steps. She can wash and dress herself and can cut her own toe-nails. When I come into the house she has one shoe off revealing her foot covered with corns and lumps.

She does some of the housework, particularly the lighter jobs – and she can still get down on her hands and knees. She cannot do any heavy lifting – her daughter does it. Mrs. Merton does most of the cooking including the midday meal for her daughter. Her daughter gets the shopping, because Mrs. Merton cannot carry it. Her daughter has been doing the heavy washing recently.

She has arthritis in her feet, hands and back. Her fingers are badly twisted but she can still use them quite well. She is working harder now than she has for a long time – since her husband died she has been doing as much housework as possible. With her husband's illness she has seen a lot of the doctor recently, but for herself only two or three times in the last year. Her only regular treatment is chiropody once every two months, and she would like it more frequently; she tries to look after her feet herself as well with a razor. She has not been in hospital in the last five years nor ill in bed at home. She could have gone to bed but she likes to keep moving. She claims never to have been off work. She had a vibrous tumour removed from a breast in 1961 and a growth on her face was removed ten years ago. She goes to the doctor if she has anything serious – unlike her husband whose cancer was well advanced before the doctor knew about it. If she were ill now her daughter would look after her.

She eats quite well, although immediately after her husband died she ate little. At breakfast she has bread and marmalade and coffee. When her husband was alive she used to have a nice breakfast of ham and mushrooms – he was fond of breakfast. At midday today, she and her daughter had fish and new potatoes and peas. At tea they have cold meat, salad and fruit. At night she has tea and a biscuit. When she was at the mill 'I never had no time to have a meal. I've had a better appetite recently'. She used to have only an hour at midday and she always came back and got a meal for herself and the rest of the family. She used to eat her meal walking about the house. She now eats all meals with her daughter who can get back from the shop to eat with her at midday.

She does not want a home help; she thinks some people have home helps despite having daughters living near by. Several people in the street have helps but she doesn't know much about them. She has bi-focal glasses for knitting, reading and watching television. She can see quite well. Her hearing is good. She thinks sufficient is done for older people in the locality – people who are in need only have to ask. She thinks Government financial provision is adequate, but that she and her husband were silly to save, 'we hadn't the sense to spend it'. She is against children's allowances.

She had only two children, the son who is dead and the daughter who lives with her. Her son was married at 30 and died aged 39. He worked in a mill and died of a brain tumour. It was caused by a blow he received on his head at work, although she was not told about this until after he had died. He was suffering from double vision, but went on working and did not go to the doctor. Mrs. Merton is very upset about her son and shows me his picture. He had no children. The son's wife remarried a year after he died and she has not been to see them since the funeral of her son. Mrs. Merton knew her daughter-in-law was not going to come from the way she behaved when the son died.

Interviews

The daughter was thirteen years younger than the son. Mrs. Merton says she has never bothered with any men and she is a very good girl. She does not have any real friends to go out with but she knows people at work. When Mr. Merton was dying her daughter did 'more for him than I can tell'. She has absolutely no complaints about her daughter.

Mrs. Merton was the eighth in a family of ten children. Four died in infancy. As a small child she was one of a group of four children, the two others were already married. But they're all dead now, she was the only one who lived to 80. The only relatives she sees are one of her husband's nephews and his wife. She has about five nephews and nieces – the oldest in her 70's – but she sees little of them. All her husband's brothers and sisters had died too.

The neighbours all work and she thinks young people don't want to bother with neighbours, except to ask them to let in the gas man. She says a neighbour next door gassed himself recently. She also lists five men in the street who have died during the last year (at this point the interview becomes a catalogue of death after death).

Time for her goes rather too quickly. Her main pleasure is knitting which passes a lot of time. When her husband was still alive she did a good deal of reading; he didn't read books himself, but he liked her to read. Since his death she has switched from reading to knitting, 'I sit a lot, knitting, and watch folks go past outside. I'm getting that way when you don't want to go out again.' She recently knitted a complete suit for her daughter which she shows me (a very determined effort considering her arthritically bent fingers). She watches television most evenings but can't mention any favourite programme; she likes good plays but there haven't been any recently. She sometimes listens to the radio. Her main activity apart from knitting is domestic work; if she weren't talking to me she would be scrubbing the back yard. They have one newspaper every day, the *Manchester Evening News*. When her husband was alive they also had the *Daily Express*.

She had no time to belong to anything when she was younger but more recently she belonged to the local old folk's club with her husband. He didn't go to the meetings and she didn't go often. They gave it up six years ago when he was getting too ill.

Groups at Risk

The main interest for both of them was going on holidays and they went to Weston-super-Mare, Great Yarmouth, Torquay and Bournemouth – all with the old people's club.

They rent the house from the National Coal Board; it previously belonged to the private pit owner. The rent, including rates, is £1 a week. The house has two bedrooms, a front sitting-room, a back kitchen and sitting-room. There is no bath and the toilet is outside. She and her husband have spent a lot of money on the house in fifty years, and recently they put in two new fireplaces. She thinks the Coal Board are good landlords; she is quite satisfied with the house and doesn't want to move, although it's cold in winter.

Her husband died of cancer. He was ill for six years from the age of 75 onwards. Two years ago he had a prostate operation and then deteriorated slowly. He went into hospital about eight weeks before he died. He was in hospital for six weeks before they operated on him. He was in much pain before he went into hospital because of 'bladder trouble – the cancer was in his stomach'. In the operation his bladder was removed and 'a thing was strapped to his leg'. He asked how long he would have to pass water in this way and when he was told it was permanent he said 'is that all you can do for me?' She says 'it broke his heart'. He died two weeks later. The funeral was attended by herself, her daughter, her husband's nephew and his wife and nobody else. Before he went into hospital she was looking after him night and day at home. For the last three weeks he was at home she didn't once take her clothes off. She sleeps quite well now and even drinks coffee before going to bed at night. She says she knows nothing about young people being widowed but in her experience as an old person 'it's bad enough'. They were married for fifty-nine years. People say she at least has her memories, but memories are no use.

Her husband used to drink a bottle of beer at home in the evenings, but he seldom went to a pub in later years. He was always at home with her and he always liked 'going' with her. When he was dying of cancer he felt very cold and they had a fire burning throughout the summer. After he retired he mostly just sat in the kitchen; she talks particularly of this time when she was with him twenty-four hours a day. After he retired they went away on short holidays four times a year but 'it didn't last long'. Her daughter was very good in nursing her father and would devote her evenings when she came in from work to looking after him – she nicknamed her father 'Tom Trouble'. Mrs. Merton says 'he didn't want to die. The doctor told me six years ago it would be slow. He had a lot of pain in him.' He never knew he was suffering from cancer.

Of national assistance she says she knows 'nowt about it'. All she has is the £3 7s. 6d. pension; she didn't keep up her own stamps when she was working, otherwise she might have had a slightly higher pension in her own right – 'I didn't know what was going to happen in those days'. They spent most of their savings after her husband retired, and when he died there was very little left. He didn't leave a will, the only thing left was a few hundred pounds' worth of insurance policies. Her total income is £3 7s. 6d. but the daughter goes out to work full-time.

Her father was a coal miner and he died at 65. He would come home dirty from the pit and he got drunk on Saturdays at the pub after he had divided the money with the other members of his gang. She says those days were awful and she was not a happy child. Her mother lived to be 73 and was going to come and live with her, but she died in hospital. About her life she says 'it's not been bad. Hard like, especially at the beginning.' The happiest time of her life was certainly not when she was young. It was round about the time of retiring, for a few years at the beginning of her husband's retirement before he became ill. 'There wasn't much pleasure till I got older.' She wouldn't like to live her younger life over again. She was her father's favourite child and when drunk he used to tell her that if she had been a boy he would have wanted her to come and work in his gang. 'If I'd been a boy I'd have had to have gone down the pit with him.'

Groups at Risk

Mrs. Leach   Oldham
Aged 84   Lives with husband
Married to retired   Intermediate social contact
  butcher   (28)
High incapacity (8)   Never lonely
Housebound (4 years)   Intermediate anomia (2)

She is upstairs lying in a double bed, and has been housebound
for about three years. Her hair is neatly brushed and she looks
quite healthy. She gets up in the afternoon, and is suffering
mainly from arthritis. Her husband when he stands still looks
a splendid figure with his upright stance and white moustache.
When he walks he has a very bad arthritic limp; his eyesight is
failing – but despite his age of 86 he does most of the domestic
work and the cooking. The semi-detached house was built by
the council in 1947, but the Leachs now own it; it is in a quiet
street next to a football field, and Mr. Leach keeps it very tidy.
Downstairs there are pictures of Highland cattle and upstairs
large photographs of the children taken about thirty years ago.

She was born in a village in Yorkshire, where she met her
husband. He was running a small hill farm, which is now
farmed by one of their sons. She has lived in the Oldham district
most of the time since she was married in 1904, at the age of 24,
but they lived back in Yorkshire on the farm for a few years.

Since his marriage, Mr. Leach worked mainly as a butcher
in Oldham. Mrs. Leach helped him in the butcher's shop.
Before marriage she worked for her mother in the dressmaking
shop in the North Yorkshire village where her husband also
grew up. Her husband only completely stopped work at the
butcher's shop when he was aged 82; but some years ago he
handed over the business to one of the sons. The son has now
sold the business but he lives across the street from them.

She cannot walk outside, although she can climb the stairs
with some difficulty; they have a hand-rail on both sides of
the rather steep staircase. At one time she was unable to
climb the stairs at all, and for about three years slept on the
ground floor – 'I couldn't get into the kitchen to make a cup

124

of tea; it was prayer that improved me'. Now she can move about reasonably well on the ground floor; she has to hold on to the furniture, and says she has made handmarks on all the walls. She has some trouble getting in and out of bed. She can wash herself quite well now, although two or three years ago she couldn't. She can dress herself all right, except she can't put the stocking on her left leg; her husband has done this for her, for some years now. She only wears slippers and can get these on quite easily. She can't do her toe-nails, and a chiropodist comes every eight weeks. She keeps saying 'you've got to persevere'. She does light jobs, particularly the washing-up, which her husband doesn't like doing and the dusting, because his eyesight is not good enough. She can't do any heavy cleaning, her husband cleans every day and her daughter comes once a week to do other jobs. She can't stand up long enough and when she does some cooking, sits down for it. Most of the shopping is delivered twice a week by the local shop. 'If we run out, we have to do without.' All the heavier washing goes to the laundry, although she does some of the light things. Her husband won't make the bed, so she herself straightens it out each day and her daughter turns the mattress and puts on clean sheets when she comes.

It is difficult to determine exactly how long she has been housebound, but it seems to be about four years. She gets taken out by car; a friend of their son comes to fetch her and her husband and take them to church on Sunday evenings. They're really Church of England, but he goes to a chapel and they are happy to go with him there. Their son across the street has a car which he uses in his business and he takes her out every few weeks; her husband goes out with him more often. She is housebound for the simple reason of rheumatoid arthritis – which she has particularly in her feet and hands, but also in her knees and back. It is painful sometimes, but not when she is lying in bed – as she does all the time except for a few hours in the afternoon. She can stand up quite well with a stick, but only for a few minutes, after which she has to sit down. She can raise her hands and do her own hair, feed herself, and attend to her own toilet. Getting out into the garden is a struggle because there are three steps. She went out a few weeks ago and pegged up some washing on the line; after this, she was trembling all over. Asked what is the worst thing about being housebound, she says how difficult it is to get stamps and get letters posted. She also misses shopping. When I ask whether there are any compensations she can't think of any. Asked whether enough is done for older people who are housebound, she says she doesn't know – she receives nothing from anyone except the calls of the chiropodist. Asked about the Government's help for housebound people, again she doesn't know: 'we've always been used to pain'.

She hasn't seen the doctor for four years. 'I don't need him. He said there was nothing he could do for arthritis.' She has never bothered with doctors much. When she last saw the doctor four years ago she was worse than she is now. But she is weaker – 'a wind could blow me over'. Since being housebound she has lost about one stone in weight. The chiropodist comes once every eight weeks but she would like him to come more often. 'My toe-nails grow so quick, and I've got corns that hurt.' Her feet are sore and swollen and she has rheumatism in her toes. She has never been in hospital in her life. After a very bad bout of arthritis four years ago, she began sleeping on the ground floor and, despite the doctor telling her nothing could be done, she rubbed herself with olive oil; she thinks this eventually relieved her arthritis.

She doesn't have meals-on-wheels and would not want them. 'He'd rather cook his own.' She has tea and toast for breakfast. The midday meal is normally cooked by her husband and consists of meat, potatoes, vegetables, and a sweet. She has a light tea and a hot drink at night. The food is delivered twice weekly by a shop they have dealt with for many years. They get their bread from this shop, also only twice a week. Sometimes they run out of things and then they have to do without. Although their son lives across the road and the neighbours have offered to help, nobody in fact buys them food. The husband does almost all of the cooking. Some days she has her midday meal in bed and sometimes downstairs with her husband; she has tea with him and comes up to bed again in the late afternoon or early evening.

For five years they had a private domestic help. But she ceased coming a year ago, when she was 60. The husband employed somebody else for a short time, but then decided that it

Interviews

wasn't worth the money – 10s. a morning. The new cleaner asked for a Hoover and Mr. Leach said he could push a Hoover as well as any woman – 'he's very independent'. The only person she knows who had a home help was her daughter-in-law, and her help was good.

She wears glasses, but has some difficulty with seeing. She sent her glasses through the post to the optician, but he sent them back – saying he couldn't improve on them. Her eyesight got worse when she was about 70, but it has since improved, at least for reading. She can't remember when she last had her eyes tested, but thinks it was about thirty years ago. She hasn't got a hearing aid and admits some difficulty with hearing. I talk loudly from about six feet away and have to repeat a sentence every now and then. She says 'sometimes I wish I had a hearing aid. I wish my husband had one, too. We always shout at each other. If anyone hears they'll think he must be fighting.' I suggest that if she wants a hearing aid she ought to consult her doctor, but she doesn't think she will.

Asked about services for older people in general in the locality, she doesn't know about them, but she herself can't grumble. 'We've never worried anybody. But people are very nice and kind.' This seems to refer to neighbours who have offered help. About the pension, she says she doesn't know anything; she and her husband don't have a pension. She doesn't know how much money the old age pension is, nor does she know anything about children's allowances.

She has four children, all of them alive. The eldest is a son, aged 59, who is working the farm which she and her husband still own in North Yorkshire; he has four children and she last saw him a year ago when they went over to stay on the farm for a month. She has two daughters, one of whom lives about twenty miles away, also on a farm, and is married with three children; she comes to see her mother and father about once a month, a journey involving three bus changes. The third child is another married daughter, with three children; she lives about half a mile away and comes to see her mother once a week – she then does the heavier cleaning jobs and some washing, but she doesn't bring any shopping. The last child is the son who lives across the street. He also is married with three children.

Groups at Risk

After giving up Mr. Leach's butcher's shop the son now drives round markets in Lancashire, selling materials. He is away quite often, but he comes in to see them once or twice a week, and Mr. Leach is able to walk across the street sometimes to see him. Mrs. Leach likes her daughter-in-law, but the children are fairly young and the daughter-in-law goes out to work. The only regular help they receive from their children is the housework which the daughter does once a week. They receive no financial help, but the eldest son is renting his farm from them at £2 a week. They went to stay with him for a month last year, but are not going again this year. Both of them have got weaker since last year and it is difficult because the son has to be out working all day and they are left in the house with the daughter-in-law. Mrs. Leach has thirteen grandchildren and four great-grandchildren.

She herself was the third in a family of five children. The two eldest died long ago and the youngest is also dead. She has one sister still alive in New Zealand, who is 83 years old and married; the sister came over six years ago on a visit, but Mrs. Leach doesn't expect to see her again.

They see one of her husband's brothers about once a month or so. She has quite a number of nephews and nieces, including four who live in her native village. When they were visiting her son last year, all four took them out for drives, but they don't see any nephews or nieces regularly. They also see very little of their grandchildren. They are on speaking terms with the neighbours, but since Mrs. Leach never goes out, she seldom sees them. Both the next-door neighbours have offered to do things, and recently one neighbour, a school teacher, told them that in any emergency, they must knock on the wall. Mrs. Leach was very relieved to hear this, although normally they don't bother the neighbours at all. There is one friend who pays occasional visits. But her social life consists almost entirely of living with her husband and seeing her children.

Time never goes slowly. Her main pleasure in life is a good book. They have some old books in the house and she likes the old ones best, especially 'a good love tale'. (In fact, I suspect that she doesn't read very much now.) She doesn't bother with newspapers, although her husband has the *Daily Mail* and the local weekly paper. About two years ago she read a story about two elderly sisters being attacked by a burglar; it frightened her and she didn't want to read newspapers any more. They had a second-hand TV, but she thought it was 'demoralizing and disgusting', and they had it taken away. She listens to the radio, especially the news. She sews a little, but her arthritis prevents her from doing much. Rubbing her limbs seems to be about her major activity. Her husband used to be keen on reading, but his eyesight is failing now. He can only read the headlines of a newspaper, which is a big loss to him.

She has never joined things and says, 'I stay at home.' When you're in a shop and you have children you don't have any time. She thinks that old people's clubs are all right, but she herself has always been a home lover. She would like to have a wheelchair. She wonders if I could help her to get one. But her husband and children say she would get killed in the street if she had one. Her husband comes in at this point and says earnestly that he would like her to have one if he thought she would be safe with a wheelchair, but he does not. They write about once a fortnight to one or other of the children. She can use a telephone, but they do not have one.

They own the house, which has three bedrooms, two other rooms, plus kitchen and bathroom. They find nothing inconvenient about the house. It is not too large, and they don't want to move.

She knows nothing about national assistance, and they don't have it. They have no contributory pension, because when her husband went into the butchering business he never bothered with the self-employed stamps. He says their joint income is £6 10s. a week. The main source of income is from four houses which he owns and which bring in about £4 10s. a week rent. He has sold four other houses, and they are spending the proceeds of this. His other income is £2 a week which his sons pay him for the hill farm in Yorkshire. He says their income remains stationary, they spend their savings, and prices go up.

Her father died when she was 7 and her mother was left with five small children to bring up. I say to Mr. Leach it seems strange his wife has not seen the doctor for four years, and he comments on doctors in general that they only say 'What do you expect at your age?' so then you don't bother with doctors any more.

Chapter Six

SINGLE

I. SINGLE AND ALONE

The single state is associated with social isolation (Table 3.4), and the single are more likely than old people in general to live alone (Table 2.1). Whether or not a single old person lives alone is connected with the availability of siblings; but the four-area survey indicates that the single mainly live with *single* siblings. Of single women who had a single brother or sister alive, two-thirds were sharing a household with one; however, of those with only married or widowed brothers and sisters alive, only a sixth were living with one.

Although there is a sharp correlation with living alone and isolation, the single state does not predispose old people to loneliness; 28 per cent of the single and the same proportion of all old people are often or sometimes lonely. Elderly bachelors may be somewhat more lonely than old men in general; but 28 per cent of single women are lonely against the larger figure of 34 per cent of all old women (Table 4.3).

The single in general are less anomic than all old people, but this difference is particularly striking among single women; only 4 per cent of elderly spinsters are anomic, against 14 per cent of all women and 19 per cent of all old people (Table 5.4).

The smallness of the group of single men makes caution necessary. But there is some evidence here of a difference between single old men and women.

Of the 538 old people in the four-area survey only 58 were single; 55 of these – 11 men and 44 women – completed the second interview, in which further questions were asked about being single.[1]

[1] The four-area survey with 58 single out of 538 and the cross-national with 260 out of 2,500 compare as follows:

Why Single?

2. WHY SINGLE?

The single women had a median age in 1914 of 25 years; the youngest had been 17. Granted the shortage of men resulting from the 1914–18 war, some women were certain to remain single. But do any particular characteristics seem to have predisposed women or men to remain single?

One of the major concerns of old people throughout their lives has inevitably been their work. Only two of the forty-four single women had not been out at work for most of their lives. The biggest category, factory work, consisted mainly of women who had worked in the Oldham cotton industry or the Northampton boot and shoe industry. The two next largest categories are domestic service and teaching which together account for a third of all the single women. Those in domestic service had mainly been resident servants in large houses in London or in the country, and all began work before 1914. In these houses they saw few young men, apart from the odd groom, gardener, or butler; they worked long hours, were only allowed out briefly in the early evening, and went home to visit their parents once or twice a year. The women teachers' work similarly cut them off from young men. Two of the eight taught in adult educational institutions, but the rest – from primary teachers to the headmistress of a girls' grammar school – worked in schools where the other teachers were entirely or mainly women.

Another common factor between teaching and domestic service is an atmosphere of social rising – and women who do such work may be reluctant to marry 'down' socially, and thus to reject the only men available to them. Several of the teachers reported a difficult struggle to go to training college or university (two went to London and one to Cambridge). The domestic servants when they started work, were considered fortunate to

	National	Four-area
Proportion of women who are single	14·2%	14 %
Proportion of men who are single	4·7	5·7
Proportion of single who are lonely, often or sometimes	27·8	38
Proportion of single women who live alone	46·5	59

On the proportion of single men the four-area survey is closer than the national survey to the 1961 Census – which shows 7·6 per cent of old men to be single. See Table 2.2.

Single

get the job – one said she was the envy of all the other girls in her village.

An hypothesis suggested by some previous evidence was that single women would come from a particular position in the sibling order; the youngest daughter might be reluctant to get married if this meant leaving an ageing parent to live alone. However, the four-area survey suggests that sibling position is not a significant variable. The median situation was having four live-born brothers and sisters with the single person being third – exactly in the middle. But probably the whole hypothesis is based on a false assumption – namely that children married and then left the home. However, at the beginning of this century many young married couples lived in one of the parental homes after marriage,[2] consequently, a young woman who was living with and determined to look after a frail surviving parent might, in fact, be able to do so more effectively if she married and brought her husband to live in the home. How many of these single people were looking after parents in early adulthood? Unfortunately there is no systematic evidence on this point, but there is information about the ages of the old people at the time when their own father and mother died. At the age of 25, 38 per cent had lost their fathers and 25 per cent their mothers; at this age, 44 per cent had *one* parent alive – while the remainder had both or neither. At the age of 20 it was only 34 per cent. Not all of these young people with one parent alive were the only child still unmarried – half of them come from families of five or more children. Were this the real factor in remaining single one would expect a number of only children – unable to pass on responsibility for their parents to other siblings – to appear in the single group. In fact only children were under-represented, making up 2 per cent of the single elderly in the four-area sample.

True, some single old people say they stayed single because of responsibility to their parents, or because their parents tried to prevent them marrying. But this is a fairly obvious rationalization; moreover, parents often resist children getting married to particular people or at a particular age.

Most single old people are extremely devoted to the memory

[2] For instance, see Seebohm Rowntree, *Poverty: A Study of Town Life* (1901), pp. 16–25.

of one or both parents. When speaking of their parents' deaths they sound strangely like widows talking about their husbands dying. The majority have continued to live with their parents, and then the one surviving parent, until the latter died. The median age for this single group when their *second* parent died was age 43; seven-tenths lost their second parent between the ages of 35 and 55. It is hardly surprising that a single woman should have been especially devoted to a parent (usually her mother) with whom she had lived for forty-three years – especially in the absence of spouse or her own children. Given, further, that the death of this second parent often left the single person living alone for the first time in her life, and since the loss so often occurred near the time of the menopause, the second parental death becomes a unique watershed in the single person's past.

Bad health is another obvious factor which may prevent people from marrying. The old people were not asked specifically about this, but some information was obtained about ill-health in youth. There were cases of polio in infancy, an unspecified major operation 'which made a mess of me', nervous illness, eyesight too poor to allow the child to go out to school or work, a partially club foot, and St. Vitus dance. Four other spinsters had had 'nervous breakdowns' or mental illness. Three had breakdowns at ages 30, 34 and 40; one was in a mental hospital from the age of 19 onwards. A quarter of the single group had had severe physical or other illness in youth. In one case (polio) it almost certainly did affect marriage prospects, and in the others it may have.

What about personality or other presumably relevant factors, such as appearance? One is nearly as difficult to investigate as the other. Appearance might be the easier, since the old people frequently have photos of themselves in early adulthood. There is certainly a different atmosphere in interviews with spinsters compared for instance with widows. Some spinsters say they have always been shy, and often they do appear shy and with-drawn. But obviously this may be result, not cause of their remaining single.[3]

If would be difficult enough to investigate why people *did* get married forty, fifty or sixty years ago. But *not* getting married

[3] For a discussion on personality, see Chapter 12.

is something which spreads over a much longer time period, during which the social and other circumstances of the individual may have radically changed.

The positive evidence about particular occupations such as domestic service and teaching is tentative. So also is the evidence about illness in early adulthood. There does not seem to be one basic social factor. The shortage of men in the relevant age-groups seems to have meant that a wide variety of women remained single.

3. WHAT DO THEY SAY ABOUT BEING SINGLE?

Despite the lack of evidence about the impact of sibling position or responsibility for parents, when the single were asked 'Does it have anything to do with your parents or with being the oldest or youngest child?', two-fifths of the spinsters answered in the affirmative. Some said, quite simply, that their parents had required care and attention:

'My mother came first. I nursed her.' *Dressmaking worker, Harrow.*

'I couldn't find the heart to leave father. I felt my duties were at home. I wouldn't have done if there'd been another girl.' *Baker's assistant, Oldham.*

Others talked of their parents being possessive and generally hostile to marriage:

'They didn't like me having a young man at all. Perhaps they wanted me to look after them. My elder sister was a real old maid. She and my father didn't like my Canadian man friend.' *Smallholder, Norfolk.*

'Her mother "always stood in my way" and was strict and interfering. When she had a week-end off her mother was very insistent that she should go back home for the week-end.' *Domestic servant, Norfolk.*

'I had a very strict father. He told me not to talk to men on the trains.' *Teacher, Harrow.*

'I was brought up by my grandmother. She wouldn't let me talk to no boys. She was very strict.' *Discharged mental patient, Norfolk.*

Another single woman said that conflict between her parents had disillusioned her about marriage:

What Do They Say About Being Single?

'My father was a drunkard. I saw what he did to my mother. I used to say to him "Some day I'll kill you."' *Domestic servant, Harrow.*

Despite this, however, the majority of single old women did not think their staying single had anything to do with siblings or responsibility to parents:

'I am the eldest. But when I was engaged, my father was unselfish, and never stood in my way.' *Domestic cleaner, Northampton.*

'My mother wanted me to get married and was sorry when I didn't.' *Teacher, Harrow.*

When asked 'Was there somebody you were engaged to or nearly married?' a full third of the single women answered in the affirmative – nearly as many as gave a firm negative reply.

Some women mentioned a specific man who was killed in the 1914–18 war:

'She was aged 18 in 1914. Her fiancé was killed on the Somme.' *Machine operator, Northampton.*

'Yes. I was engaged to one boy and then to another – both were killed in the war. What could you do when all the best young men had been killed?' *Teacher, Harrow.*

Others met men from abroad during the First World War and were then parted from them. Two were reluctant to emigrate to an unknown life:

'There was a boy I could've married. He went to Canada and came back for me. But I didn't fancy going to Canada.' *Machine operator, Oldham.*

Some of the intermediate replies went like this:

'I wasn't engaged, but I did have a romance.' *Teacher, Harrow.*

'A lot of men asked her to go out, but since she was in domestic service she was not allowed to. She did go out with a gardener and thinks she could have married him if she had wanted, but she changed to another man, didn't like him so much – and was too proud to go back to the gardener.' *Housemaid, Norfolk.*

Before either of these two questions, another more general one was asked: 'How was it that you did not marry?' Few of the single women point to parents or family reasons – only a

135

tenth mention this spontaneously against a third who give an affirmative answer when asked specifically about it.

Nearly half of those replying never came near getting married. About a third mention a man or men in their lives, while a smaller number give family reasons or ill-health as the explanation.

When asked whether being single affects the ordinary social life of an older person, the majority of answers are negative. But there is difficulty in replying – a third made no definite reply. Some single old women feel that other people expect a single person to lead a quite different form of life:

'Some married women used to say that single women were different. I hated that. It's not true. I helped my mother bring -up the younger children and I helped with my sister's delivery.' *Domestic servant, Harrow.*

'A lot of people think you're not the same. Assume you didn't have the chance. But I know what to say to them – "You weren't such a good picker yourself."' *Teacher, Harrow.*

'What I don't like is when they look at you as if you've never lived. You haven't had children and haven't had a man about the house, but you're no different.' *Cotton worker, Oldham.*

A few single women do say that being single affects their social life:

'Yes. At church they often invite married couples out, but not us single ones. We always laugh at it.' *Cotton worker, Oldham.*

'Yes. It's quite a different life, when you think of your married sisters with families. But it must be worse for widows.' *Home nurse, Harrow.*

However, the majority of those who answered denied that their single state affected their social life.

The single were also asked whether there were any compensations for staying single, such as being more independent. Only a quarter of those who answered thought there were none: the majority thought there were compensations – especially negative ones such as avoidance of an unhappy marriage. But there was little sign of the single state being viewed as a positive opportunity for a woman to pursue her own career and develop her own interests. None said it had been necessary to remain single to develop her full potentialities as a machine operator,

What Do They Say About Being Single?

or for that matter, as a schoolteacher. The others spoke of compensations rather than positive advantages:

'You can do as you like. If I'd married a bully . . .' *Machine operator, Oldham.*

'Your money's your own.' *Cinema usherette, Oldham.*

'I wouldn't have been able to go to Australia if I'd been married – I went to visit my sister. Marriage is limiting in a way.' *Teacher, Harrow.*

'Yes, there are advantages. Men aren't always clean about the house.' *Boot and shoe worker, Northampton.*

The single were also asked whether they would have liked to have had children. Two-thirds of the spinsters who gave any answer said they would have liked children. Only a fifth were against having children.[4] With some of the single women, children were definitely more popular than husbands.

But a few women were not attracted by the idea of children:

'I've never been fond of children. I held a child for one of my sisters – it was born prematurely, weighing 3½ pounds – after that I never cared for children.' *Smallholder, Norfolk.*

'I've never liked small children a lot. I prefer ones age 15 to 16 – the age I taught them at.' *Teacher, Harrow.*

In contrast, those who would have liked to have had children were more enthusiastic:

'Married life's not much without a child. They're handy for you when you're older.' *Boot and shoe machinist, Northampton.*

'Yes. I like children. And when I see women with their grown-up children around them, I regret it.' *Dressmaker, Harrow.*

'Yes, I'd leave off if there weren't any children. I liked all my nephews and nieces when they were small – I made things for them. They're not interested in me now.' *Teacher, Harrow.*

The strong preference for having children is the most clear and unanimous attitude of these elderly spinsters. About a third were once engaged or nearly married to men, while a slightly higher proportion claim that their family background had something to do with their staying single. Most single women minimize differences between themselves and women

---

[4] One of the forty-four single women re-interviewed had a child. See also Table 2.1 which shows 2 per cent of all single old people to be living with their children.

Single

who have been married, with the one major exception that most of them would have liked to have had children.

4. SINGLE MEN

The most socially isolated person in the whole sample is a single man – with a social contact score of zero:

He is aged 69, and lives by himself in a tumbledown cottage, half a mile from a hamlet, a mile and a half from a large village. To reach his cottage you have to walk from the road across a field about 400 yards. He has no electric power, no piped water, an outside chemical toilet and uses paraffin for cooking and heating. He is a very thin, rather anxious man, with a projecting red nose. In his sitting-room there is almost no furniture, no tables or cupboards, just three upright chairs and large neat piles of old newspapers on the bare brick floor.

He worked on his father's smallholding in Essex. In recent years he has had his own smallholdings in several different places in East Anglia. Four years ago, when he was 65, he gave up his last smallholding and retired to this cottage and half an acre of land, on which he keeps thirty chickens. He is in good health, apart from being deaf. He saw his doctor about this a year ago. The nearest neighbour lives a quarter of a mile away.

He was one of six children. Two are dead, and he has two single sisters who live together on the south coast and who write to him on his birthday and at Christmas; he has not seen them for thirty years. He thinks the brother, a clergyman, is still alive – but has not seen him for many years. He occasionally chats (but not in the last month) to two farmers who live in his vicinity. He does not use the one local shop, but every day walks a mile and a half to the large village to buy his food, paraffin and his newspaper. His other main activity is looking after his chickens and growing vegetables. He has no TV or radio.

He thinks he manages all right and is probably best being single. He was never engaged. He lived with his parents, but this wasn't why he remained single. His unhappiest time was when his mother died – he was 35. His only income is the £3 7s. 6d. old age pension, and he has a small amount of savings which he does not touch. He seems to avoid talking to people in the village, and is only vaguely known at the local shop – which is visible through his dirty windows. Apart from being deaf, shy and rather nervous, he shows no obvious signs of physical or mental illness.

Single Men

The bachelors as a group, however, do not provide many sharp differences from the spinsters – with the obvious exception of the sort of work they have done. Of the eleven single men, the majority have siblings alive, don't think being single affects an older person's social life, were not engaged or nearly married, do not think it had anything to do with their parents, but would have liked to have had children.

5. THE WORLD OF THE SINGLE

Single old people live in a separate world from most contemporaries who are married or have children. Almost all of the single have spent the greater part of their lives out at work – but now in retirement, half of the elderly single in this sample are living alone and most of these are socially isolated. When they retire they are cut off from a major, or the major, source of social contact in their lives.

But even before retirement, many of the spinsters have been living in a single world; women in this sample who taught in schools where all of the teachers were women, or those who were in domestic service, are perhaps the extreme examples. The two spinsters in the sample who had done clerical work both commented that before the Second World War their firms never employed married women. Others did, of course, work alongside married women; in Oldham there is a long tradition of married women in the cotton industry, and in the Northampton boot and shoe industry, the single had worked alongside the married women. However, in this respect the present sample is probably somewhat biased – and it remains true that in the population of elderly single women, many will have had comparatively little contact, even at work, with other than single women. One must remember here that the boom in employment for married women after 1940 came only near the end of most of these women's working careers.

When they retire nearly half of all single old women live alone. Most of those who share a home do so with single or widowed siblings. Out of forty-six spinsters in the four-area sample only two live with a married couple.

Of course the single do have social contact with others,

including married and widowed people. They have even sometimes played a major part in bringing up children:

'She used to take her sister's children around London a good deal – "That's why I never went away on holiday."' *Dressmaker, Harrow.*

'Her nephew was left with three children, aged 5, 7 and 11, and she helped him bring them up.' *Cotton worker, Oldham.*

'She says that her sister was living at home, so she helped bring up the niece. Later when the niece had an illegitimate child, she had the baby for a year.' *Catering worker, Oldham.*

'Her sister died in childbirth. She and another sister looked after the two children. She visited the home every day, bathed the children, and bought them clothes. "That's why I didn't bother with getting married."' *Machine operator, Oldham.*

A tenth had had this major role in bringing up children. Another task performed by some single women was nursing relatives on their sick-beds or death-beds. A third reported having done protracted nursing (usually for a year or more).

Miss S. is aged 78 and lives alone. The interview takes place in a back sitting-room with an unmade double bed – on which her sister died two months ago. The sister was 88, had been widowed for some years and had been left some money by her husband. The sister spent her time in an arm-chair sitting on top of some envelopes, each of which was full of five-pound notes. She threw grape pips on the floor and meat for the cat. 'But when they're like that, what can you say? Her mind was gone.'

Miss S. had to lift her sister on to the commode. Then the sister would become anxious about the money, and to calm her Miss S. had to hold up the envelopes so her sister could see them from her position on the commode.

Miss S. says her own arthritis has got worse since nursing her sister. She can get out to the shops, but she was not well enough to attend the funeral. After her sister died she used to walk around talking to herself and asking the cat where her sister had got to. 'For several weeks I didn't have the wireless on. I forgot I had it.' *Northampton.*

A fifth of the spinsters had done protracted nursing of their mothers. Since the father tends to die first, they are more often nursed by the mother, whereas mothers get nursed more by children.

The World of the Single

Death looms close to many spinsters. If sibling and parent–child relationships are the closest, the typical elderly spinster may have only one sibling and no other close kin still living. In contrast, a married or widowed old woman has a quite different picture because the typical person will have children. Moreover, as deaths occur among siblings, and other contemporaries, they are seen against a background of birth – as grandchildren and great-grandchildren appear. But the typical spinster has no prospect of acquiring new close kin and most or all of her close kin have already died.

Chapter Seven

RECENTLY WIDOWED

I. RECENT WIDOWHOOD

Widowhood makes an old person more likely to live alone, to be socially isolated, or to feel lonely. Forty-one per cent of the elderly are widows and widowers; but widowhood plays an even bigger part in old age because half of the 48 per cent whose spouses are still alive will eventually survive them. Thus those who are already widowed and those who will be widowed together constitute almost two-thirds of the elderly population. Moreover since the longer life expectation of women is so marked – and so well known among old people – married women can realistically regard their eventual widowhood as a normal part of the process of growing old.

Among the widowed there are old people in widely differing circumstances. Some have been widowed very recently and are still suffering from shock and perhaps loss of sleep; others have been widowed many years ago. A sizeable group of women were widowed during the 1914–18 war. Some of those, especially if they had no children, have much in common with single women; like the single they tend to have spent most of their lives going out to work.

The present chapter concentrates on the recently widowed group, those whose spouses died less than five years ago. In the four-area screening operation sixty of these recently widowed old people were interviewed, and fifty-four were re-interviewed by the author.

Recently widowed women as Table 7.1 shows are younger than other widows. Of old women widowed less than five years 72 per cent are aged under 75, against only 43 per cent of women widowed at least twenty years ago. The median age of recently widowed women is about 72 years, whilst those

Recent Widowhood

TABLE 7.1 WIDOWED WOMEN: DURATION OF
WIDOWHOOD AND AGE

| Age | Duration of widowhood | | | | | All old women (including single and married) |
	Up to 5 years	5–9 years	10–14 years	15–19 years	20+ years	
65– 9	36	28	22	23	15	34
70–74	36	34	27	28	28	29
75–79	15	21	25	23	22	19
80+	12	17	26	25	34	18
Total	100	100	100	100	100	100
Number	138	154	128	94	29	1496

Source : National survey.

widowed for at least twenty years have a median age of around 76 years.

The median duration of widowhood among those widowed up to five years appears to be less than 2·5 years of widowhood; quite apart from the question of whether being widowed in itself reduces an old person's life expectation any group of people with a median age in the early seventies must suffer attrition by death. Among those widowed less than five years, the four-area survey indicates a median duration of widowhood of just under two years.

2. LONELINESS AND SOCIAL ISOLATION

The widowed in general have a bigger chance of being lonely (Table 4.3) than married or single old people; they are also more disposed to social isolation than are the married (Table 3.4). Recent widows are more anomic than other widows (Table 5.4). The following are percentages of particular groups of old women saying they are often or sometimes lonely:

Recently widowed	52 per cent are lonely
Widowed 20 years or more	39 per cent are lonely
Single	28 per cent are lonely
Married	22 per cent are lonely

(National sample – 1,496 women)

143

Within the recently widowed group, old women who had seen a child on the day of interview or previous day were less likely to be lonely (48 per cent) than those who had not seen a child so recently – 57 per cent of whom were lonely (national).

But recently widowed women have broadly the same pattern of interaction with their children as do widows of longer duration; 84 per cent of recent widows have at least one child alive. Of those who have any children alive 89 per cent have seen at least one in the last week (national). Since children are the main source of contact for all widows, recent widows as a group would be expected not to differ greatly from other widows on social isolation. The four-area survey shows 35 per cent of the recently widowed of both sexes to be isolated against 32 per cent for all widowed old people.

3. TO LIVE ALONE OR WITH OTHERS?

Over two-thirds of married old women live only with their husbands; when the husband dies they are left living alone. Table 7.2 shows 68 per cent of married women living with their husband only and 54 per cent of recently widowed women living alone.

As compared with the married, however, there are some types of household more common amongst the recently widowed. Only 4·5 per cent of married old women share a household with married children, but this rises to 14 per cent among the recently widowed.

The proportion of the recently widowed living with un-married children is not higher; this may be because most of the old women who have unmarried children available are already sharing a home with them before the death. However, there is an indication of the recently widowed being somewhat more likely to live with a sibling or a non-relative.

At least half of all recent widows are left living alone by the death; however, the data do not indicate the household type of the recently widowed before their husbands died. In the four-area survey recent widows were asked about their house-hold circumstances before widowhood; within the limitations of the much smaller numbers of the recently widowed (sixty) involved, however, it seems that about three-quarters have

To Live Alone or With Others?

TABLE 7.2 WIDOWED WOMEN AND HOUSEHOLD TYPE

Household Type	Married	Duration of widowhood*					All † widows
		under 5 years	5–9 years	10–14 years	15–19 years	20+ years	
With spouse only	68·0	–	–	–	–	–	–
Living alone	–	54	50	36	38	40	44·6
Married daughter	3·7	10	17	16	16	22	16·6
Married son	0·8	4	6	5	6	7	5·6
Unmarried child	21·2	19	19	34	28	22	23·5
Sibling	2·4	7	3	3	4	4	4·0
Grandchild	1·4	1	1	2	1	1	0·9
Other relatives	1·2	1	1	1	3	1	1·3
Non-relatives	1·4	4	5	4	3	3	3·5
Total	100	100	100	100	100	100	100
Number	510	138	154	128	94	229	773

Source : National survey.

* Excludes, † Includes divorced and separated

stayed in the same home – with no change apart from the death of the spouse. In the remainder of cases the old people have mainly either moved in to live with married children, or another person – such as a widowed sister, a friend, or a lodger – has moved in to live with them.

Of recently widowed old women who do not live alone, about half live with just one other person – most commonly a single daughter. The rest live with two or more other people – most usually a child and child-in-law.[1]

[1] The four-area survey with 40 out of 328 old *women* being recently widowed and the national survey with 138 out of 1,496 compare as follows:

	National	Four-area
Proportion of all old people being widowed (+divorced and separated)	41·2%	43·7%
Proportion of old women being recent widows	9·2	12·2
Proportion of recently widowed women being lonely	52	57
Proportion of recently widowed women living alone	54	50
Proportion of recently widowed women having no living children	16	15

145

However, only 14 per cent of the recently widowed live with married children (Table 7.2) against 73 per cent who live alone or with an unmarried child. Why don't more live with married children? The majority of the recently widowed do have married children available, and a number report that the children would like them to move in. This whole matter is inevitably surrounded by extremely complex feelings on both sides. Elderly widows make clear their fear of losing independence. Often they are worried as to just how sincere and deeply felt the invitation really is. Even if she is completely convinced that the child does want her to move in, the old widow cannot but wonder what such intimate household contact will be like. What will the son-in-law think? Will the teenage grandchildren be too noisy and tiring? In particular elderly widows are uneasy about giving up their homes and cutting themselves off from any practicable alternative place in which to live.

Table 7.2 shows that women who have been widowed for longer periods (and are as a group older) are more likely to live with children. Meanwhile over half of all recently widowed women live alone. Some of them undoubtedly are oppressed by many doubts and fears on this score – turning over and over in their minds the pros and cons of going to live with a married child, or having someone to come to live with them; these thoughts compete with others inevitably associated with the recent death.

4. THE IMPACT OF DEATH

No answer was obtained from a full fifth of the recently widowed as to the cause of their spouse's death – mainly because such distress was apparent that it was felt impossible to ask the bald question about cause of death. Among those who did reply cancer, heart disease, haemorrhage, clots, strokes, and thrombosis accounted for the great majority. Old people whose spouses had died of cancer seemed unable to hold back at least a few tears as they said the word. 'Cancer' is one of the most emotive terms in the language, and it evidently summoned up with great immediacy images of pain, suffering, and loss. The causes of death indicated that a high proportion of spouses had

The Impact of Death

either died after much pain or had suffered some major sudden blow such as a heart attack or haemorrhage. In either case there had often been an impact of shock on the part of the surviving partner.

Many recent widows when asked about the cause of death went on – without any further questions – to describe the circumstances of the death, tending to quote the exact time of day, the last words or sentences spoken by themselves and by the dying person.

> He complained at 1 a.m. of bad pains in his chest. She wanted to call the doctor, but he told her to wait until the morning. He seemed better when she gave him his early morning cup of tea. However, when he sat up, or rather hauled himself up, to drink the tea, he fell over backwards and after gasping for a few minutes – she imitates the sound herself – he was dead. Her son was by this time leaving the house to fetch the doctor and she ran down the street to tell him his father was dying. *Northampton.*

> His wife died four years ago of a clot. He gives the exact time of her death; she was unwilling to see the doctor, and he tells how he brought her a cup of tea in bed. She said he had got his braces twisted at the back. The next time he went back into the room she had fallen out of bed and was lying dead on the floor. *Harrow.*

> He died three years ago of a cerebral haemorrhage. On the morning he died she asked him what he wanted for breakfast, and he said 'The usual thing'. She says he then passed her in the passage three times – meaning he went to the toilet three times in quick succession. Soon afterwards, she walked into the room and found him dead. *Northampton.*

Many of the recently widowed say they did not wish to sleep in the house alone for the nights after the death – a feeling which seems to be widely recognized by relatives. But some old people find their new state of isolation quickly and harshly underlined, when they are left to sleep alone in an empty house. However, most either have relatives staying in the house or go to stay with relatives.

'Her husband died of a stroke last winter. She went to stay with her son for a fortnight; she had to come back because she was worried about the house, and thought the pipes might burst. She says if she had not come back then, she would not have wanted to come at all.' *Oldham.*

5. AFTERMATH

Immediately after the death there is the funeral, and a flurry of other activity. It had been intended to ask a question about who attended the funeral, but the question tended to cause undue distress or to produce rather evasive replies. This reluctance to give details may have been partly due to the small number of persons attending most funerals. There was an impression of only about half a dozen people (and sometimes less) attending the funeral. Usually these would be children, a sibling or two and the widowed partner; some of the newly widowed did not feel fit enough to attend the funeral.

After perhaps a fortnight spent at the home of a child, the recently widowed person has to settle down to life without the marriage partner – in the majority of cases living alone in a home filled with memories. For most there was some element of shock, even though the marriage partner may have been ill for a long period. For some the death brings respite from a long and exhausting vigil. While most of the recent widows speak only in praise of their dead spouses, others offer some criticisms, and a few are quite harsh.

But even those who say they had little love for the dead one tend to say the death caused them at least a temporary sense of loss; though they may claim to prefer being alone, nevertheless it is evidently never easy to adjust to the loss of one's marriage partner in old age. Three of the fifty-four report sleeping better after the death – they slept badly before the death because of nursing and other duties. But a full third say they sleep less well since the death; and some of those who now sleep well, did not do so at first.

'I make myself sleep. I tire myself out with odd jobs.' *Woman, aged 72, Northampton.*

'Sleep is my salvation. But I didn't sleep at all well at first.' *Woman, aged 85, Northampton.*

'I always did sleep well. Now I wake early and think about my wife.' *Man, aged 76, Northampton.*

'I sleep poorly. Have had no sleep for six months. I've got

rims round my eyes and lie awake at night listening.' *Woman, aged 71, Harrow.*

'How d'you think you'd sleep when you've always been used to sleeping next to him?' *Woman, aged 71, Oldham.*

A similar pattern emerges from the recent widows' replies as to whether their health has altered since their spouse's death. Of those who replied, half said their health was the same, but about two-fifths thought their health had declined. Some reported such specific complaints as influenza, bronchitis, and rheumatism while others thought their health had suffered a general decline.

However, this is self-rated health, not a doctor's assessment. Moreover, the majority of recent widows were over 70 years of age, and some general decline in health is to be expected quite apart from widowhood. Nevertheless, since health plays such an important part in old people's lives, it is of some interest that two-fifths *think* their health has declined since widowhood.

6. ATTITUDES, MEMORIES

The recently widowed old person's attitude to the spouse's death will obviously be affected by the nature of perhaps fifty years or more of the marriage. The years immediately preceding the death are especially important. If the spouse was dying slowly and painfully of cancer, the memory of the dead person cannot but be coloured by this. Those who claimed to have had an especially happy time in retirement seemed to have the biggest sense of loss.

> Her husband was a factory foreman. His few years of retirement were the best time of her life. She did more with him and he used to help her with the housework. . . . When she was widowed four years ago it did affect her health at first, but afterwards she 'bucked up'. For three months she didn't dress all day and lost interest in life. *Woman, aged 72. Northampton.*

Many of the recently widowed were prepared to talk at some length about how and when they missed their spouses.

> He was a jobbing gardener, and he still does a few hours of paid work each week. . . . His wife died a year ago. . . . He misses her when he comes into the house from having done his small

149

stint of work and finds no tea waiting for him on the table, no fire burning in the grate. Recently, when he dressed up to go out in his best clothes, a button came off his shirt; he then had to undress completely and sew the button on himself, since his wife wasn't there to do it for him. *Man, aged 76, Northampton.*

'On the anniversary of her husband's death she usually tries to do something to stop herself thinking about it – she goes to visit a child or one of the neighbours.' *Woman, aged 70, Harrow.*

Others have their memories involuntarily jogged by external circumstances.

He was a lorry-driver and chauffeur. His wife died two years ago, and she left her body to be used for medical work. He says they keep bodies for about two years and recently he has received an official letter saying that her body is only now going to be buried. This has made him go over all his old memories again. However, in the will where she left her body she also said that she had had a very happy married life. *Man, aged 65.*

The recently widowed were asked whether they had any especially vivid memories of the dead spouse. Of those who answered, nine out of ten said they had vivid memories.

'She gestures towards what was evidently his chair: "When you've been married forty-four years you're bound to have memories."' *Woman, aged 67, Oldham.*

'I see him many times a day. I talk to him. Perhaps you'll think it's odd, but today I heard him say to me "You're tired again, aren't you?" I replied "Don't worry."' *Woman, aged 84, Oldham.*

'Her husband died of a heart attack last year, but the morning before he was walking about, quite well. She heard a noise in the kitchen, and thought her husband had dropped something. When she went in she saw him collapsed against the grate. Now whenever she goes into the kitchen she sees again his fallen body slumped against the grate.' *Woman, aged 65, Northampton.*

'Sometimes I have a fit of it. I've moved the chairs round so now I sit on his chair and I don't see it empty in front of me all the time.' *Woman, aged 71, Northampton.*

The small minority who claimed to think little about their

Attitudes, Memories

dead spouses tended also to express dissatisfaction with their marriage.

He doesn't think about his wife much. He thinks more about another girl he knew over fifty years ago, before he ever met his wife. He says he probably would have done better to marry the other girl. The happiest time in his life was when he was seeing her – they went dancing several times a week. But he moved away to work for a couple of years (around 1910) and never wrote to her. The next time he did meet her, he was walking down the street with his wife. *Man, aged 79, Oldham.*

Although most recently widowed old people admit to thinking a lot about their dead partners, these memories seem to cause them few feelings of guilt.[2] Three-quarters said they did as much for the dying person as they would have liked. Not one of the recently widowed replied in the negative, although some said they would have liked to have persuaded their dying spouse to go to hospital; others regretted not having got their partner out of hospital to die at home. A number reported staying up all night for several or many nights in a row, straining their backs with lifting the spouse, and in other tasks. Even those who had done little to nurse their spouses did not say that they would have liked to have done more. The replies gave a strong impression that the deaths were regarded as inevitable and natural – and in most cases little blame could be attached to anyone.

7. GRIEF

The recently widowed were asked whether one could get over the grief of losing one's spouse.[3] Of those who answered, only about a quarter said flatly it was impossible.

'He's been dead a year, and I miss him as much now as I did at first.' *Woman, aged 76, Harrow.*

'No. When they've been so good, you don't get over it.' *Woman, aged 80, Northampton.*

[2] Younger widows tend to feel guilty according to the Bethnal Green study. Peter Marris, *Widows and their Families* (1958), pp. 18–20.
[3] Peter Marris, *Widows and their Families* (1958); C. Murray Parkes, 'Grief as an Illness', *New Society* (9 April 1964), and 'Bereavement and Mental Illness', *British Journal of Medical Psychology*, Vol. 38, Nos. 1 and 13 (1965); Geoffrey Gorer, *Death, Grief, and Mourning* (London: Cresset Press, 1965).

151

Recently Widowed

Of those who said they had got over the worst of their grief, or would eventually do so, some were perhaps being over-optimistic:

'He has been widowed about nine months. He thinks he will get over the grief. "But not yet. Little things bring tears to my eyes. Like getting letters at Christmas still addressed to Mr. and Mrs. And when one of my nieces comes to see me I just cry – but they take no notice."' *Man, aged 74, Norfolk.*

A number of those who thought one could get over grief made short blunt statements to this effect:

'Yes. But it takes some doing.' *Woman, aged 66, Norfolk.*

'You mustn't "talk" to him. You'd go off your dot.' *Woman, aged 72, Northampton.*

'At first I never thought I could get over it. But I've always weathered storms.' *Man, aged 74, Harrow.*

'Yes, you can. She wouldn't wish different.' *Man, aged 65. Northampton.*

8. IS WIDOWHOOD WORSE FOR MEN?

Previous research has suggested that widowhood may strike a more severe blow at old men than at old women.[4] Some old people themselves say that widowed old men are liable to be helpless. Looked after by their wives during their working days, they are suddenly left at an advanced age to do their own cooking and cleaning. A number of widowed women say they are glad their husband died first, because he would never have been able to look after himself.

This chapter has concentrated primarily on dealing with the impact on both sexes and emphasizing the ways in which widowhood is similar for men and women. The four-area survey suggests recently widowed old men may be more likely than old women to live alone and be socially isolated. However, quite apart from the very small numbers involved (twenty men, forty women) other factors might explain these differences. For instance, the men are slightly older than the women and have been widowed slightly more recently (as expected in view of the men's shorter life expectation). When age is held constant, no clear difference emerges.

[4] Peter Townsend, *The Family Life of Old People* (1957), pp. 178–80.

Is Widowhood Worse for Men?

The general social expectation that old widowers will be worse off than old widows may also affect the situation – both in terms of compensating action on the part of relatives and others, and in the kind of replies the old people will give to questions. In addition there is the basic methodological problem that the survey deals only with *survivors*. Any recently widowed person who pines quickly away to death will not appear in a sample of old people who have been widowed an average of about two years.

Widowed old men have a sharply higher death-rate than married old men. However, here again there are basic difficulties in the evidence – such as the problem of cross-infection from the dying to the surviving marriage partner, and the greater vulnerability of men's health.[5]

Nevertheless old men probably do experience a different impact in widowhood from that experienced by old widows. While some widowers manage to organize themselves domestically with great efficiency, others indeed fall into a state of domestic anarchy and confusion. Moreover, the psychological position is very different for men, since widely accepted norms of emotional and social behaviour in our society make it more acceptable for women to weep, to express grief and to receive comforting and consolation – but less acceptable for men. In some interviews a strong impression emerged that when they do find themselves overcome with grief, when the tears do begin to flow, old men feel additionally distressed by the embarrassment of showing such signs of weakness.

Despite the rather negative argument of this section, recently widowed men evidently do suffer a severe loss on a number of levels. It is the magnitude and complexity of this loss which basically makes the phenomenon difficult to pin down, both because of the problems involved in questioning the old people and the difficulties of comparing old men and old women when there are so many variables involved.

But even if further research does not indicate that old widowers suffer a greater loss, the loss experienced by elderly widows is great enough.

[5] M. Young, B. Benjamin and C. Wallis, 'The Mortality of Widowers', *The Lancet* (31 Aug. 1963), ii, p. 454.

153

Recently Widowed

9. SPECIAL FEATURES OF WIDOWHOOD FOR OLD PEOPLE

The old people were asked whether they thought widowhood was different for an older and a younger person. Of those who answered, half thought it was worse for the old, while a quarter thought it was worse for the young. Another quarter said they didn't know, some indicating it depended on the circumstances. The most frequent comment of this sort referred to children, especially the difficulties of a young widowed woman with dependent children.

Children are a crucial variable in any comparison. In Peter Marris's sample of London widows, with an average age of 39, no less than two-thirds had dependent children.[6] None of the recent widows in this sample of old people had dependent children. A fair proportion of the young widows go out to work soon after being widowed, in sharp contrast to the elderly widows. While young widows tend to have their time taken up by both work and dependent children, the elderly widow has neither, and consequently plenty of time for thought.

Some old people believed the young found it easier to get over a loss, and indeed Marris's study shows that a number of younger widows re-marry within two years of the first husband's death; this proportion fell off very sharply among older women;[7] among people who are widowed past the age of 60, re-marriage is rare – despite popular ideas to the contrary, sometimes expressed by old people themselves.

Old people, when discussing marriage (or re-marriage) tend to stress 'companionship' – as against the more physically based marriage of a young couple. Some old people say this makes the loss all the greater, implying that a marriage based on companionship is purer and deeper than one based on sex. From the point of view of the sexual relationship, widowhood will undoubtedly be different for a younger person than for an elderly one. However, it is inaccurate to suggest that no old people show (or profess) an interest in sex. Kinsey's evidence indicates that old men are more likely than old women to be interested in sex, and impressionistic evidence from this study

[6] Peter Marris, *Widows and their Families* (1958), p. 5.
[7] ibid., p. 60.

154

Special Features of Widowhood for Old People

tends to support such a finding. For some old people the sexual loss may well be important and poses problems not experienced by those widowed in their youth. There is a social expectation that men or women widowed in their thirties will retain an interest in sex. But an elderly person, who has recently lost his spouse and is seeking a sexual outlet, is confronted by the social expectation that old people will probably not have any interest in sex.[8] On the other hand some old people are reluctant to share homes with, for instance, siblings-in-law, for fear of what the neighbours might say. One man evinces both of these dilemmas.

Talking about women, he says, 'I'm still interested. I'm an old man but I'm still frisky.' He talks of a distant female relative of his wife who is willing to come and live with him as his house-keeper. He is unsure what she expects of the arrangement. 'Even if you don't go to bed with a housekeeper,' he says, 'everyone will say that you are doing so.' *Man, aged 74, Norfolk.*

Four people in the sample had each been widowed twice. Two said widowhood was worse for younger people and two said it was worse for the old. However, there is one striking difference in attitudes in widowhood in old age – the virtual unanimity with which old people seem to accept the death and do not feel guilty about it. The median age at which their spouses had died was over 70 and many said spontaneously that their spouse had had a good long life. There was little evidence of the disbelief and astonishment reported by Marris for his younger widows, or of any tendency to blame the doctor or some other person for the death.

[8] Alex Comfort, 'Sex in Old Age', *New Society*, 18 February, 1965.

155

Chapter Eight

HOUSEBOUND

Loneliness is strongly associated with physical incapacity; 43 per cent of severely incapacitated men and 52 per cent of women said they were often or sometimes lonely, against 13 per cent of men and 25 per cent of women who had no incapacity (Table 4.4). There is a similar connection for the housebound and bedfast; 38 per cent of housebound old men and 48 per cent of housebound women were lonely, against 16 per cent of fully mobile men and 29 per cent of fully mobile women (national).

What is the difference between 'severe incapacity' and being 'housebound'? In practice, not a great deal. 'Incapacity for self-care' is based on the old person's capacity to perform such tasks as climbing stairs, cutting his own toe-nails, and dressing and washing himself. Being housebound consists of not going outside the house – regardless of whether the old person might be capable of so doing. The national survey found 10·6 per cent of old people in private households to be housebound, and another 2·1 per cent to be bedfast. The four-area survey, however, found only 8·4 per cent to be housebound and bedfast – less than the combined national figure of 12·7 per cent. This was largely because in the four-area survey old people were only classified as housebound if they had been so for a minimum of six months.

How 'housebound' is defined is extremely important, since small variations in the definition may well result in widely varying percentages of the elderly being categorized as housebound. Old people may become temporarily housebound during periods of wet weather or minor illness; some old people with bad bronchitis tend to be housebound each year from about

The Housebound

November to April; to avoid returning to question such temporarily housebound old people, the six months' criterion was adopted. Thus the housebound people who were re-interviewed consisted almost entirely of *permanently* housebound old people. With such a frail group one obviously expects a high rate of failure in completing long second interviews. In fact of forty-five categorized as housebound in the screening interview only thirty-two were re-interviewed; for most of the thirteen failures proxy interviews had been taken at the first stage.

This study defines being housebound as not going beyond the garden under one's own motive power. Reaching a car at the kerb would not prevent one being housebound, but anyone who can walk down the street to a shop or neighbour's house would not be housebound. On several occasions the screening interviewer was informed that the respondent had been housebound, perhaps for a period of years, which the second interview showed to be incorrect. If she has been severely ill at home for an extended period, an old person may say she has been housebound since the onset of the illness, forgetting that she can still walk short distances down the street. Old people also sometimes report inaccurately the *duration* of being housebound. Often the physical complaint has been getting steadily worse for many years; thus becoming finally housebound – by the present definition – need not automatically have special significance for the old person, who may place greater emphasis on some other point in the history of the physical condition's progress.

TABLE 8.1 HOUSEBOUND: AGE AND SOCIAL CLASS

	Percentage who are housebound (or bedfast)					
	Male			Female		
Age	Non-manual soc. class	Manual class	All men	Non-manual soc. class	Manual class	All women
65–9	4·1	2·1	2·6	4·9	7·1	6·5
70–4	3·5	5·1	4·6	4·5	10·5	8·5
75–9	7·3	8·5	8·3	17·0	20·9	19·8
80+	10·3	7·1	8·1	33·9	32·5	33·1
All aged 65+			5·0			14·1

Total sample 4067   *Source :* National survey.

157

Housebound

An obvious reason for the large preponderance of women among the housebound is the sharply rising incidence of the housebound condition in the oldest age-groups (Table 8.1). The national survey indicates a median age for the housebound of about 77. The four-area survey suggests for the long-term housebound a median age of 80, and a median duration of being housebound of three years. This may seem a short duration, but mortality rates are very high among frail people in these age-groups; the finding on duration is also consistent with a general impression that becoming housebound is only one stage in a lengthy process of declining mobility.

The high proportion of women and the high median age help to explain the 65 per cent of widows among housebound women – against 52 per cent for all old women. Housebound men, however, do not differ much from other men in terms of marital status; 65 per cent of housebound men are married. In this respect there is a major difference between housebound men and women. Most housebound old men have wives to look after them, but most housebound old women have already lost their husbands.

There is little variation in the proportion of manual and non-manual social classes who are housebound (Table 8.1).

Why do old people become housebound? In the four-area survey half of the housebound old people said the main pre-cipitating factor was either osteo- or rheumatoid-arthritis. A more objective medical assessment is provided by Dr. Douglas Snellgrove's study of housebound old people in Luton. He found the most common complaint to be osteo-arthritis (two-fifths of all the housebound) followed by coronary disease, hypertension, rheumatoid-arthritis, bronchitis, senility and stroke. Half of the housebound had three or more complaints.[1]

2. THE HOUSEBOUND AND THEIR CHILDREN

The housebound, as Table 8.2 shows, are somewhat less likely to live alone than are other old people; nevertheless 19 per cent of elderly housebound women do live alone. Less of them live only with their spouse, which is not unexpected for women,

[1] Douglas R. Snellgrove, *Elderly Housebound* (1963), pp. 48–9.

The Housebound and Their Children

since only 25 per cent of housebound women are married –
against 65 per cent widowed. Among housebound men only
35 per cent are living with spouses only, although 65 per cent
of housebound men are married. This is probably due to the
amount of attention a housebound person requires – often from
a spouse who is too frail to supply it all unaided. Altogether
54 per cent of all housebound old women live in a household
with at least one child.

TABLE 8.2 HOUSEBOUND AND HOUSEHOLD COMPOSITION

Household type	Male		Female	
	Housebound and bedfast	All old men	Housebound and bedfast	All old women
Living alone	10	10·9	19	29·7
With spouse only	35	47·1	15	23·2
Married daughter	12	7·6	21	9·8
Married son	0	2·7	5	3·1
Unmarried child	23	20·8	28	19·7
Sibling	10	4·6	8	8·1
Grandchildren	4	0·9	0	0·9
Other relatives	2	1·7	2	1·9
Non-relatives	6	3·7	3	3·6
Total	100	100	100	100
Number	52	1,004	220	1,496

Source : National survey.

Another 10 per cent of housebound women reported seeing a
child on the day of interview or the previous day – a total of
64 per cent; and 73 per cent of the women had seen a child in
the last week. A lower proportion of housebound men, 57 per
cent, had seen a child in the last week – more of the men have
their spouses alive and do not live with children.

There is little sign of housebound old people being neglected
by their children. Of housebound old women 80 per cent have
living children[2] and of these only 7 per cent have seen no child

[2] The national survey with 272 old people out of 2,500 being housebound and the
four-area survey with 45 out of 538 being housebound – in this case for six months
or longer – compare as follows:

159

Housebound

at all in the last week (national). Any housebound person requires some assistance in order to continue living in a private household; those who get no support from children or others have a much larger chance of having to enter institutions.

The majority of the housebound report missing things which they were still able to do in the period immediately before they became restricted to the house. Comparatively few say they miss going out to work – this reflects the high proportion of women in the group, and their median age which is well beyond the normal retiring age. The worst aspect of being housebound seems to be the loss of activities such as walking outside, going to visit people, and shopping, rather than the loss of mobility itself.

When the housebound were asked about any possible advantages in being housebound, most at first could not understand what this question meant; being housebound was evidently too encompassing a condition to be treated as merely another problem. There was no inclination to see anything beneficial in being housebound.

Due to the loss of mobility, they are unlikely to meet other housebound old people. Most housebound people seem to think of their disability as being 'my arthritis' or 'my bronchitis', rather than merely in terms of the reduced mobility. Consequently, housebound old people when asked have difficulty in commenting on housebound people in general. Some say they don't know any other housebound people, and can only speak for themselves. When asked whether enough is done in the locality to help housebound old people, only half gave any positive answer, and they were divided about equally between those who thought enough was being done and those who thought too little. Most replied specifically in terms of whether they thought they themselves were receiving enough help.

	National housebound	Four-area housebound 6 months +
Proportion of all old people housebound	12·7%	8·4%
Proportion of housebound who live alone	16	18
Proportion of housebound who are lonely	46	44
Proportion of housebound with no living children	22	27
Proportion of housebound being widowed	57	53

160

Who Helps the Housebound?

3. WHO HELPS THE HOUSEBOUND?

Housebound people as a group require a good deal of help of various kinds if they are to continue to live outside an institution. They tend to be in poor health, they cannot get outside the house to do shopping and, to a greater or less extent, they lack the physical capacity to perform household tasks. Table 8.3 shows nearly all of the housebound being 'unable'

TABLE 8.3 HOUSEBOUND* AND UNABLE TO DO HEAVY HOUSEWORK, OR HAVING DIFFICULTY WITH PREPARING HOT MEALS

Who helps	'Unable' to do heavy housework			'Having difficulty' or being 'unable' to prepare hot meals		
	Male	Female	Both sexes	Male	Female	Both sexes
No help	(3)	5	5	(6)	16	13
Spouse	(34)	9	13	(53)	10	21
Child in household	(21)	36	34	(18)	40	34
Child outside household	(0)	15	12	(0)	10	7
Relative in household	(8)	7	7	(9)	16	14
Relative outside household	(5)	2	3	(3)	1	2
Other person in household	(3)	2	2	(3)	1	2
Friend outside household	(3)	6	6	(3)	2	2
Social Service help	(16)	18	17	(6)	7	6
Private domestic help	(5)	7	7	(3)	3	3
Other person outside household	(0)	1	0	(0)	0	0
Meals-on-Wheels	(0)	0	0	(6)	4	5
Total	100	100	100	100	100	100
Number	38	188	226	34	92	126
Number being able or having no difficulty	4	11	15	8	107	115

* Excluding Bedfast
Total sample – 2,500.

Source: National survey.

161

to do heavy housework (such as washing floors). Forty-six per cent of these are helped with heavy housework by their children, 13 per cent by their spouses and 10 per cent by other relatives. A lower proportion of the housebound, just over half, have difficulty with or are unable to prepare hot meals. Of these 41 per cent are helped by children, 21 per cent by their spouse and 16 per cent by other relatives.

In both cases help from relatives greatly outweighs social service help; but with heavy housework a substantial minority of those needing help – 17 per cent – do receive social service assistance, in the form of home helps. The national figure compares closely with the four-area proportion of 13 per cent of all the long-term housebound receiving home helps (Table 11.1). This is much higher than the figure for other services such as meals-on-wheels; the only 'social service' with a really substantial spread is the doctor. The four-area survey shows 29 per cent of the long-term housebound having received a doctor's visit in the last week. But the figure for nurses is much lower.

Housebound people must have their shopping done for them, unless – as is the case in Norfolk – most of the shops deliver food to the customer's home. The four-area survey shows help with shopping being provided mainly by children, spouses, and other relatives. There is also some indication of a rather larger volume of help in this sphere by neighbours – about a quarter of the housebound having had some shopping done for them by a neighbour in the last week. Often this help supplements other shopping done by relatives, but some of the housebound un-doubtedly rely heavily on neighbours for shopping; while some neighbours do this free, others are paid by the housebound old person for the service.

Cleaning, cooking and shopping are, of course, not the only things in which housebound old people require help. Some also need a good deal of assistance with their personal toilet, with dressing and so on; once again the main sources of such help undoubtedly consist of children, spouse, and other relatives, although with the bedfast home nurses also play an important part.

These are necessary services which incapacitated and house-bound old people require if they are to continue living in moderate comfort in a private household. But another obvious need for some housebound old people is occasionally to get outside the house. In the four-area survey a third of the housebound had not been out in a car during the previous year; some of them had received offers but had declined because they would be too uncomfortable in the car, found it too low and difficult to get into, or were afraid of becoming ill, sick or incontinent while in the car. But a quarter of the long-term housebound had been out in a car more than a dozen times in the last year. The median number for all the housebound was three car trips in a year. Overwhelmingly the main providers of these car rides were children and children-in-law.

4. HOUSEBOUND AND ALONE

One in about every six housebound old people lives alone. It is particularly interesting to know how they manage to function by themselves. Among seven re-interviewed housebound old people who live alone, three are not socially isolated:

1. Despite living alone she has an intermediate social contact score (38). She is aged 86 and has been widowed for forty-four years. She has been housebound for one year following a severe attack of bronchitis. She lives in a bungalow in a small village, which has two shops and is not on a main road. She has six living children, all of whom she sees at least monthly. She sees two of her daughters every day and they do all of her shopping and housework; her daughters do some of her cooking and the neighbours also help. She is never lonely. *Norfolk.*

2. She lives alone but has an intermediate social contact score (32). She is aged 71 and has been widowed for nine years. She has been housebound for nine years, following an operation on her hip, but has been lame since childhood. She lives in one of a row of four cottages, in a hamlet of about a dozen houses, two miles from a larger village and the nearest bus route. She has four children living, three of whom she has seen in the last month. One son and daughter-in-law she sees every day, and they collect her pension. But all the food is delivered by the shops and she does her own housework and cooking. She also sees a lot of her two immediate neighbours. She is sometimes lonely. *Norfolk.*

3. She lives alone, but has an intermediate social contact

score (21). She is aged 82, and has been widowed for twenty years. She has been housebound for twelve years following an accident in which she broke a hip. She lives in a red-brick house in a quiet suburban street. She has one living child, a daughter, whom she sees every day. Her daughter does the shopping, a private domestic help does the cleaning, and meals-on-wheels come five days a week. She is sometimes lonely. *Harrow.*

Each of these three old people is in daily contact with a child. Two of the three are in daily contact with two children (or child-in-law). They are a marked contrast to the four house-bound old people who not only live alone but are also isolated. Whereas the non-isolated group have an average of nearly four living children each, of the isolated group three have no children alive at all; the remaining old person has only one living child, who lives some way away and is seen only about once a fortnight. Two of this isolated and housebound group are single women:

1. She is single, lives alone and has a social contact score of only 6. She is aged 73, and has been housebound for two years, mainly due to arthritis. She lives in a detached house, near to an inter-war housing estate. For many years she worked in her brother's bakery shop. A 17-year-old neighbour does most of the shopping (for a small payment) but she does all her own house-work. Her nearest living relatives are a nephew and niece, whom she sees once or twice a week. Her only other sources of regular contact are two neighbours and a friend. She had a nervous breakdown when aged about 30 and another when about 50 – the second was due to several close relatives dying in quick succession. Her main pleasure is doing the housework. She has no television set, although her nephew offered to buy her one. She likes listening to 'proper stuff, good singing' on the radio. She belonged to a Sunday temperance group when young. Before becoming housebound she attended Wesleyan chapel and, for two years, an over-sixties club. She has no voluntary visitors or social service help; she sees the doctor only about twice a year. She is sometimes lonely. *Oldham.*

2. She is single, lives alone and has a social contact score of 16. She is aged 73 and has been housebound for seven years – with an arthritic hip. The arthritis is now more serious and she can only walk with extreme difficulty. She has four living

brothers and sisters, all of whom are too immobile themselves or live too far away to come and see her. She sees a niece about once a week, but her main sources of contact are two old school-friends. She also has meals-on-wheels five times a week. She does her own cleaning, despite being hardly able to sit down, let alone kneel. She refuses to have a home help. She claims to be never lonely. *Harrow.*

3. She lives alone and has a social contact score of 14. She is aged 88 and has been widowed for twenty-seven years. She has been housebound five years. She is very weak and unsteady on her feet; she shakes badly and her eyesight is poor. She lives in a small cottage near the centre of a large village, close to shops and the bus stop. She has no children and her nearest relatives are a niece and nephew whom she sees about once a month. Her main source of social contact is a neighbour – a married woman, aged about 40 – who comes in to see her three times a day; this neighbour does all of her shopping and cleaning, and a good deal of the cooking. She has no regular social service help, but her doctor pays a visit about once a month. Her main pleasure, she says, is knitting but, in fact, she can no longer knit, and she has no television set. Nor does she listen to her radio. She claims to be never lonely. *Norfolk.*

4. She lives alone and is extremely isolated, with a social contact score of only 3. She is aged 80. Her husband is still alive, but has been in a mental hospital for the last four years and is not expected to get better. She lives in a cottage near the centre of the small village; she makes the twenty-mile-journey to the mental hospital by taxi each week, which costs her £2 of her £8 a week income. Her only child, a son, lives about twenty-five miles away and comes to see her once a month. She has been housebound since she broke her ankle a year ago. She does all the cleaning and cooking herself. Her pension is delivered by the village post office with her grocery order. A neighbour will also bring things from a larger village, once a week. But she has no other social contacts. She has no other relatives than her son. She describes herself as 'Often lonely'. *Norfolk.*

What other factors are there in common between these four isolated and housebound old people – apart from an absence of children? All four are women. Their average age is nearly 80. They have few brothers or sisters or other close relatives available who could visit them. For shopping they tend to rely on neighbours or on having the food delivered. They receive a visit from their doctor about once a month. Two of the four use outside toilets. Two of the four have suffered mental breakdowns in the past and one has a husband in a mental hospital. But, despite this, these four do not appear to be very different in personality from many others in the sample. Overwhelmingly the main factors seem to be absence of spouse, lack of children and lack or unavailability of siblings and other contemporaries.

Part III

PRIVATE PURSUITS
AND PUBLIC PROVISION

Part III deals primarily with socially isolated old people and seeks to answer three questions: How do they spend their time? How much money do they have? What use do they make of the social services?

The use of time. Very few of these isolated old people go out to work. Nine out of ten live alone, and by the definition of isolation all averaged less than three social contacts a day over the previous week. The isolated thus spend much of their time alone. Inevitably such a wide variety of old people will find many different ways of using their time. The things which an old person may do, even alone in her own home, are almost infinitely varied, and exist on many different levels.

Money is obviously important here. The present study makes no attempt at a detailed or comprehensive assessment of the old people's income and expenditure. Rather it looks at such matters as what proportion of the socially isolated receive national assistance or have very low incomes. The general picture which emerges is that most socially isolated old people do have incomes at or not far above the national assistance scales. This complements the finding that socially isolated old people spend the great majority of their time inside their own homes.

Social services, after the contributory pension, are the major public provision for old people. For some socially isolated old people the social services provide a major source of social contact; others of the isolated are only able to continue living on their own because of social service support. However, the general coverage of the social services among the socially isolated is not much different from the coverage among the four-fifths of old people who are not isolated.

169

Private Pursuits and Public Provision

These three chapters concentrate upon the socially isolated because the three issues considered here seem of special significance to the isolated. The four-fifths who are not isolated obviously spend more of their time with other people; they mostly live with others and thus their personal financial resources do not play quite so crucial a role; moreover, old people who are not socially isolated are not so obviously dependent on social services for support.

Evidence is already available from the national study on the general question of old people's finances and the spread of social services.[1] A smaller scale investigation such as the four-area survey is perhaps best suited to provide evidence on *attitudes*. Most of Chapters 9, 10 and 11 are concerned with the attitudes of 100 socially isolated old people to the use of time, money, and social services.

Interview Reports

All of the ten interview reports in this study give some information about the old people's use of time, their finances, and their use of the social services.

Mr. Warner has more interests than most old people – he is a keen amateur painter, he reads books, watches television and has a garden. However – unlike Miss Pritchard, Interview 3, who is also interested in reading and gardening – he feels that these familiar pursuits are palling; this is mainly due to the very recent death of his wife. He has no money problems and little contact with, or need for, social services. He is, however, eager to be advised on whether he should live alone now that his wife is dead.

Mrs. Parsons does a little cooking, sewing and reading; these interests and her dog apparently make her time seem to go quickly. She complains of being severely short of money (like Mr. Thomas, Interview 1; Mr. Meade, Interview 4; and Miss Hughes, Interview 5). She goes to bed at dusk in the winter. She is very dependent on, and devoted to, her home help – who provides nearly all of her social contact. Mrs. Parsons also lives in a council bungalow. Her doctor visits her regularly.

---

[1] Peter Townsend and Dorothy Wedderburn, *The Aged in the Welfare State* (1965).

Interviews

Yet despite all this social service provision, her glasses are inadequate, a spare pair of her sister's.

Mr. *Brown* is an unusually active man for his age of 74. His main activities are going for walks and dropping into a local pub in the evening; he evidently spends little time on cooking or cleaning. Despite his very shabby home he denies wanting a home help to keep it tidy. (In this he contrasts with another widower, Mr. Thomas, Interview 1, who also has a shabby home, but would like a home help if he could get one). Like some other old people he is very reluctant to 'bother' his doctor.

Mr. Brown is an obvious example of an old person whose social isolation is connected with his personality. He has five living children, and numerous grandchildren and great-grandchildren whom he never sees. However, his attitude to his three wives and his hostile comments on his children, suggest that rather than their 'deserting' him, he alienated his children by being an inadequate father.

INTERVIEW NUMBER 8

Mr. *Warner*   *Harrow*
Aged 82   Lives alone
Recently widowed (6 weeks)   Socially isolated (19)
Retired technical journalist   Sometimes lonely
No incapacity (0)   Anomic (4)

He is a tallish man with somewhat hunched shoulders, and a middle-class accent. He is wearing a suit, white collar, and a black tie for his recently dead wife. He lives alone in a detached house in a quiet 1930's street in Harrow. He was born and brought up in Somerset, worked in Birmingham as a journalist and later he moved to Fleet Street. He has lived in Harrow for forty years, and in his present house for thirty-five.

Mr. Warner worked as a technical journalist in Fleet Street until he retired seventeen years ago at the age of 65. He was glad to stop full-time work but continued to write free-lance pieces for his old paper. Retirement made no sudden difference to his life, especially since he also had his gardening and painting. He continued to see a fair amount of people he worked with, until he stopped free-lancing about ten years ago.

Private Pursuits and Public Provision

Mr. Warner is physically quite capable. He could do the housework but the cleaning is done by the paid help who comes five days a week. She also cooks his midday meal, although he does breakfast and his evening meal each day.

Mr. Warner had no medical treatment during the last year; his only complaint is rheumatism in the shoulders. He has not once been in hospital in his life. If he were ill, he thinks the domestic help could not look after him – she has her own family. The possibility of being ill has prompted him recently to move the telephone from the dining-room to the sitting-room; he has also moved a bed into the sitting-room, but has not yet started sleeping in it. (His wife died suddenly of a heart attack.)

He says he has 'just normal meals'. He always has a cooked breakfast. Sometimes the domestic help eats lunch with him, but mostly he has been eating alone since his wife died. He has been out to meals in restaurants a few times. He normally cooks himself a meal in the evening.

His domestic help has been coming regularly for the past fifteen years. Mr. Warner's wife was not strong and she did no housework. Mr. Warner says if he were to move he could not get a domestic help like his present one.

Mr. Warner only wears glasses for reading and can see quite well with them. His hearing is good. He knows little about local services for older people but expects they are probably not much good. He thinks the Government retirement pension is adequate, although he himself does not get it. He is against children's allowances on the whole. He thinks there are no poor people these days.

His only child is a married son aged 50, with his own son aged 17. Normally the son drives over (a one-hour drive) about once a month, but since his wife's death he has stayed one week at his son's. The son also was a technical journalist, but now has an administrative job in engineering. Mr. Warner may perhaps go to live at the son's, but the invitation has not been very firm or repeated.

Mr. Warner was the eldest of three children. One of his sisters is dead but the younger sister is alive; she is a widow and lives on the other side of London, with her widowed daughter. Normally, Mr. Warner goes to see them once or twice a month; since his wife died he has stayed with them for a week.

He sees no other relatives. He is on good terms with most of the neighbours, and has seen five of them during the previous week. Recently they have been inviting him into their houses more than usual, but he has accepted only a few times. The neighbours are one of the reasons why he would not like to move away; it's mainly 'a psychological thing' – there are people you know near by even if you don't talk to them much. He really has no friends he sees regularly; but there is one friend of his dead wife, who lives a few streets away, whom he has been seeing once or twice a week. He talks about several of his own friends, but they are mostly dead now. His still living friends are mainly journalists or people he knew from a local art society – but they have all moved out of the London district; one couple have moved to the south coast, another have moved to stay with a child, and so on. The only other person he sees frequently is his private domestic help.

Time often seems to go slowly, especially from 4 p.m. to 10 p.m. 'When you're over 70, you're not producing anything. It's just existing. Young people can always look forward to things. Cooking, reading, that's just existing. There's nothing in front of you.' His main activity is reading, and when I arrive he is reading a Hammond Innes novel. Every morning he goes out for an hour to do the shopping. Otherwise he does not go for walks, although he used to when he was younger. He watches television a good deal, comments on a recent programme about airliners – and says he prefers documentaries and plays. The television is being repaired at present and he misses it; he is now listening to the radio and finds it much better than he remembered.

He has no gardener and the biggish garden looks well tended. But he has lost interest in gardening since his wife died – there is no point in gardening if nobody admires what you do. He has the *Daily Telegraph*, the *Daily Mirror*, *Motor*, *The Field*, and *Amateur Gardening*. He reads biography, fiction, and travel, and gets the books from the public library. At present he is smoking at least twenty cigarettes a day. He gave up smoking twenty years ago but has started again since his wife died. 'When you get old you get very nervous. I suppose smoking's just a nervous habit. It's a solace.'

Mr. Warner says he is not a sociable person, and he is bored

173

by politics. The only organization he has belonged to is a local
art society; he has shown pictures at its exhibitions. But he
never goes to any sort of club meeting. He thinks old people's
clubs are 'a jolly good idea' for people who want them, but 'I
can't see myself sitting in a room with a lot of old people. It's
like a hotel lounge.' He is 'not the slightest bit gregarious'. In
Fleet Street he used to drink moderately after work with his
colleagues.

He is not religious, although his wife attended the local
Church of England church; the vicar came to call on her at
regular intervals. Last summer he went on a holiday with his
wife to Eastbourne – a lovely place although not like it was –
but he will not be going this year. He takes little interest in
writing letters – he supposes this is odd for a journalist. He has
a telephone but makes few calls.

He owns the house, which has four bedrooms, a garage, two
ground-floor rooms, plus kitchen and bathroom. He sold his
car about ten years ago – he became bored with cars, and
prefers to be driven by his son. He thinks the house is too large
for him now. He is worried about the three empty bedrooms.
He doesn't know whether he wants to move. 'I wish I knew. It's
the most depressing part of living, but I don't want to think
about it.' There has been a tentative suggestion from his son
that Mr. Warner should go and live there. The son tells him that
he must decide soon about his living arrangements. The son
has a garage which could be converted into a flat, but Mr.
Warner is not sure whether this arrangement would work.
'They're always there all the time.' The other possibility is
having someone to live with him in his house, but he has no
suitable person in mind.

His wife died suddenly six weeks ago of a heart attack. She
had been to see her sister in Epsom two days previously. He
has seen nothing of her family since the funeral, but will be
seeing her sister in Brighton soon, and he is keeping in touch
with her one friend in the locality. He sleeps slightly less well.
His health has 'not outwardly' worsened, but 'I shall never get
over it'.

'Conversation is the thing you miss most. Before, I'd paint
a picture, or do some gardening. Now there's no point. You
want someone to say how good it is. It's ego, I suppose. Now if

Interviews

I paint a picture all I can do is put it away in a folder. We went everywhere together; when I was travelling to write stories my wife often came with me. The morning isn't so bad. I cook my breakfast and then the cleaner comes in. From four o'clock onwards is the worst. Each day I think I won't be able to stand this much longer. I go upstairs and start preparing it for someone to move in; but then I don't know. Somebody up there splashing about in the bathroom, getting in the way in the kitchen . . . You've got to think of all these things in advance. . . . I could spend several hundred pounds putting in a kitchen and a bathroom.'

He approves of national assistance. He thinks State provision is somewhat 'ironic' – people who 'squander' their money are able to apply for assistance. He has no contributory pension. He has a small pension from his work; it has been cut down since his wife died. He has some investments, and money in a building society, and he has not had to spend any of the capital. He is slightly surprised when I say that some older people worry a lot about money. He has no specific difficulties with expenditure, though he does say that prices continue to rise. (The market value of his house must also be about £10,000.)

His father's farm in Somerset was apparently quite large; Mr. Warner used to go over to Ireland for his father to buy cattle. His father lived to be 93. He thinks he himself has had 'an average or better than average life', especially when he was young. He went to the local country grammar school and says his happiest times were when he was young – he enjoyed fishing and horse-riding. He was not in the First World War. His unhappiest times have always been connected with his wife's health. 'She was a vivacious and sunny person.' Asked whether he will live as long as his father, he says, 'I don't know. I used to think I might live to be 70. Now you just can't believe your age.'

At the end of the interview, as at the beginning, he is still talking about whether he should stay in the house or move. His own father lived alone for about ten years, but he had the housekeeper. I suggest that he go and stay with his son for an extended visit, but he says if he went to live with the son it would mean spending about £1,000 converting the garage and building a new one. Mr. Warner can't decide whether it would

175

be worth the expense. Since his wife died, he says, he has lost interest in the future.

INTERVIEW NUMBER 9

Mrs. Parsons   *South Norfolk*
Aged 79   Lives alone
Widow (40 years) of a   Socially isolated (7)
   prison officer   Often lonely
Moderate incapacity (3)   Anomic (5)

She is a small, frail woman; her legs are thin, her body breast-less, and her shoulders as narrow as a 10-year-old girl's. But her movements are vigorous and she speaks volubly. She lives in a council bungalow in the centre of a small village and two miles from a larger village, where she was born. She has been living continuously in the area since 1945 and in this bungalow for five years.

She first went to work at the age of 13 in domestic service in London; she was paid 2s. 6d. a week plus board and came home to Norfolk once a year. She married a man who was killed in the First World War. After the war she married a second time and went out with her husband to India where he was in the prison service. She became a matron in the prison where she worked for twenty-six years, until 1945; she had six Indian matrons under her and she retired at the compulsory age of 60. Her second husband died only a few years after she reached India. In 1945 she came back to England and until 1952 kept house for a 'gentleman'. She did part-time domestic work – five days a week, until only four years ago – so she finally retired from part-time work at 75. She still sometimes sees the 'gentleman'. But she regards her twenty-six years of work in India as the major event in her life.

Mrs. Parsons can get outside but can't walk far. She can get about inside her home, wash and dress herself, and so on. She can't cut her toe-nails, which is done by her sister, whom she only sees about four times a year. Mrs. Parsons does light house-work, but all the heavier jobs are left to the home help who comes six days a week. She does her own cooking, such as it is, and collects her national assistance (she has no contributory

176

pension) from the post office in the next village where she goes by bus. Most of her shopping is delivered, but she does a little – and the rest is done by the home help.

She had a major operation seven years ago, when according to the home help (present during some of the interview) 'her intestines were removed'. Mrs. Parsons is visited by her doctor, whom she thinks is a 'darling', about once a month. She also goes to his surgery sometimes. She has several medicines, one of them a laxative. She has considerable pain if she is unable to excrete. She is afraid she must have cancer – two members of her family have died of it. She suffers from rheumatism but says this is only a minor complaint. During the past five years she has been in hospital four times, each time the trouble being 'blockage of the intestines'. She has also been to hospital with 'flu. A year ago she was seriously ill with 'flu at home, and was unconscious for four days. She thinks she must nearly have died and she was in bed for six weeks. The doctor came twice a day for several days, and the home help slept in the house for two weeks; two neighbours also provided some help.

Mrs. Parsons would not like meals-on-wheels because she lacks the appetite. She only eats small meals. Her breakfast consists of bread and milk, and midday meal of an egg and bread and butter; the meal at night consists of Ovaltine with an egg in it, milk and an apple. If she wakes in the night she sometimes eats a cake. She has eight pints of milk a week, and she likes Guinness, but can only afford about two a week.

Her home help now comes six times a week for one hour each morning. She has been having the help for about a year, and she says: 'I love her.' She knew her help before, and even had some work done by her free before she became an official home help. She sometimes goes to the help's house. The jobs done are heavy cleaning and washing of clothes. The home help is aged 52 and she works for one other person. Mrs. Parsons pays 5s. a week for the home help. She does not remember having seen the home help organizer (probably because she was too ill when the arrangement began).

Mrs. Parsons wears glasses. 'My sister gave them to me. She had a spare pair.' The glasses are in a poor state of repair. When I ask why does she not ask the doctor for some advice on how to get glasses fitted she says she would never ask him.

Private Pursuits and Public Provision

'He's a darling, but he only looks after my health.' She has some difficulty with these glasses – if she had some fitted she admits they would probably be better; but she says it is unimportant and, in any case, she can't afford to pay for glasses. She has no difficulty with hearing.

She thinks little is done for older people in the area – the village is only interested in children. She is strongly against children's allowances. The Government does not provide big enough pensions. She is a strong supporter of the Conservative Government but thinks that their only mistake is keeping the pensions too low. 'Too many old people are starving. Many a day I've not got enough money.'

Mrs. Parsons had no children from her two marriages. She thinks it sad how some people have too many children and others have none. She herself is the sixth of a family of nine children. Her six brothers are all dead, but her two younger sisters are alive. One aged 77 is a widow and lives on the coast of Norfolk, forty miles away; Mrs. Parsons sees her about four times a year – she would go more often if the bus were cheapei. Her sister's son is 'a very good religious boy' who has asked her to go and live with him. She has another married sister aged 75, who lives in Surrey over a hundred miles away and she sees her only once a year. She describes her as 'a bit cranky', and the last time this sister came to stay with her the sister's husband paid Mrs. Parsons £15 for the three weeks. The sister's husband is very wealthy but Mrs. Parsons says she gets nothing from him.

She has a number of nephews and nieces but she never sees them, with the exception of her sister's son in north Norfolk. She is on talking terms with her neighbours but sees little of them. For one neighbour who lives two doors away Mrs. Parsons gets shopping twice a week. She sews for another neighbour who in return drove her to see her sister in north Norfolk a few months ago. But she has no friends.

Time flies away too quickly. Her main pleasure is sewing and 'Of course I like a chatter'. She does not own a television set, but she listens a good deal to the radio. She gets up at seven o'clock in the morning and goes to bed at four o'clock. 'I'm late into bed if it's 5.30. Then I read books in bed.' She also reads the *Daily Express*. Someone brings books for her, and she likes history – 'I read about Napoleon, he was a darling.' She sews a little most days, but her sight makes it go 'blurry'. She finds it very unpleasant having to go to bed in the early evening – partly to save fuel; if she had a television set she would stay up in the evenings. She smokes about five cigarettes a day, 'It's very consoling here alone to have some cigarettes.' She used to smoke heavily in India.

She has never belonged to clubs. The nearest old people's club is two miles away and she can't wait about for buses at six o'clock in the evening; she would go if there was one nearer. She belongs to the Church of England and last went two months ago; when she has taken her laxative medicine there is no toilet in the church if she needs one. She would like to become a Catholic, admiring them for the work they did in India, but it's too late to change now. She does not go on holidays, being unable to afford it, but last Christmas she went to stay with her sister. She writes to this sister about once a month, and less regularly to the other sister in London, and to her former employer. She never uses the telephone, because she can't hear sufficiently.

The rent is £1 5s. a week for her council bungalow. It has two bedrooms and one sitting-room, kitchen, bathroom and piped water and inside toilet. The bungalow is convenient, but she dislikes it. She has no heating in her bedroom and two years ago the pipes burst. She dislikes the neighbourhood. People talk about her; they think she's got lots of money, and they think she drinks her money because she occasionally goes to the pub. But she does not want to move from her present home. However, she may accept the offer from her nephew in north Norfolk for her to go and live with him.

She is often lonely. 'I talk to the dog. I'm learning dog language. He comes and sleeps in my bed with me, all cuddly-uddly.' She feels lonely the whole day long, after the home help has gone at eleven in the morning. Unless by chance she talks to a neighbour on the road she feels lonely the rest of the day. She feels cold – being used to the heat in India. She does not feel lonely for anyone in particular – 'no devil want me'. She thinks going out to work always makes a big difference. Nothing can be done to help her and she will wait until she dies. 'I don't mind when I die. There's nothing much to live for now, dear.' She thinks everyone gets more lonely as they get older.

Private Pursuits and Public Provision

Going to a club would make some difference. She only feels lonely when she is by herself.

Mrs. Parsons's attitude to national assistance is somewhat aggressive. She has no state contributory pension. She is dependent on national assistance; when she first applied for it she did not tell them she had a Government pension from her job in India and they made her pay back £165 – a large proportion of what she had in the post office bank. She thinks that consequently the National Assistance people don't trust her. She now receives £2 13s. weekly, and her pension from the Indian Government is £92 a year. Her income is about £4 9s. a week. She spends 25s. on rent and 5s. on her home help. She spends 15s. a week on coal during the winter – fuel is her worst expense. This leaves her just over £2 for food and all other expenses per week. In 1945 she had about £600 in her post office savings book but now it is down to £25 – she shows me the book.

Her mother died when Mrs. Parsons was 33. Her father lived on for seven years, but by then she was in India. Her father had a building business in the next village, and her sister looked after him. She has had a good life and has enjoyed herself. The happiest times were in India, and she has also travelled in domestic service to other places. 'I've been all over, a devil for travel.' Her unhappiest time was when she married her second husband and went out to India with him: 'He was a bugger.' In those days she says men didn't respect women. She married her first husband in 1914, lived with him for only six weeks, and two years after the marriage he was killed in France.

Mrs. Parsons says she had had enough after her second marriage – and she has spent more than half of her life being a widow. Now she does not want to live much longer. The only thing she needs is more money: 'I'd like to stop the children's allowances.' She would increase the old age pension, and have more visitors for old people.

Interviews

Mr. Brown   Oldham
Aged 76   Lives alone
Widower (16 years)   Socially isolated (9)
Retired iron moulder   Sometimes lonely
No incapacity (0)   Anomic (4)

He is a thinnish man of medium height, with an unshaven smiling face and two teeth. He lives in an old working-class area, about half a mile from the centre of Oldham in a cobbled street. The front door opens direct into a filthy sitting-room. The ancient metal grate, with oven above, is full of old ash and discarded pieces of paper. On the table is the debris of a meal, a tea mug encrusted in grime, and odd pieces of clothing and smoking equipment. The kitchen table is piled high with cups, plates and other impedimenta; beside another ash-filled fireplace wood is stacked on the floor. The gas cooker is covered with the dirt of years. The floors of both rooms are littered with bones; there is a smell in the front room and the dog wets my trousers. Dust is everywhere. There is a serious leak above the window in the kitchen. The window (also filthy) looks down into a valley full of grimy factories and across to steep green hills beyond. Mr. Brown says the view would be better with field-glasses – his eyes are bad. He is physically agile, and demonstrates how he can touch his toes with the base of his hands, keeping his knees straight; he goes swimming once a week and takes long walks, despite there being hills in all directions from where he lives. The sitting-room window has been broken by a stone and is boarded up. He was out drinking when this happened and found it when he came back at 11.30 p.m. It gives the home a first appearance of complete dilapidation – but he merely says somebody must have thought he needed more fresh air.

The only time his breezy front slips is when he says doesn't want to go to hospital; two years ago he walked about outside with bronchial pneumonia, frightened only of going to hospital and losing his home – he once lost his home before through unemployment. He is obviously a difficult man to

N   181

live with, but, I would guess, an entertaining drinking companion. He says he is not afraid of dropping dead in the street – and seems determined to do exactly this.

He has lived in Oldham all his life, with the exception of a few brief trips looking for work. He has lived in his present house for twenty-eight years.

He worked as an iron moulder for a large engineering firm in Oldham. He gave up work eleven years ago at the age of 65; until then he was working full-time. He missed his work – he talks proudly about the large size of the cylinders he was moulding. He also missed the good money, and the company – he worked in a gang of men – himself and one other skilled man, one semi-skilled, and two labourers. He was one of the first people affected by a new policy of compulsory retirement and he was only told he must retire one month before his 65th birthday. They said he would get 8s. a week pension, but he decided to leave straight away – 'I wasn't going to be fired' – and he then went immediately to the National Assistance who gave him just over the 8s. He sees nothing of the people with whom he worked, three of them are already dead – one died at 70 and another was killed recently at the age of 74. He made two attempts to work at other things. He 'tried to do a bit of gardening' but he was only paid 3s. an hour for it (in 1960), which he thought inadequate; he also worked a few days doing 'a bit of white-washing'.

Mr. Brown does what housework and cooking is done, and also the shopping. He claims to do the washing, with the exception of the blankets which he sends to the laundry. Three pairs of under-pants are hanging over the fire in the sitting-room.

He does exercises each morning, swims each week, walks a good deal, and is very proud of his health. The last time he saw his doctor was two years ago when he had bronchial pneumonia. The doctor told him to stop in bed, but he didn't do so. He knew his cheeks were getting sunken but he continued to go outside. He hasn't seen anything of the doctor since; he doesn't like bothering doctors, or anyone else, unless it's necessary. He only has a cough occasionally – just the same as anyone else. He also has a touch of arthritis in his shoulder, but it does not stop him sawing wood for himself in winter. Asked about a chiropodist he says he probably ought to go; he got some bad chilblains when he had pneumonia.

He was last in hospital in 1916 when some of the bones in his feet were broken – and he got a pension from the Navy for two years. He has not stayed in bed at all during the last five years. He doesn't know what would happen if he were ill; he would probably look after himself as before. He hates staying in bed, and 'I can't brood over things'.

His meals during the last twenty-four hours have been based on a chicken which a friend gave him. For breakfast on the day of interview he had bread and cold chicken. At 2 p.m. the day before he had some chicken and a tin of baked beans and some bread. He sometimes has a kipper for tea or some cheese – he brings out a packet of processed cheese from behind some clothing and a dusty radio on the sideboard to show me. In the evening he has nothing except a pint or two of beer. Asked whether he has a hot meal he says as many as he feels like – but this seems to consist mainly of warming up meat pies. (The gas stove looks as if it has not been used recently.) He has no help with cooking meals or shopping and he eats all of his meals alone.

He does not want a home help, and says he can do it all himself. He knows of a 'young man, well he's not young he's aged 70', who has a home help. Another neighbour works as a home help. But 'I'd rather do it myself'.

He has glasses for reading and another pair for other activities. Reading causes him difficulty and when I suggest having his eyes tested regularly, he seems mildly surprised. He has good hearing – he thinks it might be better but for wax in one ear – 'but I won't trouble anyone if I can help it'.

He thinks plenty is done for older people in Oldham such as 'concerts', but the Government doesn't give enough money to older people. He is against children's allowances and thinks they are an imposition on working people. One of his daughters has a children's allowance and doesn't even spend it, she just puts it away in savings. (He is against allowances and his daughter and the practice of saving.) He dislikes Pakistanis getting children's allowances.

His first wife died when he was only 23; the second wife also died, and his third wife died sixteen years ago when he was 60. He has children from each of his three marriages. The eldest is a daughter from the first wife; she lives on the other side of Oldham, is married with three children, and he never sees her. She was only one when her mother died in childbirth, and he kept her (or his mother did) until the girl was 13; then she went to live with one of her mother's sisters. He complains that this daughter's husband is a teetotaller – a foreman plasterer – and goes in for too much 'class distinction'.

From his second wife he has two daughters both of whom live in London. Both girls are married to 'proper Cockney husbands' and they have eight children between them; he saw them last about a year ago when he went down to London with the lorry driver next door. He goes out drinking with their husbands but he says Cockneys 'don't like us' – the sons-in-law soon go off and talk to someone else in the pub. He doesn't stay with his daughters when he goes down, but he stays with the lorry driver at a roadside place.

From his third wife he had two sons both of whom live in Oldham; they are both married with three children. He never sees them, and he is especially critical of them. One son was living with him until eleven years ago when he left to get married at the age of 30. His sons are 'two rough 'uns' – while he was away in London once they stole some things out of his house. Of his children in general he says: 'I've had hell with 'em.' All of them went to their mothers and 'I never had a wage out of any of them'. But his attitude is that his children are no good and not worth bothering about. (It does not seem to occur to him that he was probably not a very good father to them.) When I suggest children are usually closer to their mothers, he shrugs his shoulders and shows no interest.

He was the eldest of six children. Three of his younger siblings are already dead. He has one sister alive in Oldham and another sister in Wales about whom he knows nothing. The Oldham sister lives about one mile away and is single; the last time he saw her was seven months ago when he met her in the street. His eldest daughter goes to see her quite often; he implies they are both against him. His sister is 'a straight talker' – he almost seems to admire this – and she has never been willing to accept any nonsense from a man.

He has seventeen grandchildren and he claims never once to

have seen any of his eight great-grandchildren. He seldom sees any other relatives. He knows most of the neighbours but he never asks them for anything, and nobody offered to do his shopping for him when he had bronchial pneumonia. The only neighbour he sees much of is the lorry driver next door. He goes out with this man drinking sometimes and also calls in for a chat. He has one other friend, a younger man who works at pipe-laying and with whom he goes drinking; this man gave him the dog and also helped him by bringing firewood when he had pneumonia – the only person who gave him any help then.

Time sometimes goes slowly, particularly the early part of the evening from about 5 to 8 p.m.: 'It seems half a day.' Then he goes for a walk round and stops off at a pub – he usually only has half a pint at a time. 'You must keep exercising. It's no good sitting pining. There's a man up the street – I told him he should be exercising. I told him he was suffering from self-pity. He's never spoke to me since.'

Last night he walked about three miles with the dog. He had an old television which his pipe-layer friend gave him, but it's broken down and he's given it away – the licence was too expensive and he only likes boxing and horse racing. The woman at the pub down the street lets him watch boxing on the pub TV set. Neither of his radios work. He reads the *Daily Express* and the *People*. He used to read a lot but now 'too much reading hurts my eyes'. He used to 'study' the *Reader's Digest*; he brings some of these *Digests* out of a drawer – the last is two years old. He smokes a pipe, one and a half ounces a week; but he thinks too much smoking is bad for his eyes. He goes to a music hall once a month, because he likes the old tunes.

He used to belong to several fraternal organizations, but he hasn't been to any of them for some years. He thinks old people's clubs are good for 'lonely people who are left out', but they have nothing to offer him. 'I won't have it. All they want to know is too much of your business. They asked me to come.' He mentions cups of tea and charabancs, and says he doesn't want a lot of old women. He thinks some old men who go to clubs are worse than women; old men ought to think about the horse races they have been to in their younger days, and not worry about how 'they're going on' in the future.

185

Private Pursuits and Public Provision

He hasn't been to church since, as a boy, he sang in church choirs; when he was older he sang in pubs on Saturday nights. He has not been on a holiday for several years, apart from his trips to London. The last letter he wrote was over a year ago before he visited his daughters in London. 'I never worry about letters – none comes.' He can use a telephone, but never does.

He pays 18s. 9d. a week rent for his house, which has two bedrooms, one sitting-room and a kitchen. There is also a cellar, and a small attic which he says is falling down; the landlord won't do anything about the house. There is no bath – he goes out to the public baths once a week. His toilet is outside, down six steps which is no trouble for him – although he knows it would be for some old people. He likes the house and does not want to move. The house is cold in winter and draughty. The kitchen window gets very wet when the wind blows from that direction. Then he lights a fire in the kitchen instead of in the sitting-room. He has coats hanging over both front and back doors and he says these are to keep out the draught (even in May when the interview takes place).

He thinks people sponge on National Assistance. He himself gets 11s. 6d. a week. He has the same amount throughout the year. He has had one extra item during the last year, £2 for a pair of 'shoes' he bought – they are Army-type boots. He accepts the National Assistance officers and has no criticisms of them. He told the last one who came that some people were being given blankets and clothes and selling them in pawn shops or giving them away to relatives. He is wearing a jacket given him by the pipe-laying friend, as was another jacket he has. The friend jokes about it saying he gives him his clothes when the buttons come off.

He receives £3 7s. 6d. pension. He spends not more than 17s. 6d. a week on beer and tobacco. After paying his rent this leaves him just over £2. He spends about £2 a week on food. A man in a near-by factory gives him pieces of wood. He carries them up the hill to his home and he saws up the wood in his cellar. He never pays anything for this wood – and there is a pile of neatly chopped wood in the kitchen. He says his worst expense is food.

His father worked in the cotton industry. Both of his parents lived to the age of 78; he did not look after them at all in their later years. He himself has had 'a real good life'. His happiest time was between the age of 25 and 40. He was first married when he was 21 and his wife died when he was 23. His mother looked after the child, but he had difficulty in finding work. He claims to have walked to Leeds, to Liverpool, and to Barrow looking for work. When the war began in 1914 he joined the Navy. The unhappiest time was after the First World War when he was unemployed again. He had to give up his house and he slept in a lodging-house for six months. Then he got married again in the 1920's. Asked how long he wants to live he says he would like a long life. 'If I can keep walking . . . can't stick being in bed.' He is frightened of dropping down ill in the street because he thinks the doctor would send him to hospital and he would lose his home again; also his sons would come and steal things. But he is not afraid of falling dead in the street.

Despite several probes, he will say little about his wives; the first died in childbirth, but the second wife is particularly shadowy. However, he makes it quite clear that all three of his marriages were somewhat stormy.

Chapter Nine

USE OF TIME

Questions about their use of time will inevitably seem emotionally loaded to some old people who know they are leading lives now rather empty of activity. The most thorough method is to get the respondent to account for all the time spent in the day or week in question hour by hour, but there is still a serious 'recall' problem. The diary method is also unsatisfactory with random samples.[1]

Any method of measuring the old people's use of time would be subject to serious drawbacks; the method adopted here provides evidence which should be treated with caution. Three questions were asked. Firstly, 'What is the main thing in life out of which you get pleasure?' – an open question producing replies varying from an old woman who enjoyed going dancing and an old man who liked driving himself in his new car on lengthy trips across England, to an old woman who said 'My budgerigar' and an old man who said 'Going to bed at night.'

The second question, 'What activity occupies most of your time?' produced much confusion – revolving around the words 'activity' and 'occupy'. But this question acted as a useful bridge to the next: 'What activities did you engage in last week?' The old person was asked the number of days last week upon which he or she engaged in particular activities. Table 9.2 shows the proportions of the old people in the sample who had engaged in the activity on at least *one day* in the previous week. In Table 9.3 are given figures for those who had engaged in the activity on at least five days in the previous week; this has a dramatic effect on the figures for an activity like (clothes) washing, which two-thirds of the sample had engaged in at

[1] See above, p. 64.

188

TABLE 9.1 WHAT IS THE MAIN THING IN LIFE OUT OF WHICH YOU GET PLEASURE? (BY SUB-GROUPS)

	Socially Isolated			Often Lonely			The Single			Recently Widowed			The Housebound		
	M %	F %	M&F %	M %	F %	M&F %	M %	F %	M&F %	M %	F %	M&F %	M %	F %	M&F %
Reading	18	18	18	–	21	16	–	33	26	29	12	18	17	24	22
Knitting and/or sewing	–	17	13	–	24	19	–	24	19	–	21	14	–	19	15
Watching TV	9	10	10	–	10	8	9	7	8	24	15	18	17	19	19
Listening to radio	9	6	6	12	7	3	–	7	6	6	6	6	17	5	7
Housework	–	18	14	–	7	5	9	19	17	6	24	18	–	14	11
Seeing children and grandchildren	–	14	11	–	21	16	–	–	–	–	24	16	–	19	15
Gardening	18	13	14	–	3	3	9	10	9	12	18	16	17	5	7
Going out, walking etc.	9	8	9	–	3	3	–	14	11	6	3	4	–	–	–
Smoking	14	3	5	12	3	5	18	–	4	12	3	6	33	5	11
Having visitors, chat, etc.	–	4	3	12	7	8	–	2	2	–	6	4	–	5	4
Drink, pub, etc.	9	1	3	12	3	5	18	2	6	–	–	–	–	–	–
Church, chapel, etc.	5	4	4	–	3	3	–	7	6	–	–	–	–	–	–
Don't know, none, etc.	18	7	10	25	14	16	9	5	6	18	12	14	17	–	4
Total number	22	71	93	8	29	37	11	42	53	17	33	50	6	21	27
No answer number	2	5	7	2	0	1	3	2	2	1	3	4	0	3	5

least once last week, but which none had done on as many as five days.

TABLE 9.2 ISOLATED OLD PEOPLE: DOING PARTICULAR
ACTIVITIES AT LEAST ONCE LAST WEEK

	Male %	*Female* %	*Both sexes* %
Paid work	(5)	7	6
Shopping	(91)	80	83
Seeing relatives	(59)	59	59
Watching TV	(50)	55	54
Listening to radio	(73)	88	85
Cooking	(82)	96	93
Cleaning	(68)	92	87
Washing	(36)	75	66
Gardening	(32)	34	34
Morning newspaper	(73)	59	62
Evening newspaper	(27)	37	35
No newspaper a.m., p.m.	(14)	9	10
Magazines	(23)	33	31
Books	(23)	39	36
Sewing, knitting	(0)	51	40
Smoking	(59)	14	24
Walking	(27)	25	26
Going to club	(0)	11	8
Total	100	100	100
Number	22	76	98

No answer – 2.

Finally, in Table 9.4 the three lists are combined in order of frequency. There are some differences in the terms used between the 'main pleasure' column and the other two, but despite this several sharp contrasts emerge.

2. HOME-CENTRED ACTIVITY

The activities of isolated old people centre primarily around their own homes. Of activities taking place outside the home, shopping was done by the largest proportion of old people – 83 per cent – at least once during the previous week; but very

Home-centred Activity

few shopped as often as five days a week. Isolated old people obviously do not buy large quantities of food; they tend to prefer small local shops to the larger stores and supermarkets. The latter are often a bus ride away which, when buying small quantities, eliminates any price advantages.

Walking obviously varies greatly according to the time of year, and the locality. In South Norfolk many villages have no buses and the old person sometimes has to walk or not go at all; Oldham, on the other hand, is well supplied with bus services, and its steep hilly streets are a further disincentive to walking. Only a quarter of the sample had been on a walk during the previous week, but of these nearly half – 11 per cent of the total sample – took a walk five or more times in the week. Of all the activities conducted outside the home, walking had the highest proportion of the isolated elderly – 9 per cent – quoting it as their favourite activity.

'Seeing relatives' last week is seventh in order of frequency of activities, but it comes only tenth equal for five or more days

TABLE 9.3 ISOLATED OLD PEOPLE: DOING PARTICULAR THINGS FOR FIVE OR MORE DAYS LAST WEEK

	Male	Female	Both sexes
Paid work	(0)	5	4
Shopping	(18)	6	9
Seeing relatives	(13)	8	9
Watching television	(41)	43	43
Listening to radio	(59)	82	77
Cooking	(64)	74	71
Cleaning	(4)	30	24
Washing	(0)	0	0
Gardening	(4)	8	7
Daily newspaper	(73)	59	62
Evening newspaper	(27)	37	35
Magazines	(0)	3	2
Books	(9)	25	22
Smoking	(59)	14	24
Walking	(27)	6	11
Club	(0)	0	0
Total	100	100	100
Number	22	76	98

No answer – 2.

Use of Time

TABLE 9.4 ISOLATED OLD PEOPLE (MEN AND WOMEN):
ORDER OF FREQUENCY IN WHICH VARYING ACTIVITIES
ARE REPORTED

Main pleasure	At least once last week	Five or more days last week
1. Reading	Cooking	Radio
2. Housework ⎤	Cleaning	Cooking
⎬ 2 =		
3. Gardening ⎦	Radio	Newspaper (morning)
4. Knitting/sewing	Shopping	Television
5. Seeing children	Washing	Newspaper (evening)
6. Television	Newspaper (morning)	Smoking ⎤
		⎬ 6 =
7. Going out, walking	Seeing relatives	Cleaning ⎦
8. Radio	Television	Books
9. Smoking	Smoking	Walking
10. Church, chapel	Sewing/knitting	Shopping ⎤
		⎬ 10 =
11. Having visitors ⎤	Books	Seeing relatives ⎦
⎬ 11 =		
12. Drink, pub, etc. ⎦	Newspaper (evening)	Gardening

last week. 'Seeing children' comes only fifth in the table for main pleasures – and is quoted by 11 per cent of the isolated. Partly, this low figure is accounted for by 54 per cent of isolated old people being childless.

Such outside-the-home activities as going to cinemas, theatres, pubs or clubs are fairly infrequent for isolated old people. The evidence on pubs may not be very accurate; however, in the open question about pleasures, only 3 per cent of the men and women quoted pub-going or 'having a drink' as their main pleasure in life. Eight per cent had gone to a club in the previous week, but none had gone as often as five times.[2]

Gardening might be classified as either inside or outside the domestic sphere. Many of the houses – especially in Oldham and Northampton – have no gardens, but a third of all the isolated elderly have done some gardening during the previous

---

[2] Clubs are dealt with at greater length below, pp. 218–223. Table 11.1 shows a higher proportion attending clubs. This discrepancy arises because Table 11.1 is based on the four-area *screening* interviews whereas Table 9.2 is based on the follow-up interviews.

Home-centred Activity

week. Gardening is second equal as a favourite activity – being the favourite of 14 per cent of the sample. Gardening evidently gives great satisfaction to some active elderly people, and is engaged in equally by isolated men and women. It provides a variety of forms of exercise, and a chance to be creative; it can be a useful source of food. It may involve social contact as well – many old people report seeing more of their neighbours during good gardening weather. But although gardening provides satisfactions for some elderly people, for others it becomes a source of severe anxiety. While a garden can be a satisfying indication of an old person's continuing physical powers, an unkept garden full of weeds clearly indicates another old person's physical decline. Old people are less likely than others to be able to afford a gardener. Of course, old people's gardens are often cared for by others – sometimes a son or nephew; another common arrangement is for a neighbour to take over an old person's garden and to use it, in effect, as an extension of his own. But isolated old people, because of their very lack of a full family and social life, are less likely than others to get such help with their gardens. So strong is their antipathy to the possession of an untidy garden that some isolated people strain their already severely limited physical capacities in order to do a minimum of gardening.

The activity engaged in at least once a week by the highest proportion of isolated old people – 93 per cent – is cooking; it also has the second highest proportion doing it at least five times a week, 71 per cent of the isolated elderly cook that frequently. Another domestic activity, cleaning, features second on the at-least-once-a-week list, being done by 87 per cent. On this list, washing (clothes) comes fifth, so the three housework activities have a dominant position. A fairly high proportion also clean as often as five times a week. Perhaps slightly more surprising is that the blanket category of 'housework' ranks second equal in the list of main pleasures. Housework is a main source of pleasure for 14 per cent of the sample, all of these respondents being women; some of them refer to housework as 'my work'.

Another domestic activity which features high on the list of main sources of pleasure is sewing and/or knitting – reported by 17 per cent of the women; during the previous week half of

193

Use of Time

all the isolated old women had sewn or knitted. Some said it kept them occupied through the long hours of the day. It is also another indication of physical ability; some old women show their swollen arthritic fingers in explanation for not sewing or knitting.

Another major home-centred activity is consuming the offerings of the mass media – which isolated old people engage in overwhelmingly in their own homes.

3. THE MASS MEDIA

The importance of the mass media is most strikingly shown in Table 9.3 which gives the proportions engaging in activities five or more times during the previous week. Listening to the radio is first in frequency and, after cooking come morning newspaper, television and evening newspaper. The figures on main pleasures give a somewhat similar picture. 'Reading' is quoted by the most old people – 18 per cent. Television comes sixth in the list, being reported as a main pleasure by 10 per cent of the old people.

Leaving school at 13 or even younger and going out to work for long hours, many old people never learnt to read books:

'She watches television every evening. She has the *Daily Mail* and the local weekly paper. She says she could no more read a book than fly. She was the youngest of six children. . . . When she was a girl her mother used to stop her reading books and tell her to do something useful.' *Woman, aged 80, South Norfolk.*

Others complain of the lack of a library in the immediate vicinity. This is a particularly severe problem in the country:

He spent about half his working life as a coal miner and the second half as a farm labourer. He reads the *Daily Mail*, the local weekly and the *News of the World*. He likes reading cowboy books, but can't get them in the village. If there were a village library he would take books out of it, but he can't afford to buy them. (He gets National Assistance and has £3 4s. a week after paying rent.) So he does not read as much as he'd like. His main pleasures are watching the village football team and television. He takes his dog for a walk every day. *Man, aged 69, South Norfolk.*

194

The Mass Media

Some of the isolated old people do read a good deal:

> He was a machine operator, retiring at 71. He spends a lot of time on his allotment. He listens to the radio more than watching TV. He also reads the *Daily Express* and the local paper and he has a pile of library books – claiming he reads six books a week, many of them Westerns. He is a 'regular customer' at the local public library. *Man, aged 77, Northampton.*

However, the book readers are in a minority. Twenty-two per cent of the isolated elderly had read a book at least five times last week, and 36 per cent had read a book at least once last week. These figures may be slightly inflated; to most of the people in the sample the word 'book' means magazine, especially women's magazines. The comparable figure for magazine reading are 2 per cent and 31 per cent which is markedly lower than for book reading. However, both these forms of reading are undoubtedly much less widespread than is newspaper reading. The great majority of the isolated elderly have either a morning or an evening daily newspaper. Sixty-two per cent of the sample had a morning newspaper, the most popular paper being the *Daily Express*, followed by the *Daily Mail*, and then the *Daily Mirror*, *Daily Telegraph* and *Daily Sketch*.[3] There was only one *Daily Herald* reader, the same as for the *Daily Worker*. A number of people read the one popular provincial morning paper in the four sample areas, the Norwich *Eastern Daily Press*. Thirty-five per cent of these isolated old people read a local evening paper – such as the Manchester *Evening News*, the Oldham *Evening Chronicle*, and Northampton *Chronicle and Echo*, the Norwich *Eastern Evening News*, and the London *Evening News* (in Harrow).

Fifty-four per cent watched television in the previous week, and 43 per cent saw it on at least five days. The favourite programmes or type of programme most frequently quoted was 'plays'. The most frequently named programme was 'Coronation Street', followed in order by 'Emergency Ward Ten', 'detective', 'Here's Harry', boxing, 'Black and White Minstrel Show', 'Tonight', travel, religious services, and documentaries. Perhaps the most noticeable point is the very wide range of choice:

[3] Readership surveys indicate that the *Daily Express*, *Daily Mirror* and *Daily Mail* are the daily newspapers read by the highest proportions of all people in Britain aged 65 and over.

Use of Time

no less than forty-two different programmes or types of programmes were quoted as favourites.

Among those who watch at all, extensive viewing is usual;
a number of isolated elderly people reported having the TV
on for five hours or more each day. Some isolated old people,
who do not go to bed early, watch children's programmes in
the afternoon and continue watching right through till 11 p.m.
or later:

> Her husband was a machine minder in the cotton industry
> and she also worked in it till she was 50. Her only social contacts
> are her son, brother and niece, each of whom she sees twice a
> week. She reads the Manchester *Evening News* and knits a certain
> amount. Six months ago her son gave her a television. She
> watches it every night and says it gives her a lot of pleasure.
> Asked about her favourite programmes, she says, 'I like it all,
> I'm not funny.' *Woman, aged 74, Oldham.*

For one blind man and for several others with very poor
eyesight, television had less appeal than the radio. No standard
question was asked about this, but the non-viewers seemed to
be about equally divided for and against television. Those who
are against television give a variety of reasons:

> He has worked as a farm labourer and gardener and lost a
> leg in the First World War . . . He has lived alone since his wife
> died a dozen years ago . . . He describes himself as 'practically a
> hermit'. Asked about his main pleasure he says 'What can that
> be?' then he says religion and books. He has no newspapers,
> radio or television. 'I don't like 'em. I like me own life.' He goes
> to bed at 6 p.m. on winter evenings. *Man, aged 65, South Norfolk.*

'She lives alone; her husband, a building worker, died twenty-
eight years ago . . . Her chief pleasure is housework . . . She has
no TV set. "I don't believe in it. Where's the £4 coming
from?"' *Woman, aged 87, Oldham.*

For those who would like TV, the cost is the major obstacle.
Most of those who have no television do have a radio – and
indeed some of the isolated old people who retire to bed at dusk
on winter evenings lie awake listening to the radio:

> Married twice, she was both times quickly widowed. She
> worked for many years as a district nurse, and attributes her
> arthritis to bicycling in wet weather. . . . Now her eyesight is

196

The Mass Media

failing. She drops the stitches badly when she knits. Her other main pleasures are playing patience and 'I live for my wireless'. She goes to bed at dusk, 4.30 at this time of the year (December), taking the radio with her. She lies in the dark listening to the radio until the 10 p.m. news. She uses the electric light very little. *Woman, aged 73, South Norfolk.*

Listening to the radio is the activity which the largest proportion of the isolated elderly – 77 per cent – do at least five times a week; 85 per cent listen to the radio at least once a week. The most popular programme was *The Archers*, mentioned specifically by a fifth of the heavy listeners. The agricultural content of this programme appealed especially to isolated old people in South Norfolk – and several urban dwellers said that *The Archers* reminded them of their childhood spent in the country. Next in frequency of mention among radio programmes came plays, music, church services, 'Mrs. Dale's Diary', 'Any Questions', and orchestral concerts. Again there was a large spread in the types of favourite programmes.

The mass media appear to affect isolated old people in two separate ways. Some of these old people are very well informed about recent political events and trends in popular entertainment. Some of the interviewing took place at the time of Mr. Profumo's resignation and later that of Mr. Macmillan; isolated old people often spontaneously expressed considerable interest in these events and referred to how the politicians appeared on television.

On the other hand, another strong impression formed in interviews is that the mass media serve to emphasize to these old people their own isolated state. There are a good many grumbles that the papers, TV and radio don't have anything interesting in them any more – everything these days is for and about young people. Newspaper stories and broadcasts are quoted as examples of young people's delinquency, lack of respect for parents and older people, and so on. Quite frequently, the old people contrast their own childhood with present-day pop singers or other entertainment stars. But more than age differences, the mass media seem to project images of change, activity, social intercourse – which inevitably contrast sharply with these old persons' everyday isolated existence.

4. OLD MEN AND OLD WOMEN

Fifty-one per cent of women have knitted or sewn once in the last week, and no men report this activity. Less men wash their own clothes. Although over a third of men had washed clothes in the last week, the proportion of isolated old women was nearly twice as high. The women are also much more likely to do house-cleaning at least five days a week, although on house-cleaning at least once a week the men are not far behind the women.

More women read books – especially the isolated spinster school-teachers in the sample. The women also favour evening newspapers more while more men favour morning newspapers. This may be because old women prefer the local evening papers – especially the local deaths, births and marriages – while men prefer the national morning papers for sport and politics.

More men are smokers – over half of the isolated men smoke, against only 14 per cent of the old women. A standard complaint from the men is the cost of tobacco. (One old man said he sometimes rolled himself a cigarette filled with tea leaves.) Shortage of money plays a large part in the basically similar ways in which the old men and the old women use their time.

All but 14 per cent of the men and all but 9 per cent of the women read either a morning or an evening newspaper. Frequency of watching television is similar among men and women and in general they like the same sort of entertainment and variety programmes. There is a great similarity in domestic activities. Two-thirds of the men did some cleaning last week; and a higher proportion had done both cooking and shopping. As with women, a third of the men had done some gardening. On the negative side, the vast majority of the isolated old men – like the old women – were not in paid work and did not go to clubs.

Simply because the old men and old women engage in roughly similar activities, the two sexes do not necessarily regard these activities in the same light. Although isolated old men perform many of the same household activities as the women, none of the men quoted housework as a main source of pleasure, whereas 18 per cent of the women did. Nevertheless, isolation – for both men and women – means primarily isolation within the old person's own home, where his or her main activities are most likely to be cooking, housework and consuming the mass media.

Chapter Ten

MONEY

I. LOW INCOME

Socially isolated old people in the four-area sample as a group clearly have low incomes. Although at one extreme is a man who recently sold his business for £60,000, at the other extreme is an old woman who is living off a small and rapidly declining amount of savings and whose only income is under a pound a week. But the median income of all 100 socially isolated old people is a little over £4 a week. The great majority are very close to this figure: 68 per cent have an income below £5 a week and 80 per cent have an income between £4 and £7 a week.

The State contributory retirement pension forms the bulk of most of these old people's incomes. At the time of interviewing (1963–64) the standard rate of pension for a man retiring at 65 or a woman at 60 (with ten full years of contribution) was £3 7s. 6d.[1] The typical isolated old person had about this amount of State pension and one further pound of income either from having worked beyond the minimum qualifying age[2] or from some other source.

Eight per cent of the group had no contributory retirement pension. They had a median age of 82 and had been too old to pay any contributions; half of them were receiving national assistance.

Comparatively few – only 15 per cent – had any kind of pension other than the contributory State retirement pension; mostly these were occupational pension schemes. The recipients were mainly public service employees such as clerical workers or railwaymen or teachers. A quarter of the isolated men had these

---

[1] This amount has since been increased.
[2] A man who worked until age 70 or a woman to 65 could get a maximum total pension of £4 2s. 6d.

Low Income

other pensions, but only one-eighth of the isolated women. To repeat: 85 per cent of these socially isolated old people had no pension other than the State one; a number reported that their firms had introduced occupational pension schemes in recent years – but the respondents had been too old to qualify.

Another source of income is, of course, interest on invested savings (and in one or two cases rent from property). But few have substantial income from such sources; only 13 per cent of the isolated group have a total income, including the State pension, of £7 a week or over. Forty-four per cent of isolated old people are receiving national assistance – which is only allowed with a very low level of savings. Even more striking, the median income of the 56 per cent who are not receiving national assistance is no higher than the income of those who do receive it. While those who receive national assistance have a median weekly income of £4 6s., the non-recipients have a median income of only £4 4s. This apparently paradoxical situation arises because national assistance is allowed to old people primarily to help them pay their rent.[3] Nine-tenths of those receiving national assistance were paying rent, while only three-tenths of the non-recipients were paying rent; 43 per cent of the whole isolated group owned their homes or other-wise paid no rent. The 57 per cent, who paid rent, paid a median rent (including rates) of exactly £1 a week. There is a good deal of regional variation in rent levels; the median rent in Harrow is £1 10s. a week, but in South Norfolk among the elderly isolated it is only 10s. a week.

No systematic investigation was conducted into how these isolated old people spent their money. However, for the great majority who had incomes around the median figure of just over £4 a week there was obviously little to be spent on anything other than rent (or rates), food, and fuel. All the isolated respondents were asked if they had any 'special difficulty' paying for food, clothing, rates, or fuel. Fifty-nine per cent reported difficulty with at least one expense – two-thirds of whom

[3] At the time of the interviewing the National Assistance Board's ruling was that a person living alone would 'ordinarily be regarded as needing £3 3s. 6d. a week (or £2 15s. if he is not a householder) plus an allowance for rent . . .' The ruling on capital was that 'no grant will ordinarily be payable if the value of the capital is more than £600 . . . no account is taken of the value of an owner-occupied house or the first £375 of "War Savings".'

Money

said fuel was a difficult expense. Although the interviewing took place right round the year (mid-1963 to mid-1964) it did follow the severe cold months of early 1963 – and this may partly account for the majority referring to fuel, most of whom actually said 'coal'. A quarter of those replying quoted rates (and rent). A fifth said clothing was a special difficulty; this group had a median age of 74 – a reminder that clothes can wear out after ten years of retirement.

2. NATIONAL ASSISTANCE

Of the socially isolated who receive national assistance, three-fifths are widowed women. Five-sixths of the whole group are women. Only a third of the isolated men, but a full half of the isolated old women, receive national assistance. This is to be expected in view of men's greater chance of having occupational pensions and the preponderance of widowed women in the isolated group. It is more surprising, however, that 44 per cent of all the isolated receive national assistance. This is double the proportion in the whole population of old people.

Among all old people about half as many against as receive national assistance would probably be entitled to it, but do not apply.[4] There is no indication of such a sizeable group among the isolated in the four-area sample. At most there is another 5 per cent of the old people who might get national assistance if they applied, but the numbers are too small for this to mean much. What is quite apparent is that national assistance is a major factor in the financial existence of isolated old people. A number of those not at present receiving national assistance have applied without success, and others say they will apply soon when they have spent a little more of their savings and come within the qualifying limit. Thus among these socially isolated old people 49 per cent either currently receive or are entitled to receive national assistance; if those who have already unsuccessfully applied to get it, or expect to receive it in the future, are added, then more than half of these old people are involved.

The isolated old people were asked what they thought about national assistance – in particular whether it was 'a charity' or whether 'everyone has a right to it'. Many of those who received

[4] Dorothy Wedderburn and Peter Townsend, *The Aged in the Welfare State* (1965).

National Assistance

national assistance gave somewhat ambivalent replies. Most of the old people said firmly that people had a right to national assistance – if their need was sufficient; the uncertainty was as to how and why need was assessed in the means test operated by the officers of the National Assistance Board. There was widespread agreement that national assistance was better than the earlier system – some respondents recounted stories of 'relieving officers' telling them or their parents to sell pieces of furniture before any cash would be forthcoming; but there was a variety of opinion as to how big the change had been.

A number of old people insisted that they and their families had paid for national assistance and thus they were 'entitled' to receive it:

> She says: 'The Government gives us nothing; our sons and husbands paid for it.' She receives 15s a week national assistance. She thinks it is very different now . . . In the 1920's when her husband was unemployed the relieving officer came and told her to sell the baby's high chair and the fireguard. *Woman, aged 70, Northampton.*

Old people receiving national assistance are normally visited once every six months by an officer. Isolated old people tended to say that the officers were pleasant; comparisons with the inter-war period were invariably favourable to the National Assistance officers of the present. The great majority reported the last visit of the officer as being brief – sometimes only 'two minutes' – and the officer being a 'nice' person, or 'all right'. But one in seven of isolated old people receiving national assistance had something critical to say of at least one officer:

'He thinks most of the officers are reasonable although some are "very haughty". You never know what's going to happen, whether some money may be knocked off.' *Man, aged 76, Oldham.*

'The National Assistance officer comes in May and November; he looks at her bank book and rent book. They are usually very nice, except for one woman officer she did not like.' *Woman, aged 75, Northampton.*

The name of National Assistance itself produced a good deal of confusion; one in ten of the isolated old people could not remember the name at all or called it 'National Health'. A

National Assistance

number called it alternately 'National Assistance' and 'Public Assistance' – an obvious hangover from earlier terminology. One person put explicitly an idea that others seemed to be hinting at:

"She thinks national assistance is good 'for poor old things who need it'. She gets 5s. 6d. a week, throughout the year. She thinks National Assistance 'ought to be given a better name'. She herself refers to it some of the time as 'Public Assistance'. *Woman, aged 76, Norfolk.*

Some old people say they were extremely reluctant to start having national assistance. Receipt of national assistance is seen as a loss of independence; one man said: 'You don't want people at your door.' Others regard it as indicating a severe decline in social status, and going to collect the money may become an ordeal:

Before the war she employed a full-time maid. . . . She receives no pension from her husband's work. After he died she steadily spent her savings, and accepted national assistance only when her doctor eventually persuaded her. She gets 18s. in summer and 24s. in winter. 'It made me ill, accepting it at first. It's a bitter pill to swallow.' At the post office where she first drew the money there was a 'hostile atmosphere'. The post office to which she now goes is much nicer; they put your pension book and national assistance book together – not showing them to other customers. She would like to have the whole sum in one book, because it's so 'demoralizing' having other people looking. When she worked for a time last year she felt 'ten years younger', because she did not have to draw national assistance. *Woman, aged 65, Harrow.*

Other isolated old people reported being encouraged to apply for national assistance by their doctors, neighbours or relatives. One recently widowed old woman said her husband had first discovered their entitlement to national assistance when he read a letter in the *News of the World* from a man in similar circumstances.

When they arrived at the office for the first time some old people were startled to find themselves among not merely other old people, but also unemployed men:

She gets 4s. 6d. a week national assistance. 'I stood out against

Money

it; I only had it because I was drawn in.' She describes her first visit to the National Assistance officer and the number of people waiting, 'blacks and whites'. There was a man shouting at one of the officers. When she talked to an officer, she tried to pull up her chair to the table, but the chair was 'fast to the floor'. The officer told her this was because some people got so angry they wanted to pick up the chair and hit him with it. *Woman, aged 73, Oldham.*

There is a good deal of confusion as to how the additional discretionary grants are made for such things as clothing. A number of old people are confused by the way in which extra allowances are paid for fuel in winter; often the old person can quote a case of someone in apparently similar financial and health circumstances who is receiving a different amount of money from the National Assistance Board. Nevertheless despite general confusion as to how the regulations are applied in detail, there is a fairly widespread understanding among those on national assistance that, for instance, if their rent is increased the amount will be reimbursed by national assistance. On the other hand a few isolated old people on national assistance lack even a general idea of how the system works; they seem to regard national assistance as totally unpredictable.

These isolated old people's experience of national assistance is probably different from that of old people who are not isolated. Old people with children often receive financial and other help from them; through their children or other social contacts they may be better informed about how State provision for old people functions.

Undoubtedly national assistance plays an important part in the lives of the 44 per cent of those isolated old people who receive money from it. A number brought up the subject spontaneously early in the interview, as did some others who were not at present receiving national assistance.

3. POVERTY AND SOCIAL ISOLATION

Does poverty predispose some old people to social isolation? Isolated people almost all live alone – whereas most of the non-isolated live with others. Thus isolated old people tend to pay more rent (because they do not share it with others in the

204

Poverty and Social Isolation

house). On the other hand the State provides bigger pensions for widowed or single women than for married women; and those with higher rent obligations will get more from the National Assistance. But if receipt of national assistance is taken as an indication of poverty, then a higher proportion of these isolated old people are living at the poverty level than is the case with the elderly population at large. But being qualified for and receiving national assistance is hardly in itself sufficient to predispose old people to isolation. However, living alone (and paying rent alone) not only predisposes old people to social isolation but also plays a part in qualifying them for national assistance.

This is the basic connection between low income and low social contact: old people are predisposed to both states by living alone and a number of other factors. Old men as a group are better off financially than old women, while widowed and single women have particularly low incomes.[5] Similarly, lack of a husband correlates strongly with social isolation. The same is true of children – they are a source both of social contact and often of a variety of small payments and gifts. Some isolated old people also receive support from children:

'Her television is paid for by her children, as is her washing machine and newspaper bill; her son and daughter sometimes buy her groceries. She pays 12s. a week rent to her daughter who is the landlord; some structural work has been done on the house recently.' *Woman, aged 83, Northampton.*

However, childlessness is a major factor in social isolation (Table 3.3); so lack of children not only cuts off old people from one form of financial help, it also predisposes them to social isolation.

Paid work also is a source both of income and of social contact. The socially isolated are unlikely to be working full-time (Table 3.8) and even those few who do some work have median earnings of only £2 10s. a week.

Increasing age also correlates both with lower income and lower social contact. Social contact declines with age because of the increasing proportion of widows, the death of siblings

[5] Dorothy Cole (Wedderburn), *The Economic Circumstances of Old People* (1962), pp. 53–7; Peter Townsend and Dorothy Wedderburn, *The Aged in the Welfare State* (1965).

and so on. These changes similarly affect income; the older age-groups are also less likely to work, and have had more time to spend their savings. Among the socially isolated those receiving national assistance have a median age of 75, whereas those not receiving assistance have a median age four years younger.

The same factors which contribute to social isolation also contribute to lower incomes. It is impossible to say any more on the present evidence about the connection between poverty and isolation. However, 44 per cent of the socially isolated are on national assistance, with a median income of £4 6s. a week; most of them pay about £1 a week in rent (and rates). Those not on national assistance often own their own houses, but have a median income of only £4 4s. If the National Assistance Board's scales are accepted as an official definition of poverty, the great majority of the socially isolated are at no more than £1 a week above the poverty line.

Chapter Eleven
SOCIAL SERVICES

I. THE GENERAL SPREAD OF SERVICES

Table 11.1 gives information from the four-area survey on the coverage of some of the more important services among different categories of old people. None of the services has a very high coverage even among the groups with which this study is particularly concerned. The general medical practitioner service has easily the widest coverage. Next come clubs, and the domiciliary services are lower still. The housebound are the most likely to have seen their doctor in the last week and to have a home help.

The relationship between these categories may be complex. The highly anomic, for instance, tend to have a low level of contact with the social services. The anomic group's negative attitudes to 'public officials' might perhaps lead them to avoid the social services; on the other hand lack of the services may contribute towards the anomic attitudes.

The social services constitute possible sources of social contact; anyone who has contact with these services increases his social contact score and has less chance of being socially isolated. But few old people score more than two or three contacts a week from these services. Moreover in view of the high age of the socially isolated and their general lack of social support, they might be expected to have more contact with the social services than does the elderly population at large. However, in fact, the socially isolated have about as much contact with these social services as do old people in general.

2. DOCTORS

In the four-area study 13 per cent of socially isolated old people saw their doctor in the previous week. This is less than the

Social Services

TABLE 11.1 PROPORTION OF OLD PEOPLE IN CERTAIN
CATEGORIES RECEIVING SOCIAL SERVICES

	Living alone	Socially isolated	Often lonely	Highly anomic	Single	Recently widowed	6 months housebound	All old people
Doctor last week	15	13	(18)	10	19	12	(29)	16·7
Home help last week	7	8	(4)	5	7	8	(13)	4·5
Nurse, Health Visitor, Blind Visitor last week	3	3	(0)	2	3	3	(9)	1·7
Meals-on-wheels last week	3	4	(2)	1	5	0	(4)	1·3
Old people's club last week	9	10	(9)	4	12	3	(0)	7·8
Non-old people's club last week	12	11	(7)	7	19	8	(0)	11·3
Voluntary Visitor last week	1	2	(2)	0	0	0	(2)	0·9
Minister or Vicar last week	4	2	(2)	2	7	12	(4)	5·4
Seen Minister, Vicar last week but not been to church in last month	0	0	(0)	1	0	0	(2)	1·3
Total	100	100	100	100	100	100	100	100
Number	151	111	45	96	58	60	45	538

16·7 per cent for all old people in the four-area sample, but the same as for the national survey (12·9 per cent).[1] Of the socially isolated 22 per cent had not seen their doctor in the last year, as against 30 per cent for all old people of both sexes in the national survey.

Sixty per cent of socially isolated old people in the four-area study saw their doctor three times or less in the previous year.

[1] Proportions of old people receiving social services in the two samples:

	National	Four-area
Proportion of all old people seeing doctor last week	13.0%	16·7%
Proportion of all old people having home help last week	4·4	4·5
Proportion of all old people receiving meals-on-wheels last week	1·1	1·3
Proportion of all old people attending old people's club last week	6·6	7·8
Proportion of all old people attending any kind of club last month	23	25

Doctors

A sizeable minority see their doctor something like once a month; this reflects a common habit of general practitioners – several of whom showed the present writer a short list of elderly patients whom they visited about once a month.

The great majority of contacts with doctors take place at the doctor's surgery. Only 30 per cent of socially isolated old people had received a home visit from the doctor in the previous year. Only 20 per cent had received two or more home visits in the previous year. Of all the home visits paid by doctors to the socially isolated, 83 per cent of the visits were to only 10 per cent of the old people.

What old people think of their doctors cannot be reliably deduced from a sample obtained from doctors' lists. The old people were told in the screening interview that their name was one chosen from their doctor's records. Most of the old people had a strongly positive response to this information. Frequently during the follow-up interviews the old people referred to how satisfied they were with their doctors; many of them – especially the working-class old people – appeared to view their doctor with some reverence and awe. Things which the doctor had said years ago about the old person's health were repeated at length. Of course most old people are keenly interested in their health, whether they think it good or bad.

A number of old people said that when they were children before the First World War, you only went to your doctor in extreme emergencies. The National Health Service did not arrive until most of these old people were in their fifties and sixties, and some old people say they are still reluctant to go to a doctor unless there is something seriously wrong with them. The odd ache or pain is often not regarded as sufficient reason for seeing the doctor.

A typical comment from an old person about attending the doctor's surgery is: 'I go to see him every two months to get my pills.' Many doctors' consultations appear to be very brief and physical examinations are rare – this impression is supported by medical studies which report substantial proportions of old people suffering from severe conditions unknown to the general practitioner.[2]

[2] J. Williamson, I. H. Stoke *et al.*, 'Old People at Home: Their Unreported Needs', *The Lancet* (23 May 1964).

Social Services

Many old people seem to regard their doctor as the most powerful and important person with whom they have contact. In the sphere of social services this has some objective support; and, of course, in the field of ill-health, the doctor's word carries great authority. However, there are signs of some isolated old people feeling resentment against their doctors:

> She would like to see her doctor more frequently than the two occasions on which she saw him this year. A few months ago she wrote asking him to call. But he did not come – 'that made me feel awful.' Now she won't call him again whatever happens. Her previous doctor arranged for her arthritis to be treated at the hospital – electrical treatment, wax, and injections. But her new young doctor said such treatment would no longer help her. She is worried and puzzled, claiming her arthritis has got considerably worse since last year. 'I've never liked going to a doctor. I hate going even more since this young doctor came here'. *Woman, aged 71.*

Four per cent of the isolated old people said they would like to see more of their doctors; this group had seen their doctors an average of twice each during the previous year. But to most of these isolated old people the idea of agreeing or disagreeing with a doctor's actions appears to be meaningless. The overwhelming impression is that isolated old people's attitudes to their doctors are primarily of respect and acceptance.

3. OTHER MEDICAL SERVICES

Social isolation among old people might be related to poor sight or poor hearing which made social intercourse especially difficult. In follow-up interviews the old people were asked whether they had any difficulty with sight or hearing, but no marked difference emerged between the socially isolated and other old people. Socially isolated old people might still have less good sight and hearing – but be unaware how bad it is. A note was kept of old people who did not admit difficulty with hearing but nevertheless appeared to have difficulty. However, when an isolated old person seems to hear badly it might be due to mental confusion or lack of practice in carrying on extended conversations. Similarly when an old person appears to have especially bad eyesight, this may be due to life-long difficulty

Other Medical Services

with reading or to some quite different mental or physical condition. Nevertheless among the socially isolated, as among other elderly people, there is undoubtedly a heavy incidence of difficulty with both sight and hearing – much of which is not being treated. Moreover, difficulty with sight and hearing will probably pose severer problems for old people living alone and in isolation.

Ninety-four per cent of old people wear spectacles (national); 36 per cent of the socially isolated reported having either 'a lot' or 'a little' difficulty with seeing – and 3 per cent had difficulty but possessed no glasses. Four per cent of the socially isolated were wearing glasses originally fitted not for themselves but for a daughter, sister, husband or neighbour. At least 3 per cent, and probably more, of the socially isolated wore glasses but had not had their eyes tested in the last five years; 3 per cent said they needed to have new glasses. Thus at least 13 per cent of the socially isolated required attention for their eyes.

A number of others had been receiving eye treatment – in particular cataract operations. There was substantial dissatisfaction with National Health provision of spectacles, and a general perplexity in dealing with the system:

> She has 'a little difficulty' with seeing with glasses. She recently had her eyes tested at the hospital and went to collect two new pairs of spectacles from the local optician. But the new glasses made her eyes run badly, so she went back to the optician; he said the prescription had been followed accurately, and that the test in the hospital must have been incorrect. But she has not been back to the hospital – saying she doesn't want to 'show up' the man there who tested her eyes. Meanwhile she is not using the new spectacles for which she paid £5. *Woman, aged 66, Oldham.*

In contrast to the situation with spectacles, relatively few old people possess hearing aids. Only 3 per cent of the socially isolated had a hearing aid and only 2 per cent used them regularly. But 19 per cent of the socially isolated admitted having difficulty with hearing and another 2 per cent were noted to have unadmitted difficulty. Why such a small fraction of people with hearing difficulties use hearing aids is not clear;[3]

---

[3] Peter Gregory, *Deafness and Public Responsibility* (1964).

negative attitudes to hearing aids in general and National Health aids in particular were readily expressed. However, there is a widespread attitude that hearing fails in old age and cannot be alleviated.

Many old people have trouble with their feet – such as thick nails and corns. Arthritis, fatness, poor eyesight, breathlessness and dizziness make it difficult for other old people to attend to their own feet. The socially isolated group may be expected to have a somewhat bigger physical need than other old people, since they are somewhat older, and a markedly bigger social need for chiropody – since an old person living alone with little social contact is less likely to have anyone who will regularly help him with cutting toe-nails, treating corns, or simply washing his feet. However, only 19 per cent of the socially isolated receive chiropody – the same as for all old people (national). Another 3 per cent had had regular chiropody in the past but were no longer doing so; and 9 per cent of the isolated were not receiving regular chiropody but said they wanted to do so. Some receive subsidized chiropody for 2s. 6d. or 3s. 6d. a session, while others do not have the service because they find the full price too high:

> She suffers from an arthritic spine, and high blood pressure; not long ago she had an operation for a duodenal ulcer. She tries to walk a half a mile or more every day. She has seen her doctor six times in the last year; she has been to a chiropodist once for a corn on her toes. But at 12s. 6d. a time, she thinks chiropody is too expensive; if it were cheaper she might go more often . . . She has £3 12s. a week after paying rent. *Widow, aged 65, Harrow.*

Sixty-nine per cent of the socially isolated have not had chiropody recently and say they do not require it, but on an objective medical test some of these probably would be regarded as requiring chiropody:

> Hardening of the arteries and high blood pressure affect his feet. He wears bedroom slippers. His swollen feet, he says, are the main reason he goes out very little. His grandson, whom he sees once or twice a week, cuts his toe-nails. Because he complains about his feet I ask about a chiropodist: 'No, you have to go right up about a mile, and it's only a lady who does it.' When his feet are particularly swollen he bathes them either in vinegar

or in Epsom Salts and water. He sees his doctor once a month and gets a new supply of pills for his blood pressure – 'made with Horlicks', he comments. He has little faith in doctors. While still running his coal delivery business, fifteen years ago, he injured his foot and the doctor said he would never walk properly again. When he came back from hospital in the ambulance, he picked up a sack of coal and carried it up and down the lane. Not only does he get no chiropody, he has no glasses, but shows me how he reads with the aid of a large magnifying-glass. He also never wears his false teeth – they don't fit well. He is a bit deaf and puts vaseline in his ears for this. *Widower, aged 76, Oldham.*

Of all old people 1·7 per cent saw a home nurse, a health visitor or a blind visitor in the last week (Table 11.1). The home nurses' visits were concentrated among the housebound group. One isolated, but not housebound, old woman was receiving visits from a nurse:

> She had a severe stroke about two years ago; she sleeps on the ground floor and seldom goes beyond the corner shop just down the street. One of her hands was badly affected by the stroke and this makes washing difficult. A nurse comes once a week to wash her feet and cut her toe-nails. She looks forward to these visits. *Widow, aged 75, Northampton.*

Two per cent of the socially isolated are registered as partially sighted and receive regular visits from blind visitors. Three per cent of the isolated see health visitors; one health visitor was calling on an old woman who had had a growth removed from her breast recently, another woman had previously been suffering from malnutrition and a third did not know for what specific reason the health visitor called.

The great majority of socially isolated old people have spectacles – which seems also to be true of dentures (not dealt with in this study). But apart from about a fifth who have chiropody, other contacts with medical auxiliaries have a very low coverage. No other medical service comes near the spread and frequency of 78 per cent contact in one year – achieved by general medical practitioners among isolated old people.

Social Services

4. THE HOME HELP SERVICE

4·4 per cent of old people have a local authority home help and 9 per cent have a private domestic help. Another 5·7 per cent are not receiving, but want a domestic help (national).

The four-area study shows that those living alone, the socially isolated, the single, the recently widowed and, of course, the housebound are more likely to receive the home help service. Nevertheless of 538 old people interviewed in the four-area survey twenty-four had home helps; only a quarter of these recipients were housebound and less than half lived alone.

Socially isolated old people are twice as likely to receive a council home help, but less likely to have a privately paid domestic help, than the elderly population at large. Some old people live in large households where a private domestic help is paid for by a child or other relative; the socially isolated, most of whom live alone on low incomes, are apparently recognized by local authorities to be in greater need of home helps.

In the lowest social class (R.G. 5) 4·5 per cent of old people have local authority home helps while only 1·6 per cent have private domestic helps; in the highest social class (R.G. 1) 42 per cent have private domestic help while only 1·2 per cent have council home helps. Of old people who receive home helps about a third have a home help one day a week, a third have one two days a week, a third for three or more days a week (national).[4]

In the four-area survey nine socially isolated and five non-isolated old people who received the home help service were re-interviewed (fourteen out of twenty-four recipients from the screening interviews). The median of these fourteen was an old person having a home help coming three days, for a total of five hours' work a week. All the helps were doing heavy cleaning work, and half were doing light jobs such as dusting or washing-up. A third were shopping for the old people and a third were washing clothes. Most home helps are told not to clean windows, but one was doing so regularly; and one home help was cooking midday meals three times a week for a blind old man.

[4] Peter Townsend and Dorothy Wedderburn, *The Aged in the Welfare State* (1965.)

The Home Help Service

Old people receiving the service tended to be frail and in the higher age-groups; the median old person had been 78 before she first received the service and was now aged 81. During the years she had been receiving the service she had had a total of two or three home helps.

A hard-core of home helps are very stable – several old people had only had the one help coming regularly. But another group of home helps only do the job for a short time – one old person had had five different home helps in three months.

The old people were asked their home help's age and they often knew it precisely – the median being 41 – half the age of the old person. The majority thought the home help was good at understanding the needs of old people, and that she did the work cheerfully:

'My God yes, she sings all the time. You have to tell her to knock off.' *Man, aged 65, Northampton.*

'She's my own type – working class. Some of them prefer the expectant mothers, but she loves old people. She stays past the time to have a chat.' *Woman, aged 90, Harrow.*

On the other hand one old person in five was severely critical of the home help – for gossiping too much, not working enough, or stopping early:

'The home helps are shocking. People don't want to do housework. They're a poor lot. Most of them prefer to work in the factory. She's a busy-body – she knows everybody's business, and never has a good word to say for anyone.' *Man, aged 81, Norfolk.*

Those who are paying part or all of the cost of the home help are usually visited by a 'collector' who calls every four or six weeks. Some old people confuse this person with the 'home help organizer', the local council official who administers the service. Old people receiving the service on a regular basis are apparently only visited infrequently by the organizer.

'The organizer goes mostly to the ones who need looking after. She comes here about once a year – for a minute or two – just to say she's been.' *Woman, aged 80, Harrow.*

'When the organizer came I thought she was the new home help. All dressed up, she was, with a car outside. I told her to to get stuck into the housework. That got rid of her quickly.' *Man, aged 76, Oldham.*

Social Services

Five per cent of the socially isolated did not have, but wanted, the service. All five live alone; one is housebound with minimal social contact. Four of the five are aged 80 or over, and three of the five are extremely isolated. Four of the five had had a major illness in the last few years with an extended period in bed at home or in hospital.

Three per cent are living alone in extremely filthy conditions and yet deny needing a home help. Two of these three are men, and the third is a woman who is suffering from severe arthritis and poor eyesight. In addition some others only manage to do without a home help by tremendous effort and determination.

> She lives alone in a one-bedroom flat on the first floor of a large new block. She has been housebound for seven years and her arthritis is making any movement steadily more difficult. She is 'severely incapacitated' (9). Throughout the interview, she hobbles back and forth on her huge, swollen feet with the aid of two sticks; her hands shake badly and she cannot sit down without severe pain. It takes her five minutes to reach the front door. In the morning she has to exercise her limbs for an hour before she can get out of bed. Her doctor, who calls about once a fortnight – sometimes on Sunday – wants her to have a home help. 'Sometimes I think I'll have one . . . but I don't know. They say you never know which day they're coming.' She has meals-on-wheels five days a week. Her niece comes once a week to clean the windows. But she herself claims to be able to do all the rest of the cleaning. She has dish mops for cleaning the hearth and the floor; she puts paraffin rags over the end of the mop. The flat is very clean. 'I'm rather determined,' she says.
> *Woman, aged 73, Harrow.*

Among those who do not use the service the most commonly expressed attitude is one of indifference. The next most frequent attitude is of approval – the service is very good for people who need it. The third most commonly expressed attitude is that 'it depends who you get'. These old people usually know either from old people who are home helps or from other people receiving the service that individual home helps vary considerably. Another attitude is expressed by old people who know ex-home helps; these old people say that the service is excellent, but the old people it serves – especially the old men – are too dirty.

Mobile Meals and Visiting

But strong criticism is confined to a minority of all isolated old people. The majority are either indifferent or enthusiastically in favour of the home help service.

5. MOBILE MEALS AND VISITING

A range of other domiciliary services for old people scarcely show up on a sample of the four-area size. No attempt was made to ask people about such services as the special laundry services (primarily for the incontinent and infirm) which are operated by some local authorities. However, a good study of the meals-on-wheels service already exists.[5] The national survey found that meals-on-wheels were being delivered to 1·1 per cent of all old people in private households. None of the sub-groups, not even the long-term housebound, were receiving this service in any substantial proportion. Four of the 100 socially isolated people re-interviewed in the four-area study were receiving meals-on-wheels – in all but one case, two meals a week. The great majority of the isolated said they knew nothing about the service and were not interested.

Table 11.1 shows a more substantial proportion of the socially isolated who have seen their religious minister or vicar in the last week, 5·4 per cent; but the majority were seen at a religious service or some other church activity – 17·3 per cent of all old people say they have been to a religious service in the last week (national). Table 11.1 also shows the proportion of old people who have not been to a religious service in the last month but have seen a minister during the last week. Only 1·3 per cent of non-church-going old people have seen a minister in the last week, and no isolated old people at all. There is thus little evidence of old people receiving domestic visits from religious ministers.

'Voluntary Visiting' is also shown in Table 11.1. Just under 1 per cent of all old people and 2 per cent of the socially isolated had seen a voluntary visitor in the previous week. None of the other categories of old people has a higher level. Altogether five old people out of 538 had seen a voluntary visitor; three of those five were not living alone and four of the five were not housebound.

[5] A. Harris, *Meals on Wheels for Old People* (1960).

217

Social Services

6. CLUBS FOR OLD PEOPLE

After doctors, clubs are the community service with the widest coverage among old people (Table 11.1). All the other services in the four areas have a roughly equal coverage among old men and old women, but old people's clubs are mainly frequented by old women. Only 4·5 per cent of old men have been to an old people's club in the last week, against 8·1 per cent of old women. However, somewhat more old men than women have been to a club not restricted to old people. Three-quarters of all old people have not attended any kind of club in the last month.[6]

Apart from the housebound, the other sub-groups of old people considered in this study show much the same attendance level as the elderly population at large. Three in every ten old women attending an old people's club are isolated. But socially isolated old men are extremely unlikely to attend either kind of club.

Only 27 per cent of those attending old people's clubs in the last week were old men (national). Old men who go to the clubs are mainly married men going with their wives; three-quarters of the men going to other sorts of clubs were married old men.

Old people's clubs seem to appeal particularly to widowed and single women, but by no means exclusively. The groups they appeal to least are single and widowed old men. Old people of both sexes attending old people's clubs are somewhat younger than the elderly population at large; only 19 per cent of regular attenders at old people's clubs are 75 years or older, against 34 per cent in the elderly population at large. Old people attending other kinds of clubs are also drawn predominantly from those under 75 – which suggests that the frailty of

[6] Figures based on the 538 of the four-area sample and 2,500 of the national sample compare as follows:

	Four-area			National		
			Both			Both
	M.	F.	sexes	M.	F.	sexes
Old people's club last week	3%	11%	7·8%	4·5%	8·1%	6·6%
Any club in last month	22%	28%	25%	23·8%	22·4%	23.0%

218

TABLE 11.2 SOCIAL ISOLATION AND CLUB ATTENDANCE

	Old people's club last week			Other club last week			Any club all last month			All old people		
	Male	*Female*	*Both sexes*	*Male*	*Female*	*Both sexes*	*Male*	*Female*	*Both sexes*	*Male*	*Female*	*Both sexes*
Isolated	(0)	(31)	(26)	(7)	(29)	20	(4)	31	22	14	25	21
Intermediate	(57)	(46)	(48)	(33)	(47)	41	(46)	46	46	49	57	54
High contact	(43)	(23)	(26)	(59)	(24)	39	(50)	23	32	37	18	26
Total	100	100	100	100	100	100	100	100	100	100	100	100
Number	(7)	(35)	(42)	(27)	(34)	61	(46)	91	137	210	328	538

those over 75 is the major reason for their lower participation. Social class provides one of the sharpest differences between clubs for old people and other clubs. More working-class old people attend old people's clubs and more middle-class old people attend other types of clubs. This is especially so among old women. Only a fifth of women attending old people's clubs are from the non-manual classes against half of all old women attending other kinds of clubs – such as the Women's Institute, Townswomen's Guild and Church Social Groups.

Twenty-one old people were re-interviewed who had been to an old people's club in the last month. Only one club met more frequently than one afternoon a week, and some met only fortnightly or monthly. They met on weekdays normally from 2 to 4 p.m. or 3 to 5 p.m. The one club which met more frequently was also the only one having its own premises; it was open in the afternoon and evenings each day of the week, with special times for such groups as handicapped old people. But all of the other clubs rented or borrowed church halls, community centres and village halls.

Half the members said their club was called 'Darby and Joan' or the 'Over-Sixties' club, while others gave names like 'Evergreen', 'Silver Lining', 'Cosy Corner' or such neutral names as 'Community Club'. Almost all of the old people said they had talked and had a cup of tea at the last club meeting. A third had played bingo. A few old people had had a 'singsong' or some kind of entertainment. Advertising films were also mentioned. One old woman reported having listened to a Civil Defence lecture about what precautions to take against atomic fall-out. Most clubs had a Christmas party. In the summer there were bus-trips, usually lasting nearly all day:

> She enjoyed a recent bus outing, when 120 old people went to Cambridge; what she liked most was the American war cemetery. There was a long discussion among the old people as to whether the bodies were actually buried in the cemetery. She thought the Cambridge colleges were dirty, and she didn't like the fish and chips served at the cinema where they had tea. The outing cost 14s. 6d. *Woman, aged 71, Northampton.*

Some outings are to visit other old people's clubs – or working men's clubs – at a town or village elsewhere. Most of the clubs also organize a summer holiday for members. These vary from

Clubs For Old People

an out-of-season (May or September) visit to an English seaside resort, to a bus trip round Switzerland. The oldest members usually say they found these holidays – like the day trips – too strenuous.

The old people were asked who organized their club. Some said the W.V.S., or the local church or chapel; but over half gave the name of an individual, or said 'the Committee', or 'the helpers'. Only one woman criticized the organization of a club, and her reaction had been to leave and join another. Three-quarters said the usual attendance at their club was between twenty and seventy, but a few clubs were bigger. A typical reply on the cost of attending a club was: 'Tea, threepence. Membership threepence, sandwiches twopence, bingo a penny.' All the clubs expect old people to pay something for their refreshments. Most of the public announcements in the clubs seem to concern money – raffles, bring-and-buy sales, sub-sidized holidays and parties.

Asked what they get out of going to old people's clubs the members are fairly unanimous:

'Good companionship. Somewhere to go.'

'We get together and have a good laugh.'

'Takes you out when you might not bother.'

'Just the company. To feel you're getting chatting.'

Four-fifths mentioned one or more particular people they knew at the club; nearly half were either sisters or neighbours. The majority of club members say they always sit with the same group.

'I get together and have a chat with my old school friends. We sit at a table, seven of us, and we call ourselves "the dead-end kids".' *Woman, aged 71, Harrow.*

Few old people report sitting by themselves in the club, and few went by themselves in the first instance. Three-quarters say a particular person either invited them or took them to the first meeting – some were asked by club organizers or committee members, others by sisters, neighbours or friends.

In some parts of the country, for instance South Wales, one-sex clubs are common – with a larger proportion of old men than old women belonging to clubs.[7] However, in the four areas of this study only one person belonged to a one-sex club – and

[7] C. C. Harris reports this situation in Swansea (Personal communication).

he was not currently attending; the club was that rather rare thing, an all-day club:

His club is only for men over 65. 'It's companionship and it gets you out of the house.' He plays dominoes and is a reserve for the cribbage team. The club meets in a hut nearby. 'Our hut is one of the best in town.' It's open from 9.30 a.m. to 9.0 p.m. every weekday and has only thirty-five members. Usually about a dozen are there at one time. The council pays for electric light and upkeep and any old man can join. *Man, aged 84.*

Most club members belong only to one club, but a few go to more. One woman attended three old people's clubs and an all-age one; of course, some clubs which are nominally for people of all ages are in fact composed mainly of elderly members.

Ten per cent of the socially isolated have been to an old people's club in the last week and 15 per cent in the last month. There is no indication, however, that clubs make much attempt to recruit isolated members; 3 per cent of the socially isolated old people who were re-interviewed had stopped going to old people's clubs – two referred to increasing physical difficulty in getting there and back, and one man had stopped going when his wife died. None of these three club members had been encouraged by organizers to continue in active membership.

Another 12 per cent of the socially isolated have never been club members but say they would be interested in attending; they might go if they were driven, if they had a friend, or if they received an invitation:

'I haven't bothered. If I had a friend I might go, but I can't push myself. Some of these things get into clicks.' *Woman, aged 68, Oldham.*

'It's always the same gang going on the outings. They've never come to me with a cordial invitation. Some people are perpetual hangers-on. Yes, I might go if they asked me. I'm a great mixer. I've had a bit of free and easy. I like a nice sing-song.' *Man, aged 74, Harrow.*

However, 70 per cent of the socially isolated are not involved in and not interested in old people's clubs. A quarter said they preferred to keep to themselves, they didn't like mixing, or they were too immobile to get to meetings. A third of all the non-attenders were firmly critical of the clubs – saying they preferred the company of the young, that clubs were for the

Clubs For Old People

'lonely', the 'decrepit' or the 'dodderers' who talked about their ailments, their grievances and the past. Several felt 'not old enough yet'. Some people explicitly were against the passive role of the clubs or their working-class atmosphere or both:

'The local Darby and Joan's just for marrying them off. I can't picture myself sitting on a hard chair, wearing a funny hat and singing "Knees Up, Mother Brown". Old people's clubs are sterile, like Women's Institutes. They don't do anything. They ought to be marching up to London and making demands.' *Single woman.*

Another third were either in favour of old people's clubs although not personally interested, or had no opinion to express about them. However, all the socially isolated knew what the clubs were and almost all knew where at least one club met in the vicinity.

7. HOUSING

Those old people who live alone live in somewhat worse housing than do old people as a whole. Only two-fifths of those living alone have sole use of their own kitchen, fixed bath and an inside toilet; 45 per cent of those living alone have no inside W.C. – against 38·9 per cent for all old people. Eight per cent of all old people living alone have no water toilet at all, but only a chemical or other type (national).

The housing of those who live alone cannot be directly compared to the housing of those who, for instance, live with their children. This may be a comparison between one old person living in a home which is too big and in bad repair, and another old person living in a home which is in a good state of repair, but too small. (For instance, one housebound old woman had moved to live with her daughter after a severe illness – which involved one member of the household sleeping in the kitchen.)

By 1963 over 300,000 'single-bedroom dwellings suitable for elderly people' had been built by local authorities in England and Wales.[8] Of the socially isolated group in the four-area survey who were re-interviewed, 13 per cent were living alone

[8] *Health and Welfare: The Development of Community Care,* Ministry of Health (1963), p. 15.

223

Social Services

in this kind of accommodation. There were four different kinds
of local authority 'old people's housing' – small groups of
flats or bungalows exclusively occupied by old people; flats in
big blocks also containing larger flats occupied by young people
with families; and two old people lived alone in bungalows
with *two* bedrooms, which nevertheless seemed to be primarily
intended for old people.

Most of these old people said their present housing was an
improvement on what they had lived in previously. But all
except two had strong criticisms to offer. Two-thirds had some
complaint about the heating arrangements. A third had had
frozen or burst pipes since being in their special housing.
Draughts from ill-fitting windows and doors were frequently
mentioned. None of the homes had central heating – but a lack
of any planning in the heating provision was the general complaint.

> She thinks the open fire should not have been on the outside
> wall, but on an inside wall so as to warm the bedroom as well.
> She uses a paraffin heater for her bedroom in cold weather, coal
> for the sitting-room fire, electricity for hot water, and gas for
> cooking – four kinds of fuel in one small bungalow. Her pipes
> froze last winter. *Woman, aged 73, Harrow.*

The next most frequent criticism was about the baths. Six
of the thirteen were not using them at all, two were having
difficulty and only seven were having no trouble. The main
criticism was that the baths were not designed for the use of
old people:

'She doesn't use her new bath because she is afraid of falling.
When I suggest a special fitting on it she says she cannot imagine
the council liking such alterations. It is a small block of flats
for old people.' *Woman, aged 81, Northampton.*

One flat, built in 1960, had bare concrete floors. In one
bungalow a cupboard handle was eight feet from the floor, and
in a flat a woman of 87 had to stand on a chair to reach a kitchen
cupboard. Noise was another complaint; one old woman's bedroom immediately adjoined the main front door of a large block
of flats in which younger people lived. Nevertheless despite
these criticisms the old people did not want to move. They
thought the new housing could have been better, but it was
still greatly preferable to what they had before.

Housing

Twenty-five per cent of all the socially isolated said they wanted to move from their present home. They were asked if they would like to move 'into a small block of new flats specially built by the local council for older people?' Twenty-one per cent of all the socially isolated said they would like to move into such a flat – or a bungalow. (Unfortunately the bungalow option was not included in the question.) There was a strong preference for bungalows – which is supported by other evidence on old people's housing. The preference for bungalows was especially strong in the country area of South Norfolk. However, a few old people were equally strongly in favour of a small flat. One person who wanted a bungalow had never been inside a bungalow of any kind.

With 13 per cent of socially isolated old people already living in specially built housing, this type of social provision is undoubtedly having an impact on the isolated group. The present evidence does not make clear whether moving to such housing has any general effect on social contact scores. The old people living in this special housing seemed to know several of their neighbours; but this might be simply because special housing attracts those who already like interacting with other old people.

Part IV

DISCUSSION

The concluding three chapters of this book report no further empirical evidence from the four-area survey. The first discusses *personality* and its relevance to social isolation; although social isolation correlates with a number of variables there are always exceptions to the trend. Personality may play a large part here. The next chapter deals with the relevance of social isolation to general *social theory* about old age. The final chapter makes an attempt to show how *social policy* might be developed to help alleviate social isolation and loneliness.

These discussion chapters range more widely over the whole of old age. The intention is to set the empirical evidence in its general context. In each case it is suggested that insufficient attention has been paid to the substantial minority group of socially isolated old people; studies of personality in old age may paint too optimistic a picture by having ignored important minorities among the elderly. Social theory, while perhaps being somewhat over-pessimistic about old age in general, has failed to distinguish adequately the minority patterns in old age (for instance among the single and childless widows) where the evidence seems to justify some pessimism. Social policy while being vaguely intended to cater for minority groups of old people, has in practice been unsuccessful in searching out the minority group of the socially isolated.

Such inadequacies in personality studies, social theory and social policy stem in part from the extraordinary difficulty of the problems involved. It is much easier – once a definition of social isolation has been decided – to find out what proportion of the socially isolated live alone, or go out to paid work than to answer questions like: What part does personality play in an old person becoming socially isolated? The problems of concept and method are complex indeed. Even the definitions of old age

Discussion

and ageing are major hurdles. In those societies where few people live to 65, can old age be said to exist at all? Moreover, in social policy a whole new series of chicken-and-egg questions can be posed about what constitutes 'need'.

Value judgements inevitably enter into discussions of any of these issues. In studying the connection between personality and ageing such concepts as 'successful' adaptation inevitably arise. Social theory in comparing old age in industrial society with old age in peasant or primitive societies, and in dealing with functions and roles within the human family also cannot avoid value judgements. The same is obviously true of social policy.

This is not to say that the early part of the present study is free of value judgements. Clearly even the choice of subject matter, here as elsewhere, involves such judgements, which continue to operate through the study. However, while they have lurked in the background to date, in these discussion chapters values come to the centre of the stage.

Chapter Twelve
PERSONALITY

I. SOCIALIZATION IN OLD AGE

The problem of studying the personality of a seven-year-old child whose social experience is limited to contact with his parents, his siblings and play- and school-mates is obviously more simple than examining the personality of a seventy-year-old widow – whose past is so much longer and more varied and who may not always be willing to co-operate with a more youthful investigator. A key question is to what extent personality is regarded as being fixed in childhood, which in turn depends on how 'personality' is defined. James E. Birren writes:

> 'Personality' is a difficult term to define, since there is such a wide variety of theories and measurements. In general, 'personality' refers to the distinctive behaviour patterns of individuals . . . While there is measurable continuity in personalities from early childhood onward, continual evolution of the personality over the life span would seem to characterize the healthy, adaptive adult . . . The adaptive person continually modifies his behaviour over time, thus aging successfully.[1]

If the basic personality is set in early childhood, with subsequent changes or adaptations, the question now revolves around the extent to which social isolation in later life may be connected with personality patterns set in the early years, and the extent to which it may be associated with changes in later life, such as failure to adapt successfully.

As a biological process ageing appears to take place at a fairly steady pace. Despite these important biological changes the social roles which individuals perform, especially in their work, remain comparatively stable. Retirement comes rather abruptly.

[1] James E. Birren, *The Psychology of Aging* (1963), pp. 231, 248 and 249.

Personality

For men, retirement is accompanied by other important changes – such as loss of income, and loss of status. Social ageing thus tends suddenly to present the older person with the problem of adapting to new patterns of behaviour. Old age is for each individual who reaches it a new experience. The ageing man or woman may have thought of reaching old age, just as the adolescent may have thought of becoming an adult. But in each case he has not been here before. There are new patterns or behaviour to evolve or to learn. It is thus legitimate to refer to 'socialization' in old age. Robert Merton defines socialization as 'the learning of social roles'.[2] Just as medical students have to learn the social role of doctor, so ageing people have to learn the social role of the old person.

Because retirement from work usually happens rather abruptly, and since work tends to mean so much to men, adapting to old age may be more difficult for men than for women. But retirement is not the only crisis connected with old age. Especially for the socially isolated and the lonely there have often been other crises, such as widowhood. Friends and brothers and sisters themselves retire, become less active, and die – so the level of social contact tends to decline. The old person may face other new problems – such as the departure of the youngest child to get married. For the housebound, reduced physical capacities tend to produce severe limitations on social activity. Some old people experience none of these crises, but pass from a state of full social engagement – in work, marriage, and good health – straight into death. However the old people with whom this study is particularly concerned do face some or all of these crises.

For these old people the socialization in which they are involved has a large negative aspect. They experience what American sociologists call 'role loss'. They lose a variety of roles – as spouse, as employed person, as wage-earner, perhaps also as friend, sibling, neighbour. The housebound lose their role as physically active person. The socialization of old age is concerned with learning such new roles as widow, retired person, pensioner; the housebound have to learn a version of the 'sick role'.

[2] Robert K. Merton, George Reader and Patricia L. Kendall, *The Student-Physician* (Harvard University Press, 1957), p. 287.

Socialization in Old Age

Some old people take up new roles such as club member; those who join old people's clubs or in other ways become actively involved in meeting with or working for other old people as a group have been termed the 'Ageing group conscious'. They tend to associate more with their own age-group, and when with them to discuss health and old age problems more than do other old people.[3] This is one process by which an ageing person may adjust to his or her new roles.

Just as a child learns to behave as a schoolchild by going to school and mixing with other children, so an old person learns about being an old person if he or she goes to an old people's club or otherwise takes part in old people's activities. But only a small minority of old people go to old people's clubs; isolated old people often have no friends, or brothers and sisters with whom to interact. A married couple can learn about the problems of old age to some extent by growing old together – but a widow or a single person lacks even this aid to old age socialization. Many widows interact only with their children or other young people and have few contacts with elderly people. Some old people must learn to adapt to old age by themselves or with their children (who in turn often have no previous intimate experience of old people); many old people are surprisingly ignorant of basic facts about old age and are unable to see their own problems in perspective. Thus the more isolated an old person is the more difficult it may be to adjust to old age – simply from lack of the socializing influence of people of the same age.

This brings us to the question of success and failure in ageing, If one is to discuss how the individual *adjusts* to his new circumstances, how he *accepts* his losses of familiar roles, how he *socializes* himself to new roles – then some old people will obviously do this more successfully than others. Broadly there are two main theories as to how successful ageing may be achieved. One is the 'activity' approach – which says that the individual should keep at work, join clubs, continue to see people. The other main approach proposes that a more passive style leads to successful ageing; the more passive style of ageing

[3] Arnold Rose, *Group Consciousness Among the Aging*, Paper at International Social Science Seminar, Markaryd, Sweden, 1963.

has been called 'disengagement',[4] or the 'rocking-chair' pattern.[5] Some social scientists believe these active and passive approaches are not necessarily mutually exclusive – there may be more than one way of ageing successfully.

In what does unsuccess consist? The authors of *Aging and Personality* categorize those who are bitter, 'angry', or 'self-haters' as being unsuccessful. Richard H. Williams has suggested 'Autonomy' as a criterion of success. 'Independence' is another possibility, but a category which it is very difficult to define in practice.[6] Those who seek to pin down success are driven back to using scales of 'morale', such as that conceived by Kutner, or Leo Srole's scale of anomia. The authors of *Growing Old* admit, however: 'It can be argued that these items ask only for expressions of placidity or contentment which might actually be apathy.'[7]

Discussion of success and unsuccess inevitably involves value judgements. Cumming and Henry criticize the 'implicit theory of aging' which recommends an old person to keep active; they criticize naïve conceptions in the popular literature such as that a person abruptly enters old age at one point in time. Cumming and Henry suggest on the contrary that ageing is a process – 'an inevitable mutual withdrawal or disengagement, resulting in decreased interaction between the aging person and others in the social systems he belongs to.' They argue that 'we can describe the process by which he becomes so, and we can do this without making assumptions about its desirability.'[8] However, Cumming and Henry also talk about 'successful aging' at some length.[9] One could argue that to say something is successful is merely to observe that it has reached a certain objective, but surely in this context the authors are 'making assumptions about its desirability' – or do they regard successful and unsuccessful ageing as equally neutral?

Cumming's and Henry's book is an extremely important pioneering work in the field of personality and ageing where the

---

[4] Elaine Cumming and William E. Henry, *Growing Old: The Process of Disengagement* (1961).
[5] Suzanne Reichard, *Aging and Personality* (1962), pp. 129–35.
[6] Elaine Cumming and William E. Henry, op. cit., p. 129.
[7] ibid., p. 129.
[8] ibid., p. 14.
[9] ibid., pp. 128–42.

Socialization in Old Age

conceptual problems are far from easy. The problems of method are even more difficult; but before discussing these perhaps it is worth considering in more detail two works in this field – one of them Cumming's and Henry's.

2. RETIREMENT

This section discusses a study conducted at the Institute of Industrial Relations of the University of California (Berkeley). *Aging and Personality* by Reichard, Livson and Peterson is a study of eighty-seven older men, half of them retired and half still at work. The men, mainly skilled manual workers, were each interviewed for about nine hours in weekly sessions, concluding with a series of psychological tests. The influence of E. H. Erikson is acknowledged: 'Erikson regards the achievement of integrity as the crucial task of the final stage of life.'[10]

The study indicates that the real personality crisis comes immediately before, not after, retirement. It is those not yet retired who are most worried about retirement, most concerned about their health, and most anxious about death. Cumming and Henry agree: 'Those who find the thought of death most alarming are the men under sixty-five.'[11]

Among married older men, successful adjustment does not depend greatly on having children or seeing them; the role of husband is more important than the role of the father. The better adjusted tend to be better off financially and to like travel. Men who enjoy release from the pressures of work adjust better. Those who have stable work records and are satisfied with their occupational careers are most willing to accept growing old. 'It may be that the key to successful aging is held by one's past – or, more precisely, by one's view of the past.'[12]

The study reports five main patterns of adjustment, three successful and two unsuccessful. The *Mature* are involved in warm personal relationships and welcome retirement as an opportunity for more interaction. They have a sense of humour, are relaxed and enjoy hobbies. They are independent, but not

[10] Suzanne Reichard *et al.*, *Aging and Personality* (1962), p. 4.
[11] Elaine Cumming and William E. Henry, op. cit., p. 71.
[12] Suzanne Reichard *et al.*, op. cit., p. 108.

235

rigid. Happily married, they are flexible and realistic – especially in appraising themselves. They accept their pasts and after a life full of satisfactions they approach death calmly.

The *Rocking-chair* men are much more passive and dependent, often married to a domineering wife. They do not go out to see people but prefer to stay at home. Unambitious, they didn't like work and welcome retirement. They are fairly satisfied, have no feeling of failure and appreciate the freedom to enjoy leisure which ageing brings them.

The *Armored* men are the third of the categories who adapt successfully. They over-control their impulses, are rigidly, fiercely independent and are unwilling to discuss intimate matters. They had a stable work career, are afraid of being idle and are reasonably satisfied with their past, but they talk somewhat defensively about their wives and are reluctant to face death.

The *Angry* men adjust badly. They are hostile to other people, and blame others for their own lack of success. They are highly aggressive and prejudiced, projecting hostility on to other racial groups and on to women. They had unstable job histories, and exhibit rigid negative attitudes to retirement. They fight against growing old, are dissatisfied with life, and are anxiously preoccupied with death.

The *Self-haters* are the second poorly adjusted group. They admit their lack of success and were poorly adjusted at work. Unhappily married, they reject their wives. They openly despise themselves, and have failed to come to terms with their own past. They welcome the idea of death as a release from an intolerable existence.

The study was designed as an exploratory one. Not all of the men with whom interviews were completed fell into one of the five categories. Only a minority are placed into the three 'successful' categories – which has rather pessimistic implications, since as the authors say: '. . . the men we studied were not incapacitated by the most acute problems of aging – poverty, illness, and social isolation . . . they did not adequately represent the despondent, the sick, the isolated among the elderly.'[13]

Moreover, this study deals only with men, whereas poverty,

[13] Suzanne Reichard *et al.*, op. cit., p. 169.

Retirement

illness and social isolation are mainly concentrated among old women. Retirement also involves women. Single women who have worked all their lives and some women who have been widowed for many years are often deeply involved in work. Retirement affects other women indirectly. For if their husband's death is the major loss of old age for many women, the husband's retirement is another important loss – financially and in status. For some women – such as the wives of the 'mature' men – their husband's retirement will have its compensating advantages. But for other women – such as those married to 'angry' men or 'self-haters' – their husband's retirement is probably most unwelcome.

3. DISENGAGEMENT

This section deals primarily with Elaine Cumming's and William E. Henry's *Growing Old* which Professor Talcott Parsons calls in his foreword 'Probably the most serious attempt so far to put forward a general theoretical interpretation of the social and psychological nature of the aging process in American society.'[14]

Growing Old is based on a study conducted in Kansas City. There were two samples, one of men and women aged 50 to 70, and a second of people aged over 70. The chronically ill and certain other minority groups were excluded; the main sample were interviewed for a total of seven to eight hours each. Several measures were made of the process of disengagement between the individual and society. The 'Role Count' deals with the number of active roles a person has – such as household member, kinsman, neighbour or worker. While Role Count deals with variety of interaction, the 'Interaction Index' measures density of interaction, in particular the amount of time spent each day in social intercourse. A third measure, 'Social Life-Space', is a quantitative estimate of the numbers of 'discrete contacts' with others which the respondent has in a month. On all three measures of social involvement a fairly abrupt decrease was found – it occurred five years earlier among women than among men. 'The aging person sees fewer kinds of people, less often, and for decreasing periods of time as he grows

[14] Elaine Cumming and William E. Henry, op. cit., p.v.

237

Personality

older.'[15] However, according to the theory, not only does society disengage from the ageing person, the individual also disengages from society. At the personality level there is a falling off in ego energy: '. . . with increased age there is less ego energy available for responding to the environment. The older person tends to respond to inner rather than outer stimuli, to withdraw emotional investment, to give up self-assertiveness, and to avoid rather than embrace challenge.'[16]

The disengagement theory proposes that a mutual severing of ties takes place between a person and others in his society. Because interactions support social norms, decreasing social interaction leads to increased freedom from everyday norms of behaviour, which becomes a self-perpetuating process. Since the central social roles of the sexes differ, disengaging from these roles differs for men and women. Disengagement may be initiated either by the individual or by the society through such mechanisms as age-grading and industrial retirement policies. If only the society or only the individual is ready, disengagement probably results, but when both society and the individual are ready disengagement is always completed. The abandonment of men's central work role and women's marriage and family role leads to loss of morale and crisis, unless different roles are available, appropriate to disengagement. A shift in the quality of relationship occurs in the remaining roles. Vertical relationships such as those involved in responsibility for children are abandoned, and a shift takes place towards more horizontal relationships which are less demanding and more optional.[17]

The disengagement theory fits closely with the Reichard 'Rocking-chair' men. There is the same stress on sensuality, and satisfaction with a greatly reduced level of activity, the same decreasing involvement with a variety of people and increasing interest in self. Richard Williams and Claudine Wirths also stress the importance of disengagement; they suggest that television has become the medium of disengagement. William Henry agrees that American TV programming allows an older person to sit in complete physical and psychic immobility

[15] Elaine Cumming and William E. Henry, op. cit., p. 51.
[16] ibid., p. 127.
[17] ibid., pp. 210–18.

238

Disengagement

contemplating and re-examining many values of his earlier life and of the society at large.[18]

Anyone who has done any interviewing of randomly selected old people – even when the interview is not directed towards personality – will agree that the phenomenon described under the name of disengagement does exist among old people. *Growing Old* has a number of strengths, not least of which is the presentation of old age as a process, developing over time. The key question about disengagement is not whether it exists as a process among old people, but to how many old people it applies.

It is difficult to avoid the conclusion that Cumming and Henry have overstressed their differences from 'problem-oriented' writing about ageing.[19] and have thus become unrealistically optimistic. Of the very old they say:

> To sum up, we suggest that, given an adequate income, the very old enjoy their disengaged existence. They have reduced their ties to life, have shed their cares and responsibilities and turned to concern with themselves. They lead static, tranquil, somewhat self-centered lives, which suit them very well and appear to provide smooth passage from a long life to an inevitable death.[20]

Even if this picture of happiness is not exaggerated it is strange, if an adequate income is – as these authors suggest – the only prerequisite for happiness in extreme old age, that they give so little consideration to the variable of income. In fact, Cumming and Henry say that their sample are wealthier than the general aged population in America.

Another example of Cumming's and Henry's tendency to gloss over some of the aspects of old age which are less obviously easy to 'enjoy' is their treatment of widowhood. The disengagement theory of course encompassed widowhood – a dramatic example of role loss. The authors, however, seem to think the problem of widowhood capable of solution:

> In the first place, widowhood is an honored state . . . In the

[18] William E. Henry, *The Theory of Intrinsic Disengagement*, Paper at the International Social Science Seminar on Social Gerontology, Sweden, 1963.
[19] Elaine Cumming and William E. Henry, op. cit., p. 16.
[20] ibid., p. 209.

Personality

second place, widows are identified to a large degree with their late husband's careers, and though they may lose financial status, they do not need to lose such prestige as their husbands had at the time . . . Finally, widows have a ready-made peer group in other widows, and there is reason to believe that they join this very happily.[21]

This may be true of some, but it is clearly not true of many other widows in America and in Britain.

The whole question of social isolation is not adequately dealt with in the disengagement theory. The theory emphasizes that the logical termination and completion of disengagement is death. It might therefore seem logical that the stage previous to death would be institutionalization or social isolation – evidence of the continuing loosening of social ties.

It may be well to regard the disengagement theory as an adequate description of ageing as experienced by many, perhaps most, fairly healthy and economically secure old people. But it is not acceptable as a picture of ageing among other important groups of old people, such as the housebound or the extremely isolated.

4. PERSONALITY AND SOCIAL ADJUSTMENT IN OLD AGE: COMPLEXITIES

Little research has been conducted on personality in old age, especially compared with the amount on personality in child-hood. What constitutes the 'normal' social development of a child in a given society and time is comparatively clear cut. Events such as starting in school, or puberty, take place within a fairly narrow margin of years. But social development in old age conforms to no such clear norms. Even retirement for men varies to some extent and such other crises of old age as widowhood, or severe physical illness, follow no 'normal' pattern.

There is no agreement as to which the key years are for the personality of old people. A basic problem of old age research is that the elderly population are *survivors*; and certain types of personality may be associated with early death before old age.

[21] Elaine Cumming and William E. Henry, op. cit., p. 33.

240

Personality and Social Adjustment in Old Age : Complexities

The departure of children, retirement, decline in health, loss of friends and siblings, and widowhood – all call for adaptation by the old person. But this cannot be regarded merely as a one-way connection. The personality of the ageing person may also affect and shape these crises. An obvious example is of children moving out of the parental home, which some ageing people resist. Health and retirement can be affected by personality; some types of personality refuse to retire, while others are eager. Loss of contact with age-mates may also be affected by an old person's changing attitudes, or, for instance, his decision to move home to live elsewhere.

Personality also contributes to a person's marital status; certain types of young personality are obviously more predisposed to marriage than are others. Separation and divorce presumably also do not occur on a completely random basis from the personality point of view. Nor can widowhood be regarded as quite independent of personality. For instance, women who marry men ten years younger than themselves can be expected to differ in personality, as a group, from women who marry men ten years older than themselves. The second group, of course, are much more likely to suffer widowhood in old or middle age.

A two-way connection is also likely between old people's personality and other sorts of social contact, such as the social services. Two old people may objectively have an equal need but while one old person persuades the doctor she needs a home help, the other old person may be too proud, or otherwise reluctant, to ask. The same is probably true of institutionalization. Some kinds of personality are much more determined than others to avoid going into an institution.

5. PROBLEMS OF METHOD

Cumming and Henry say: 'The ideal way to study a process is to watch it happen and measure its extent.'[22] In practice, the social scientist usually has to settle for something a little less ambitious. Watching disengagement happen would be a long business, if, as Cumming and Henry, indicate, it can last for up

[22] Elaine Cumming and William E. Henry, op. cit., p. 24.

to forty years in one individual. The Kansas City studies used two samples, one based on a random sample of people aged 50 to 70, and the second a quota sample of people aged 70 to 90.

A basic difficulty of this type of research procedure is that differences in attitude or personality between one sample of people with an average age of 60 and another with an average age of 80 cannot be attributed solely to one group being twenty years older than the other. Quite apart from the problem of sample attrition through death some differences may be due to the two groups having gone through childhood and come to adulthood at times when typical social values in the society were not the same. In the Reichard *Aging and Personality* study there is also, despite the more narrow sampling, some hint of this type of difficulty. The 'Armored' men had an average age of 73,[23] whereas all the men of the other four personality groups combined were about ten years younger.

Perhaps the most severe problem of method in studying old people's personality and using – as both the *Aging and Personality* and the *Growing Old* studies do – a series of long interviews is the loss of respondents through refusal and for other reasons. In the Cumming and Henry study in Kansas City the initial health questionnaire suffered a 5 per cent loss; after a controlled reduction on certain grounds there was a loss of 17 per cent of the remainder. At the second round of interviews 91 per cent of these were successfully interviewed, followed by 82 per cent at the next round, then 74 per cent and 66·2 per cent at the fifth round.[24] With interviews being spaced about six months apart, some of the loss was inevitable, because of death or removal from Kansas City. Nevertheless, the total loss by the fifth interview is of almost half the sample originally approached in the screening interview – quite apart from other groups which were intentionally dropped.

In the Reichard study the interviews took place at a time interval of only one week. Nevertheless, of the men who met the study's sampling criteria only 71 per cent agreed to participate. Moreover, the original group were not approached through a systematic sampling method. The majority of the retired men

---

[23] Suzanne Reichard *et al.*, op. cit., p. 136.
[24] Elaine Cumming and William E. Henry, op. cit., pp. 233–5.

were contacted through unions, while the majority of non-retired men were contacted through employers.[25]

Because of the multiplicity of difficulties involved in studying personality in old age there is pressure to cut out some of the major variables. The Cumming and Henry study excluded all Negroes, who of course are a sizeable minority group in the United States. They also decided to reduce the class variable: 'We decided to eliminate the lowest and highest layers of the class structure. Lower-class people are difficult to communicate with and require special interviewing techniques.'[26].

The Reichard study is also based on a sample of men 'somewhat better off, in all probability than the average retired manual worker.'[27] This is important since the study indicates that adequate finances play a part in adjustment to old age. For instance: 'Travel was more frequent among the well-adjusted than among the maladjusted. All but one of those in the well-adjusted group mentioned travel as a recreational activity.'[28] Both studies excluded people who were chronically ill.[29]

The 'disadvantaged', as they are referred to in these studies, are particularly reluctant to submit to a series of personality-oriented interviews. Reichard comments: 'Indications of depression, apathy and resignation were frequent among those who refused to participate.'[30] Cumming and Henry report that the 'suspicious and isolated' bulked large among the refusals; they also note a larger loss from the panel of people with a low level of interaction.

Probably less than two-fifths of those with low social interaction from the original sample of old people continued to the last interview reported in *Growing Old*. The authors indeed comment that continuing through the rounds of interviews may be connected with narcissism: 'In short those people who like to talk about themselves to outsiders remain while those who find this distasteful fall out. . . .'[31]

---

[25] Suzanne Reichard *et al.*, op. cit., pp. 16–18.
[26] Elaine Cumming and William E. Henry, op. cit., pp. 232–3.
[27] Suzanne Reichard *et al.*, op. cit., p. 24.
[28] ibid., p. 78.
[29] ibid., p. 15. Elaine Cumming and William E. Henry, op. cit., p. 230.
[30] Suzanne Reichard *et al.*, op. cit., p. 25.
[31] Elaine Cumming and William E. Henry, op. cit., pp. 34–35.

Personality

6. PERSONALITY AND ISOLATION

The argument of the two preceding sections has been largely negative. The intention, however, has not merely been to criticize *Growing Old* and *Aging and Personality*. These two studies represent some of the best recent research on personality and ageing. Both studies are primarily exploratory, designed to build up useful concepts and hypotheses. Their failure to deal with important minority groups of old people arises largely from the extremely difficult problems involved in studying these groups.

Simply because an old person is isolated, he is not necessarily maladjusted. Reichard argues convincingly, for instance, that one particular single man who led an isolated life had adapted successfully: 'Retirement allowed Mr. C. the independence he found so essential and the isolation that protected it.'[32]

In the four-area survey the majority of isolated old people are neither 'often lonely' nor anomic. Nevertheless isolation seems unlikely to make their problems of personality and of adaptation to old age any easier. If an old person becomes isolated as the result of widowhood the adjustment to the loss is more difficult than if he still retains an extensive network of social relationships. James Birren writes:

> Generally it would be predicted that the more adequate the interpersonal relations of the individual, the more likely he is to have an appropriate social input to help manage the reaction to loss . . . Being isolated means fewer available effective outlets to compensate for the loss and less social restricting of behaviour to help overcome the uncertainty.[33]

In the studies of retirement and disengagement discussed in earlier sections the general picture presented is of the old person adapting to the changes of old age and adjusting, with more or less success, his relationships with other people. The personality of an isolated old person is presented with a somewhat different problem, for although he or she may have experienced a number of the major changes or crises of old age, there are –

[32] Suzanne Reichard *et al.*, op. cit., p. 91.
[33] James E. Birren, *The Psychology of Aging* (1963), p. 285.

244

Personality and Isolation

because of the fact of isolation – comparatively few social relationships which exist and call for adaptation. The socially isolated old person is short of people to talk to most of the time.

Reminiscing is, of course, a common form of behaviour among old people. One American study suggests that reminiscing is positively associated with successful adaptation to old age and freedom from depression.[34] James Birren writes of a period in the lives of old people when they review their pasts and attempt various kinds of reconciliation:

> The tendency to think more often about the past and to talk about it to others can be easily misinterpreted . . . More than must a young person, the older individual must see and reconcile his past place in the world of people, places, and things. He is under pressure to integrate his views of his past . . . As he comes nearer the end of his life, the aged person needs more and more psychological support from fewer and fewer available individuals. His ability to secure this *rapport* and support involves not only his skills, but also the capacity of his listener to discern what he is doing and saying, both manifestly and latently.[35]

The socially isolated old person is much less likely to have anyone to help him with this review of his past life and to listen to his reminiscences. If this form of behaviour does indeed help adaption in later life, then clearly the isolated old person will find adaptation the more difficult.

Although there is very little evidence specifically about the connection between old people's personalities and social isolation, personality, however defined, probably does play a part in predisposing some old people to isolation; it also seems likely that when an old person is socially isolated this provides special problems of personality adjustment.

It may well be some years or even decades before satisfactory studies have been completed. Some solution must be found to the basic problem of the especially high refusal rates of isolated old people in personality studies. When that solution is available

[34] Arthur W. McMahon and Paul J. Rhudick, *Reminiscing: Its Adaptational Significance in the Aged.* Paper at the World Congress of Gerontology, Copenhagen, 1963.
[35] James E. Birren, op. cit., pp. 276–8.

245

it may be possible to conduct longitudinal studies of middle-aged and elderly people as they grow older; since one of the problems in this type of study is of geographical moves made by respondents, it might be easier to organize such studies in small countries like Britain than in the huge area of the United States.

Chapter Thirteen
SOCIAL THEORY

I. SOCIOLOGICAL THEORY AND OLD AGE

The major social theorists have paid little attention to old age. Tönnies, for instance, devoted only one brief section to old age in *Gemeinschaft und Gesellschaft* and even this deals with contrasting old age and youth:

> ... we find between youth and old age the same relation as between feminine and masculine beings. The youthful woman is the real woman; the old woman becomes more like a man. And the young man has still many feminine elements in his nature; the mature, older man is the real man.[1]

One suspects that Tönnies had not thought very much about old age.

Talcott Parsons in his introduction to Elaine Cumming's and William E. Henry's *Growing Old* welcomes it as the first important theoretical contribution.[2] Here Parsons appears to have diverged from some of his earlier writings. In three publications on the family Parsons developed an important theory of the conjugal family and dealt only very briefly with the role of the aged in the family. It is worth returning to these brief references because – even though Parsons himself has modified them – his formulations on the conjugal family have been accepted uncritically by many sociologists.

In two essays 'Age and Sex in the Social Structure of the United States' and 'The Kinship System of the United States', published in 1942 and 1943, and in his later *Family, Socialization and Interaction Process* Parsons elaborated his concept of the 'isolated' conjugal family – consisting only of a married couple

---

[1] Ferdinand Tönnies, *Community and Society*, translated and edited by Charles P. Loomis (Michigan State University Press, 1957), p. 156.
[2] Elaine Cumming and William E. Henry, op. cit., p.v.

and their dependent children; it is the 'normal' household unit of American society, and is 'segregated' from both pairs of parents as well as being economically independent of both.[3] Instrumental leadership inside the family rests with the man, who derives it from his occupational role in the world outside the family.[4] Affective leadership resides with the woman, the principal agent in socializing the children. The marriage bond is the structural keystone, to an extent not known in other kinship systems. Institutional support of the role of marriage partner from the wider kinship system is comparatively unimportant; more emphasis than in other systems is placed on romantic love between the marriage partners.[5] For Parsons, conjugal families are 'factories' which produce human personalities:

> We therefore suggest that the basic and irreducible functions of the family are two; first, the primary socialization of children so that they can truly become members of the society into which they have been born; second, the stabilization of the adult personalities of the population of the society.[6]

Parsons argues that the American type of occupational structure 'requires a far-reaching structural segregation of occupational roles from the kinship roles of the *same* individuals.'[7]

How do old people fit into such a system? Firstly old age as such is not valued highly; on the contrary there is a 'romantic idealization of youth patterns'.[8] Secondly, the older generation are structurally isolated from the conjugal families of their married children. 'In a very large proportion of cases the geographical separation is considerable.' This and the abruptness of retirement from the man's occupational role means that old people tend to be 'left out of it'.[9] Parsons continues that 'through well-known psychosomatic mechanisms, the increased incidence of the disabilities of older people, such as heart disease, cancer, etc., may be at least in part attributed to this structural situation'. Despite upper and lower class and rural

[3] Talcott Parsons, *Essays in Sociological Theory* (1964 edition), pp. 183–4.
[4] Talcott Parsons, *Family Socialization and Interaction Process* (1956), p. 13.
[5] Talcott Parsons, *Essays in Sociological Theory* (1964 edition), pp. 187–8.
[6] Talcott Parsons, *Family Socialization and Interaction Process* (1956), pp. 16–17.
[7] Talcott Parsons, *Essays in Sociological Theory* (1964 edition), pp. 191–2.
[8] Talcott Parsons, *Family Socialization and Interaction Process* (1956), p. 101.
[9] Talcott Parsons, *Essays in Sociological Theory* (1964 edition), pp. 184, 194.

exceptions[10] Parsons argues that the isolated conjugal family is the dominant American pattern. In particular he contrasts the position of the aged in such an isolated conjugal family system with their status in societies based on a wider kinship pattern:

> This situation is in strong contrast to kinship systems in which membership in a kinship unit is continuous throughout the life cycle. There, very frequently, it is the oldest members who are treated with the most respect and have the greatest responsibility and authority. But with us there is no one left to respect them, for them to take responsibility for or have authority over.[11]

But are old people really accorded so much authority and respect in kinship societies in contrast to our own?

2. OLD AGE IN NON-LITERATE SOCIETIES

Only one full-length study exists of the position of old people in non-literate societies. Leo Simmons's *The Role of the Aged in Primitive Society* was published at Yale in 1945; it is based on the existing literature on seventy-one tribes from all parts of the world.

Since chronological age as such is of no significance in a primitive society an anthropologist can only roughly estimate informants' ages. Meyer Fortes in northern Ghana in 1934 used a well-remembered expedition of 1911 as a base-line and added twenty-three years to the probable age at that time.[12]

W. H. R. Rivers in his study, *The Todas*, published in 1906, reports that only 4·7 per cent of the men and 5·3 per cent of the women were over 50 years of age. Other reports of this period have similar figures with women usually outnumbering men. A study published in 1866 reports Mongol women in Mongolia as being 'middle-aged at 30, and old and wrinkled at 40'.[13]

Quite apart from the problem of deciding at what age to place the beginning of 'old age' in a non-literate society the

[10] Talcott Parsons, *Family, Socialization and Interaction Process* (1956), pp. 103, 185.
[11] Talcott Parsons, *Essays in Sociological Theory* (1964 edition), p. 195.
[12] Meyer Fortes, *The Web of Kinship among the Tallensi* (1949), p. 66.
[13] Leo W. Simmons, *The Role of the Aged in Primitive Society* (1945), pp. 16, 17.

position of the older surviving people varies radically from one non-literate society to another. Simmons deals with a number of specific spheres. Older people get more food in those primitive societies which are simply organized and less food in societies which cultivate the soil and have a more complex organization.[14] Their property rights vary greatly, but older men with property rights tend to be respected.[15] In a non-literate society oral story-telling assumes great significance and this is an important role of old people. Some older men also occupy leading roles in the political sphere and in those of magic and religion.[16] But the situation is not simply that all older people are respected:

> In primitive societies there are no signs of a deep-seated 'instinct' to guarantee to elders either homage or pity from their offspring. Whatever prestige they received was not a boon of nature; it was a product of social developments, it rested primarily upon rights, and it stemmed from the force [of] custom or the fear of consequences.[17]

In many primitive societies the most important and powerful people were often among the older men; but not all old men were powerful. Powerful old men were so because they commanded economic resources – such as land, wives and the labour of sons who would inherit the land; older men might also occupy positions of political power – but only because they could command the political support of younger men.

In primitive societies, as elsewhere, the holder of power or the respected man may use this to acquire further power or respect. Older men in many patrilineal African societies have the economic resources to marry additional young wives – who support their elderly husband and supply him with further children and economic resources. But, of course, not every older man can have several wives.

Moreover, such a system obviously places a different emphasis on older men and older women; this is important since women appear to predominate among the older surviving people in primitive, as in industrialized societies. Leo Simmons points out

[14] Leo W. Simmons, op. cit., pp. 32–35.
[15] ibid., pp. 47–48.
[16] ibid., pp. 103–4, 130, 175–6.
[17] ibid., p. 50.

Old Age in Non-literate Societies

that older women fare badly in primitive – especially patrilineal – societies on the basis of property rights; they are unlikely to be accorded much prestige – particularly in the more complex non-literate societies.[18] In the sphere of magic and religion older women are often at a severe disadvantage – since older women are often accused of witchcraft, an event which may involve a violent death.[19] Among the Tallensi of Ghana, for instance, the traditional system was for a woman accused of witchcraft to undergo the ordeal of stabbing herself in public with a poisoned arrow.[20]

In some primitive societies feeble old people were put to death. Sometimes there was an element of mercy-killing in this, but Simmons reports the phenomenon for twenty-one different primitive societies and 'only in about half of the tribes in which the aged have been killed has any special respect or honor been associated with the event'.[21]

Killing of feeble old people was common in migratory tribes. Among the Labrador Eskimo, 'When an old woman became a burden on the community she was apt to be neglected until so weak that she would not keep up with the group.' Then three or four male relatives would retrace their steps, and kill the old woman.[22] Older people in such tribes were well fed until they became feeble, but there was no question of the movements, or even speed of movement, of the larger group being modified in order to look after a feeble or ill old person.

In most African societies old people were supported by relatives, even if not necessarily honoured. However, Leo Simmons comments:

'With the advance of herding and agriculture . . . grain supplies, property, trade, debt-relations, and slavery, support of the aged through communal sharing of food appears to have declined in importance or to have taken on features more characteristic of "organized charity".'[23]

A study directed by William Harlan (of Ohio University) in an Indian village dealt specifically with the question of the

[18] Leo W. Simmons, op. cit., p. 81.
[19] ibid., p. 230.
[20] Meyer Fortes, *The Web of Kinship among the Tallensi* (1949), pp. 33–34.
[21] Leo W. Simmons, op. cit., pp. 239, 241.
[22] ibid., p. 232.
[23] ibid., p. 35.

Social Theory

prestige of older men.[24] Fifty older men were interviewed in their own language. They reported that although the young men asked them for advice about agricultural matters, the advice tended to be ignored. Harlan concluded that the older men in the village lacked prestige and respect. Harlan's study is important because it is concerned, not marginally, but centrally, with the position of older people – and was directed by an experienced sociologist who had previously conducted research on old age in the United States.

3. OLD AGE IN A PEASANT SOCIETY

Talcott Parsons refers to Conrad Arensberg's and Solon Kimball's *Family and Community in Ireland* as providing a 'Paradigm of the Patripotestal Nuclear Family'.[25] This study, published at Harvard in 1940, was based on fieldwork conducted among peasant farming families in southern Ireland from 1932 to 1934. A remarkable feature of this family system was the long delayed marriage of the men. The son, who will eventually inherit the farm, works for his father – whose 'parental dominance continues as long as the father lives'. Until the son gains control of the farm he will not marry. 'Even at forty-five and fifty, if the old couple have not yet made over the farm, the countryman remains a "boy" in respect of farm work and in the rural vocabulary.'[26] In the Irish Free State in 1926 half of the males aged 35–40 were unmarried as were a quarter of those aged 55–65.[27] The population was, of course, in decline.

Arensberg continually emphasizes the power and prestige which the 'old fellows' wield in the Irish village. Much of it is due to property rights and inheritance – the farm normally goes complete to one son and 'In choosing the son to remain upon the farm, the father has full power of decision.'[28] Arensberg and Kimball discuss the longevity of the Irish and make this suggestion:

[24] William H. Harlan and J. Singh, *Social Status and Attitudes of Old Men in an Indian Village.* Paper at International Congress of Gerontology, Copenhagen, 1963.
[25] Talcott Parsons, *Family, Socialization and Interaction Process* (1956), pp. 344–6.
[26] Conrad M. Arensberg and S. T. Kimball, *Family and Community in Ireland* (1940), pp. 55–56.
[27] ibid., pp. 103–4.
[28] ibid, p. 65.

Old Age in Non-literate Societies

The existence of such a large proportion of the old among small farmers presents a problem in the organization of behaviour among human beings. Nevertheless, might not the longevity of peasants be after all a simple matter? In the Irish case we shall see that they live long because they have much to live for. In their own sphere of life, they are honored. They have power.[29]

In the Irish village the 'old fellows' tend to meet together regularly; from this gathering the 'boys' are excluded. The older men exert important influence through their informal deliberations. Arensberg and Kimball say, 'It is here public opinion is formulated.'[30]

Does not this study show, then, that the old indeed have a more significant place in a peasant-kinship-based society than in contemporary urban society? But let us look more closely. Arensberg and Kimball describe at some length the informal gathering of the old men in one small village; each man's family position and age are detailed.[31] Of the seven 'old men' in the meeting only one is over 65. The average age of the other six men is in fact about 55. The one over-65 who attends the meetings is given 'the place of honor in the chair to the right of the fire'. But in fact he says little – 'Usually they know he contents himself with a word of affirmation, or now and again a slow and measured judgment upon a current topic.' Only one other man over the age of 65 lives in this village (of twelve households) – he is 75 years old, is feeble and housebound, and does not attend the meetings.[32] Thus in the only village where the position of the 'old men' is described in detail – the 'old men' who run things turn out to be mainly men aged between 50 and 60; and this in a country with 9 per cent of its population over 65. Arensberg and Kimball seem to have adopted too easily the local meaning of 'boy' and 'old man'. (Two men can both be aged 55; one will be referred to as an 'old man', but the other may be a 'boy' – simply because his father is still alive.)

Even in the matter of farming, the Irish peasant men do not always retain control beyond the age of 65. At some point the

[29] Conrad M. Arensberg and S. T. Kimball, op. cit., pp. 167–8.
[30] ibid., p. 191.
[31] ibid., pp. 183–93.
[32] ibid., p. 187.

Social Theory

father decides to hand over control to his son – which is the signal for the son to marry. Afterwards, even if the old man continues to work, the 'initiative in agricultural matters' rests with the young man.[33] 'Marriage transfers the boy into the adult farm-owning man. . . .'[34] The son's wife moves into the farmhouse, where she may become involved in kitchen disputes with her new mother-in-law. In such a dispute the young husband takes the part of his wife and in the event of a breach 'it is usually the mother who must leave'.[35] There is little sign here of innate respect for the elderly.

When the old man has handed over the farm, the tactful son shows a certain amount of deference – which may be largely pretence. One young man said that each day he asked his elderly father 'what he thought I should do for the day . . . I would go then and spend twenty to thirty minutes doing what the old man said, and then go about my business'.[36] When alone together the young people express not only respect but also antagonism for the older generation.[37]

Moreover, the community as well as the family is not always so respectful of the elderly. At the time of Arensberg's and Kimball's fieldwork a Government Land Commission was distributing additional acres of land to local farmers. An official of the Land Commission told the authors : 'An old-age pensioner without a family could not be considered for an addition of land, nor could a couple of spinsters.'[38] There are also clear indications from the study that, although the wider kinship system was important among these Irish peasants it still did not support all the frail single and widowed old people : 'If, however, the new family finds the old too great a burden, the old may go to the County Home, where the poor and derelict old people are maintained.'[39]

Family and Community in Ireland indicates that, among the Irish peasants, men in their fifties were accorded considerable power and influence. However, there is a good deal of evidence

[33] Conrad M. Arensberg and S. T. Kimball, op. cit., p. 123.
[34] ibid., p. 131.
[35] ibid., p. 128.
[36] ibid., p. 126.
[37] ibid., p. 173.
[38] ibid., p. 69.
[39] ibid., p. 125.

Old Age in Non-literate Societies

that men and women (in this male-dominated society) over the age of 65 in the Irish countryside were not always accorded much respect or vested with any significant power.

4. OLD AGE IN CONTEMPORARY SOCIETY

Is Talcott Parsons justified in talking of youth being idealized? It is not quite clear what 'idealization' consists of – but there is some evidence of youth being idealized in the same way in which women are said to be idealized in societies where their objective position is one of marked inferiority.

One could argue that the societies in which young men are accorded the most prestige and power are not those of the advanced but of the underdeveloped world, especially Africa. Many leading politicians of independent African nations tend to be younger than politicians in countries with longer political traditions. But, of course, these young African politicians do not achieve respect or power solely on the basis of youth. It just happens that they have the education and the skills which independent government requires and which the older men usually lack.

'In 1799 the average age of United States Representatives and Senators was 43·5 and 45·2. A century and a half later the average age was, respectively, ten and twelve years older. In the United States Supreme Court over 85 per cent of the service rendered is by men beyond 65.'[40] In Britain between 1931 and 1961 there was only one Prime Minister below the age of 60. The median age for the British Prime Minister during this thirty-year period was 67 years. Sir Winston Churchill was already of pensionable age when he became Prime Minister in 1940 and was in his eighties before he finally resigned the office in 1955. The Trade Unions, another major power centre in contemporary society, tend to have fairly elderly leadership. There seems to be a preference among younger people for choosing fairly old men to top leadership positions. Prime Ministers, Party Leaders or Trade Union general secretaries are hard to dislodge once in office. This being so, ambitious younger men have a personal vested interest in electing older men, who will have to retire in the not too distant future. In other centres

[40] *Encyclopaedia Britannica* (1964 edition), article on 'Gerontocracy'.

255

Social Theory

of power and prestige where the average age of retirement is high, Judges and Bishops tend to be elderly and to be first appointed at a fairly advanced age. Paradoxically, the later the normal age of retirement the more reason there may be for appointing already elderly men.

At the local level also people who fill positions of prestige are often elderly. The British Aldermanic system, even if not so effective as the seniority principle in the United States Congress, tends to favour older men. Other local positions such as Justice of the Peace are often held by people over 65.[41]

The basic situation seems to be similar to that in primitive societies. There is no automatic respect paid to old people, but the most respected and powerful people in our society are often quite elderly. Nevertheless there are unique features in the position of the elderly in contemporary urban society, such as the existence of a sizeable fraction of the population over the age of 65 and the recent shortening of the average length of generations.

Although retirement is not always 'abrupt' in urban society, it obviously tends to be much more so than in a non-literate or peasant society. Moreover, as has often been noted, the increasing spread of occupational pension schemes may tend to fix retirement ages more rigidly. One important development in this connection is the existence of Trade Union support for the trend to *earlier* retirements in the American motor industry.[42] If one long-term effect of automation is indeed the establishment of massive re-training schemes, employers may prefer to induce some workers to retire earlier rather than to retrain them for only a brief remaining work span. We may move towards a standard retirement age of not 65, but 60 for men – as well as for women. With probable trends in population this would by the 1980's leave us with a retired group aged 60 and over who would make up 20 per cent of the whole population.[43]

The very concept of 'retirement' – as distinct from feebleness, senility, and physical incapacity – does not appear in non-literate societies. And retirement, as a general phenomenon not

[41] In Glossop nine out of eleven J.P.s were over 60 and four were over 70. A. H. Birch, *Small Town Politics* (Oxford University Press, 1959), p. 143.

[42] Harold L. Orbach, *Retirement Patterns of Industrial Workers.* Paper at International Congress of Gerontology, Copenhagen, 1963.

[43] See below, p. 262.

confined to one social class, is of course linked to State retirement pension schemes. State retirement pensions undoubtedly have had a vital impact on the experience of old age. Arensberg and Kimball report that among the Irish peasants the introduction of the old age pension had a number of effects on the family system: 'Receipt of the pension facilitates the maintenance of the old people and hastens the transfer of land to the son, as the farmers must divest themselves of their small farms in the majority of cases in order to become eligible for the pension.' One Irish countrywoman is reported as saying:

> Before the old age pension the father would keep the fat of the land and there would be argument between them, the young women and the old women slashing each other with tongs, the doors broke, and it would be two dwellings in the house, like, but since the old age pension, there are no rows and, if there are, then they make it up with the old people for the ten bob a week.[44]

5. ISOLATED CONJUGAL FAMILIES AND ISOLATED OLD PEOPLE

Talcott Parsons talks of the family in contemporary urban society as having only two 'basic and irreducible' functions – the socialization of the children and 'the stabilization of the adult personalities of the society'. This depends upon the definitions of 'basic and irreducible' and 'family'. Parsons appears to define the family as necessarily including children – and for such a family one might say that the only 'irreducible' function is the socializing of the children. But the second of Parsons's functions is much less 'irreducible'; a substantial proportion of families have only one parent. A recent estimate for Britain is that 'of all families with dependent children about 8·6 per cent are fatherless'.[45] The divorce figures alone are significant – Parsons himself quotes statistics which show the United States' divorce rate in 1950 running at 23 per cent of the marriage rate. Moreover, the well-known Kinsey findings on marital infidelity show that other 'stabilizing' forces than merely the marriage partner are operating on a high number of American parents' personalities.

[44] Conrad M. Arensberg and S. T. Kimball, op, cit., p. 126.
[45] Margaret Wynn, *Fatherless Families* (London: Michael Joseph, 1964), p. 18.

Social Theory

But of course to limit the 'family' to the socializing of children is to use a very narrow definition. No doubt Talcott Parsons is correct in saying that his two functions are the most basic. Nevertheless his distinction between the American conjugal family and other 'kinship' families seems excessively rigid.

Parsons surely exaggerates the extent to which the occupational sphere is demarcated from the family. The great government and business bureaucracies no doubt manage to do this. But in many occupations family ties play a part. The farm family and the upper-class pattern Parsons notes. Not only farmers but farm labourers appear to follow their fathers. Moreover, it would be hard to exaggerate the family ties between leading British Conservative families, and the Bank of England, merchant banks, newspaper proprietors and leading industrialists.[46] In the United States also this phenomenon is not entirely unknown both at the national and state level. Important family patterns also operate among doctors, in the small legal partnership and in the Army.[47] Many small businesses, shops, restaurants, building firms and the like – are family enterprises. In Britain leading firms, even in such fields as motor vehicles and electronics, are controlled by people whom one student of management calls 'Crown Princes'.[48]

Nor are the lines between family and occupation always so clear among manual workers. In one British study of dock workers, it was found that 75 per cent of dockers were also the sons of dockers.[49] Coal-miners tend to be sons of coal-miners.[50] In certain skilled trades such as printing the family tradition is legendary. The apprenticeship system and the power of some Trade Unions make this possible. The family sphere laps over into the occupational sphere in another way. The present writer interviewed a woman in Oldham who had for many years worked in the same department of the same factory as her husband.

[46] Anthony Sampson, *The Anatomy of Britain* (London: Hodder and Stoughton, 1962), p. 34.
[47] Morris Janowitz, *The American Soldier* (New York: Free Press, 1960), p. 96.
[48] R. V. Clements, *Managers* (London: Allen and Unwin, 1958), pp. 28–36, 162–3.
[49] University of Liverpool, Department of Social Science, *The Dock Worker* (University of Liverpool Press, 1954), p. 49.
[50] N. Dennis, F. Henriques and C. Slaughter, *Coal is our Life* (London: Eyre and Spottiswoode, 1956), p. 235.

Isolated Conjugal Families and Isolated Old People

Of course these sorts of connection between family and occupation are nowhere near as pervasive and general as in a kinship society where the normal agricultural team (in a patrilineal society) consists of father and son, or a group of brothers – plus their wives and children. Nevertheless the *optional* functions of the family in the occupational sphere are significant. Similarly kin beyond the basic conjugal family are often important. Among these kin are, of course, the elderly parents.

Talcott Parsons says that 'In a very large proportion of cases the geographical separation is considerable,' between the conjugal family and both sets of elderly parents. Many old people do have children a long way away; but it is no less true that the same old woman who has a son living on the other side of the world may also have a daughter living on the other side of the street. Even in the United States of all old people with any children alive 60·7 per cent have a child living within ten minutes and 76·3 per cent have a child living not more than half an hour's journey away.[51]

In Britain among married old people 26·7 per cent live in a household with a child (Table 2.1). The response of the wider kinship group varies with the situation of the old people. When the old person is widowed he or she is more likely to live with a child. In Britain 46·2 per cent of widowed old people live with children – of whom just over half are married children. Half of all widowed old people live in a household with relatives (Table 2.1). Cross-national evidence shows a similar pattern in the United States.

A greater proportion could live with their children if they wished – but they choose otherwise. True, some old people may not go because they regard living with their children as being 'unnatural' – and they may fear tensions between the generations. But, of course, tensions do not only exist *between* generations; they also exist within them. In a contemporary urban society the old person is given a choice. A widow may choose to become a household member in a home of which one of her children, or another relative, is the head. But she may choose to remain alone as head of her own household.

[51] Ethel Shanas, 'Family and Household Characteristics of Older People in the United States', in P. From Hansen (ed.), *Age with a Future* (1964), p. 453.

Social Theory

Some old people lead an isolated existence, when they would prefer to live with one of their children – but are not asked to come. Options work both ways. Nevertheless we should be careful of exaggerating the benefits which accrue to an old widow living in her child's home. One suspects that even in a 'kinship' non-literate society the position of some elderly widows is one of inferiority. According to Leo Simmons's study they are not always adequately fed. An old widow living with a married son may find herself only the third or fourth most important woman in the household; whether she is in fact exiled to an outhouse or given some status and respect may well depend upon a number of variables, including her physical capacity to perform household and agricultural work.

In Britain social isolation most affects those who are without husband or children, and in primitive societies little honour accrues to any woman who has no children. Even among the Irish peasants, Arensberg and Kimball report, a man had a right to express his displeasure if his wife was barren. He could beat her or 'bounce a boot off her now and then for it'.[52] When a childless but physically vigorous young woman could be treated in this way, presumably the position of a childless older woman was even more vulnerable.

6. SOCIAL ISOLATION AND SOCIAL OPTION

The relations of old people with their wider group of kin involve options. But there is also another kind of option involved – namely the option of the community at large. To date the only firmly established obligation towards old people which the community has decided to undertake consists of the retirement pension and attendant financial support (such as national assistance). Other sorts of support are also being provided but only in a tentative, and geographically uneven, manner.

Parsons in his writing on the family looks at the kinship system primarily from the point of view of the young conjugal family. Social theory now needs to look at the system from the point of view of the man and wife as they enter old age, and as widowhood occurs. Moreover, it must be remembered that there are other important groups such as the single, the

[52] Conrad M. Arensberg and S. T. Kimball, op. cit., p. 319.

widowed and the physically incapacitated. A start has already been made by the authors of *Growing Old* and *Aging and Personality* to show how the ageing personality changes through time. Talcott Parsons himself has already welcomed this.

But at present, the work on the ageing personality is far removed from such major variables as class, income, and physical incapacity. There has also been an unfortunate tendency for research on old age to become fragmented into personality, family, income, retirement, health, leisure, pensions, politics and so on. We need a broad theoretical approach to such typical crises of old age as retirement, widowhood, and illness; and this needs to be set in the wider framework of the community's provision for and attitude towards old age, in addition to old people's impact on the community through their voting patterns and other behaviour.

We also need to see old age as part of the whole social system – in the way in which Parsons and others have already enabled us to see childhood. In particular the connections between family and occupation – which Talcott Parsons so rightly stresses – require further investigation. To date most research on both family and occupation is recruitment-oriented. Occupational studies devote a great deal of time to how the workers are recruited, but little to how they retire; studies of the family deal at length with marriage and child socialization, even with divorce, but much less with widowhood and retirement. Nevertheless the *exit* patterns from any institution, even if less crucial than the entry patterns, presumably have some feed-back impact.

Social theorists have tended to ignore old age partly because it is a social problem area and therefore one carrying low academic status. This attitude has for too long played a part in providing one more example of Robert Merton's self-fulfilling prophecy.

Another reason for social theorists having largely ignored old age is the inherent difficulty of the subject – some of which have been indicated on the chapter on 'Personality'. Old people are probably more socially differentiated from each other than are the members of any other age-group. This poses difficult problems of theory and method.

One further possible objection to developing a body of social theory about old age is that the subject is not sufficiently

Social Theory

important. The underdeveloped countries, it is true, have only about 2 per cent or 3 per cent of their populations aged 65 and over. But 8·7 per cent of the Japanese population was aged 60 or over in 1960; this proportion is expected to rise to 13 per cent by 1985 and 25 per cent by 2015.

Moreover, the growing size of the elderly population in a large number of industrial countries already makes this too large a segment to be ignored. One European country, East Germany, is expected to have 21 per cent of its population aged 60 or over by as early as 1976. By that time countries with 18 per cent or more of their population aged 60 or over should include Austria, Belgium, West Germany, Norway, Sweden, Switzerland and the United Kingdom.[53] On the evidence of the present study, these countries can thus expect *3 per cent or 4 per cent of their total population* to be socially isolated people in their sixties or older.

7. MAJORITY AND MINORITY PATTERNS IN AGEING

The basic household pattern of old people is very similar in economically developed countries. Table 13.1 shows how closely Britain compares with Denmark, Western Germany, the United States and Vienna. In all of these countries about half the people aged 65 and over have their spouses still alive; most of them live with their spouse only. The remainder, who have no spouse alive, are split about equally between those who live alone and those who live with children or others. Of all old people around a fifth to a quarter live alone.[54]

In an important article, 'Propositions for a Sociological Theory of Ageing and the Family', Leopold Rosenmayr and Eva Kockeis argue that in the interpretation of such data, traditional sociological concepts of 'role' are unsatisfactory, as are those of 'function', including Robert Merton's 'latent function'.[55] They point out that the functional detachment of the family need not necessarily entail the disintegration of the family. They refer to the repeatedly found phenomenon of old

[53] Alfred Sauvy, 'Demographic Ageing', *International Social Science Journal*, No. 3, 1963.
[54] Vienna is not representative of Austria, as Vienna has an atypically high proportion of non-married women – the group most likely to live alone.
[55] *International Social Science Journal*, No. 3 (1963), pp. 423-4.

Majority and Minority Patterns in Ageing

people preferring to live near, but not with, their children,[56] as

TABLE 13.1 HOUSEHOLD COMPOSITION OF PEOPLE
AGED 65 AND OVER IN FIVE COUNTRIES

	Britain	Denmark	Western Germany	United States	Vienna
Married people					
Living with spouse only	33	45	35	37	33
Living with spouse and children	13	8	12	12	9
Living with spouse and other persons	3	2	0	3	2
	(49)	(55)	(47)	(52)	(44)
Non-married					
Living alone	22	28	23	21	32
Living with children	19	9	20	16	14
Living with other persons	10	8	10	11	10
Total	100	100	100	100	100
Number	2,500	2,445	821	1,734	2,784

Sources:
For Britain and Denmark cross-national survey, 1962.
Details for the surveys in West Germany (1958), U.S.A. (1957) and
Vienna (1961) are given in Leopold Rosenmayr and Eva Kockeis
'Propositions for a Sociological Theory of Ageing and the Family', *International Social Science Journal*, No. 3, 1963.

'Intimacy at a Distance'. These authors discuss the continuity of emotional family relations leading to 'functional flexibility'. This flexibility is demonstrated by the widespread determination of children to care for frail elderly parents when the latter are ill. But 'flexibility' is also evidenced by the tendency of young divorced women to return to the parental family. Another example is the desire of some married women to go out to part-time work in order to have more money to spend on their families.

Rosenmayr and Kockeis conclude by calling for an approach which will set ageing in the context of the individual's whole life cycle. In terms of household composition and daily (or near daily) contact outside the household the pattern for *women only* on the basis of present evidence is as follows:

[56] First reported by J. H. Sheldon, *Social Medicine of Old Age* (1948), pp. 195–6

263

Social Theory

MAJORITY PATTERN
(woman who marries and has children)

Ego's age	Household composition		Daily or near daily social contact outside household
5	Father, mother, brother, sister		School
10	Father, mother, brother, sister		School
15	Father, mother, brother, sister		School
20	Father, mother, sister		Work, full-time
25	Husband, children		Father, mother
30	Husband, children		Father, mother
35	Husband, children		Father, mother (work, p.t.)
40	Husband, children (Mother)	(*Father dies*)	(Mother) (work, p.t.)
45	Husband, children	(*Mother dies*)	(work p.t.)
50	Husband		Daughter (work, p.t.)
55	Husband		Daughter (work, p.t.)
60	Husband		Daughter
65		(*Husband dies*)	Daughter
70	(*a*) Lives alone (*b*) Daughter (+ son-in-law + grandchildren)		(Daughter)

Note: All relationships are to Ego.

In this majority pattern only household relationships, work and school, and daily or near daily parent-child relationships outside the home are shown. The items in rounded brackets represent *optional* features of the majority pattern. When ego's father dies, her mother may move in, but on the other hand she may be visited daily; after age 35 ego is shown as having the option of going out to part-time work. The first major change in this pattern comes when the woman marries. As household members she exchanges her parents and one unmarried sibling to live with her husband and then her own children; outside the household she stops work but retains near daily contact with her

Majority and Minority Patterns in Ageing

parents. The largest number of household and daily outside contacts comes in the middle years. These fall off as her parents die and her own children get married; however, she now sees her daughter outside the household and she may also do part-time work. The biggest change comes around age 65 when her husband dies. This shatters the majority pattern, which divides into two sub-patterns; one sub-pattern is to live alone, the other to live with a child, most often a daughter. Likely results from the point of view of social contact and social isolation are these:

(a) Lives alone, no daily contact outside   – isolated
(a) Lives alone, sees child daily   – intermediate
(b) Lives with daughter, no daily contact
     outside   – intermediate
(b) Lives with daughter, sees other child
     daily   – high contact

The minority groups with which the present study is particularly concerned do not conform to this majority pattern. From the point of view of ageing and social contacts there are two main minority patterns:

Social Theory

MINORITY PATTERN (1)
(woman who marries but is childless)

Ego's age	Household composition	Daily or near daily social contact outside household
5	Father, mother, brother, sister	School
10	Father, mother, brother, sister	School
15	Father, mother, brother, sister	School
20	Father, mother, sister	Work, f.t.
25	Husband	Father, Mother, (work)
30	Husband	Father, Mother, (work)
35	Husband	Father, Mother (work)
40	Husband (Mother) (*Father dies*)	(Mother) work
45	Husband (*Mother dies*)	(Work)
50	Husband	(Work)
55	Husband	(Work)
60	Husband	
65	(*c*) Lives (*d*) Sister (*Husband dies*)	
70	alone (+ brother-in-law)	

In this pattern, after the woman leaves her parental home she lives only with her husband; when her husband dies there are two sub-patterns. Either she lives alone or she shares a household with a sibling, usually a sister – and most often a single or widowed sister. The likely consequences for her subsequent social contacts are these:

(*c*) Lives alone, no daily contact outside – isolated

(*d*) Lives with sister, no daily contact outside – intermediate

The second minority pattern is that of the single woman:

MINORITY PATTERN (2)

(Single woman)

Ego's age	Household Composition		Daily or near daily social contact outside household
5	Father, mother, brother, sister		School
10	Father, mother, brother, sister		School
15	Father, Mother, Brother, Sister		School
20	Father, Mother, Sister		Work f.t.
25	Father, Mother		Work f.t.
30	Father, Mother		Work f.t.
35	Father, Mother		Work f.t.
40	Mother	(*Father dies*)	Work f.t.
45	(*e*) Lives alone	(*Mother dies*)	Work f.t.
	(*f*) Sister		
50	(*e*) Lives alone		Work f.t.
	(*f*) Sister		
55	(*e*) Lives alone		Work f.t.
	(*f*) Sister		
60	(*e*) Lives alone		–
	(*f*) Sister		
70	(*e*) Lives alone		–
	(*f*) Sister		

The single woman's pattern is basically different from the childless woman's and from the majority pattern, because the sub-patterns develop so much earlier for the single woman. By about age 45 both her parents are dead. The sub-patterns are either to live alone or to live with a sister (if she has one who is single or widowed).

The single pattern is also different in that full-time work usually continues throughout adult life. Although the single woman stops full-time work around age 60 her household situation is unlikely to alter at this point in time – she continues on the same sub-pattern she has already been following for fifteen years. After retirement the likely consequences for social contact are the same as for the childless woman after she is widowed.

Social Theory

These three patterns, one majority and two minority, suggest three main points of sharp change – around the early twenties (marriage), around the late forties (parents die, children leave home), and around 65 (husband dies). The majority pattern – the woman who marries and has children – involves all three of these. The minority pattern of the childless woman also involves all three of these points of change, although the second change only involves the death of parents. The minority pattern of the single woman is radically different – there being only one main point of change, around the middle forties – when the parents are both dead, and the sub-pattern which the single woman is likely to follow well into old age is established.

These patterns are obviously greatly simplified; they do not, for instance, include contact with siblings or non-relatives outside the household. They do, however, help to illustrate how the minority patterns, which are especially likely to lead to social isolation, stretch back into the past. These patterns also illustrate that while there is only one standard social contact situation in childhood (although there may be variants, for instance, for only children) there is a continual broadening in variety of patterns later in the life-cycle. The variations in pattern particularly increase around the early twenties, in the late forties and again around the mid-sixties.

Any social theory of old age must recognize these two basic complexities: firstly, patterns of ageing stretch far back into the individual's past, and secondly there is great variety in social relations in old age. However, although there is so much variation within Britain, this variation is closely paralleled in other countries. The similarity, in the total situation of old people between comparable countries, suggests that a comprehensive theory of ageing may – despite the difficulties – be established in the future.

Chapter Fourteen

SOCIAL POLICY[1]

I. SOCIAL OPTIONS AND SOCIAL DEFICIENCIES

There is little evidence that we treat our old people particularly badly, compared with primitive or peasant societies. The sorts of old people who tend to be socially isolated – especially childless women and widows – may or may not be socially isolated in such societies, but they usually have a lowly social position.

In industrial societies the State has become committed to making some provision for old people – in particular through the retirement pension. This provision is inextricably bound up with the phenomenon of social isolation. For without pensions or other State support (such as the Poor Law), old people who lack financial resources could hardly survive at all living alone and in social isolation. They would have to live as dependents in relatives' or other households or in institutions.

State financial provision is thus enough to enable old people to maintain the minimum of independence; but society has the option of providing more than this minimum. It is highly probable that substantially increased financial provision would raise some socially isolated old people out of the category altogether. Having social contact often involves spending money. Lack of money for travelling, for providing food and drink, or buying new clothes discourages some old people from engaging in social intercourse. But even if higher financial provision did not reduce social isolation, it can be justified on the ground of enabling these old people to live a little more comfortably in their isolated state.

This study was not primarily designed to deal with social services for old people and only a limited amount of evidence emerged on the subject – partly because of the very limited

[1] It is assumed that the reader of this chapter has read Chapter 11 on 'Social Services'.

Social Policy

coverage of the social services for old people. Most of what follows cannot be demonstrated from the evidence of the four-area survey. However, it hardly seems appropriate merely to utter the ritual request for more research. One can at least make informed guesses.

Apart from the rather low level of the retirement pension the gap in provision for old people which is probably best known to the general public is the substantial proportion of old people who are entitled to national assistance, but do not apply for it.[2] However among the domiciliary and other services for old people the gaps and failures in provision are on an even bigger scale. One example of the lack of thorough provision is that services for old people virtually close down at the week-end.

The insufficiency of services for the elderly is, however, nowhere more clearly indicated than in the Ministry of Health's Ten Year 'Plan', *Health and Welfare: The Development of Community Care* (1963). This document is supposed to supplement the Ten Year Plan for hospital building. The main fault of the plan is its failure to plan. The Ministry of Health merely asked local authorities what they expected to be doing in ten years' time and published the results.

Table 14.1 shows how Northampton, Norfolk and Oldham compare[3] in 1963 and in their future plans. Oldham had *three* times more home helps per population than had Northampton in 1963; while Northampton was planning only a small increase, Oldham was aiming nearly to double its proportion and by 1973 to have *four* times as many home helps per population as Northampton. Norfolk was planning to have a *nine* times larger proportion of its elderly people in special housing (small bungalows or flats) than was Northampton. While both Oldham and Norfolk were planning a big increase in special housing and only a small increase in places in Homes, Northampton was planning to double its Home places. Northampton was also planning to more than double its health visitor effort, while Norfolk and Oldham were staying fairly stable. As the plan itself says '. . . the variation in need cannot be so great'.

[2] Peter Townsend and Dorothy Wedderburn, *The Aged in the Welfare State* (1965).
[3] Figures for Harrow are in any case not available. Those for Middlesex may also not be of much value since Middlesex has since become part of the new Greater London Council area.

Social Options and Social Deficiencies

TABLE 14.1 PLANS IN THREE AREAS FOR CERTAIN
COMMUNITY SERVICES 1963–73

	Northampton (County borough)		Norfolk (County)		Oldham (County Borough)	
Proportion of population						
aged 65+ in 1963	14·0%		14·0%		12·9%	
predicted 1974		15·1%		16·0%		14·9%
Places in Homes for						
persons 65+ per 1,000						
in age group 1963	12·2		17·7		22·9	
planned 1974		26·6		20·3		26·7
Special housing, units per						
per 1,000 people						
aged 65+ 1963	2·1		7·3		2·2	
planned 1969		2·0		18·1		7·3
Health visitors per						
1,000 population 1963	0·06		0·09		0·11	
planned 1973		0·15		0·1		0·13
Home helps per						
1,000 population 1963	0·39		0·4		1·09	
planned 1973		0·47		0·58		2·01
Home nurses per						
1,000 population 1963	0·17		0·17		0·14	
planned 1973		0·23		0·19		0·2
Social workers per						
1,000 population 1963	0·07		0·08		0·11	
planned 1973		0·08		0·08		0·16

Source: Ministry of Health; Health and Welfare: The Development of Community Care. Revision to 1973–74 (H.M.S.O.) 1964.

National evidence of unmet need for old people's services is available from the national survey. Table 14.2 indicates that there is demand for a more than 100 per cent increase in those having home helps and those receiving publicly provided chiropody. For meals-on-wheels there are five people wanting the meals for every one person receiving any. In addition a high proportion of old people have hearing trouble but no hearing aid, while another large group have severe difficulty with seeing but have not had their eyes examined during the last five years.[4]

[4] This information has previously appeared in Peter Townsend and Dorothy Wedderburn, The Aged in the Welfare State (1965).

271

Social Policy

TABLE 14.2 OLD PEOPLE RECEIVING AND WANTING
CERTAIN SERVICES

	Percentage receiving public or voluntary	Percentage receiving private	Percentage not receiving but wanting
Home help	4·4	9·0	5·7
Mobile meals	1·1	–	5·9
Chiropody	7·3	11·3	11·5

Source : National Survey.

A major increase in services for old people is required. The national evidence is only based on what the old people themselves say, a method which almost certainly understates real need. No account is taken in Table 14.2 of those who are receiving a service – for instance a home help coming once a week – but want more of it. The likelihood of major understatement emerges from the replies about doctors. Only 3·5 per cent of all old people in the national survey said they wanted to see more of their doctors. However, objective evidence indicates that unmet medical need among old people is on a substantially larger scale.

2. DOCTORS

About half of all old people's disabilities are unknown to their family doctor, according to a study conducted on a sample of elderly patients from three practices in the Edinburgh area, by Dr. Williamson and his colleagues, who remark:

> One of the most striking and distressing features in the geriatric unit is that patients are so often admitted in a very advanced state of disease. Many have pressure sores or permanent joint contractures, and show signs of prolonged neglect and sub-nutrition. Yet the family doctor may write 'I saw this patient for the first time yesterday', or 'the last time I saw this old lady was two years ago when her husband died'. Careful history-taking will establish that timely medical or social intervention might have prevented much of the disability.[5]

[5] J. Williamson, I. H. Stoke et al., 'Old People at Home. Their Unreported Needs', The Lancet (23 May 1964), p. 1117.

Doctors

In Williamson's study 8 per cent of the old people were judged by a psychiatrist to be suffering from moderate or severe dementia – and only a fifth of these cases were known to the G.P. Another study among 200 patients admitted to a geriatric unit in Aberdeen found that the old men had a mean of 6·4 disorders each and the women 5·4 each. The author, Dr. L. A. Wilson, challenges the use of the term 'senility'.

> The use of 'senility' to explain general frailty is equally un-satisfactory and often covers a lack of diagnostic interest and effort. All the 'senile' patients we have examined have been ill with diseases whose number and seriousness would have produced severe disability at any age. . . .[6]

In view of this sort of evidence the Royal College of Physicians of Edinburgh in *The Care of Elderly in Scotland* say bluntly that : 'The interpretation we place on the figures we have quoted is that the usual system of self-reporting of illness, which appears to be reasonably satisfactory in the younger age-groups, is totally inadequate for the care of the elderly.'[7]

Since the traditional system of self-reporting is inadequate, some other system is required; and this implies radical changes in the conduct of general practice. The Gillie Report on *The Field of Work of the Family Doctor* (1963) also foresaw important changes in general practice. Dr. Gillie and his colleagues wanted the G.P. to become the focus and co-ordinator of health and welfare services : 'The central position of the family doctor, mobilizing for his patient all the resources of hospital and local health and welfare services, gives him an unique opportunity to bring this functional unification about.'[8]

If the general practitioner does ultimately become an effective co-ordinator of health and welfare services, this will presumably involve medical auxiliaries such as home nurses and health visitors. But even when these workers are available in much greater numbers, general practitioners will not be able to refer elderly patients to them for care or attention until some more

[6] L. A. Wilson, I. R. Lawson and W. Brass, 'Multiple Disorders in the Elderly', *The Lancet* (27 Oct. 1962), p. 843.

[7] Royal College of Physicians of Edinburgh, *The Care of the Elderly in Scotland* (1963), p. 21.

[8] Central Health Service Council, Standing Medical Advisory Committee, *The Field of Work of the Family Doctor* (1963), p. 57.

effective system is devised of breaking through the barrier of old people's failure to report their own disabilities.

The typical general practitioner has about 2,300[9] patients, of whom about 280 will be aged 65 or over. At present 49 per cent of old people have seen their general practitioner during the last three months and 70 per cent within the last year (national). Despite this contact the evidence provided by medical experts is that much simple disability goes undetected. Old people often comment that their doctor never physically examines them. Obviously a general practitioner lacks the equipment in his surgery to carry out an exhaustive series of tests. But with the 200 or so old people he sees a year he should be able to carry out a brief physical examination *at least once a year*.

But what of the 30 per cent of elderly patients who have not seen their G.P. in the last year? The doctor must attempt to contact these eighty or so people.[10] The obvious way would be to write inviting them to attend a surgery – at one of the less busy times of the year, such as the summer. Those who did not come, probably not more than twenty, could be visited in their homes and given a brief physical examination.

At a later date when the present chronic shortage of doctors is less severe it should be possible to give all or most elderly people a thorough annual medical examination including a wide range of tests. In addition to home nurses and health visitors a thorough programme of this kind will probably require special clinics devoted to preventive health work among the elderly. One such clinic has been pioneered by Dr. John Maddison in West London. Elderly people examined in his clinic had a median of *eleven disabilities* each: 77 per cent had 'incorrect glasses etc.', 70 per cent wax in the ears, 65 per cent had foot defects, 56 per cent had shrinking skeleton bones and joints, 52 per cent had diseases of the stomach and digestive system, 34 per cent suffered from anaemia, 33 per cent from thyroid deficiency, 29 per cent from heart disease, 29 per cent from artery disease, and 27 per cent from defective artificial teeth. Dr. Maddison curtly comments: 'Most of these condi-

[9] Ministry of Health, *The Health and Welfare Services*, year ending December 1963, p. 66.

[10] In a one-doctor practice it would only take a few hours to extract these names from the records – so long as the doctor's records reach a minimum level of efficiency, i.e. include date of birth, address, and details of last consultation.

Doctors

tions, with perhaps the exception of the gross heart diseases which are unpredictable, were considerably improved under preventive treatment.'[11]

The training at present received by general practitioners is heavily hospital-oriented. The Gillie Report calls for a change of emphasis: 'In the pre-clinical years education in normal psychology and sociology is as important as any pre-clinical subject and must come to occupy part of the time hitherto given to other subjects.'[12]

The Gillie Report also calls for more social and operational research on general practice. If more evidence from such research were available it might be easier to discuss how the present situation could be improved. An important point is how general practitioners can be saved from the present financial disincentive to have old people on their lists; a G.P. receives the same capitation fee regardless of the patient's age and, since old people as a group see their doctors more often, the individual G.P. is discouraged from showing the active and inquiring interest in old people which is needed if their unmet medical needs are to be remedied.

Although people aged 65 and over make up only 12 per cent of the population, they account for 20 per cent of all consultations[13] and probably a higher proportion of home visits. We need to know much more about why, despite so much expenditure of time, such a vast amount of disability and illness goes untreated. The importance of the doctor in many old people's lives – especially those of isolated old people – can hardly be exaggerated. Doctors have a higher weekly and annual coverage among old people than do any of the other social services. Without a much more adequate service from the G.P., any social policy for old age will fail.

[11] John Maddison (Area Medical Officer of Health, Area 10, Middlesex C.C.), *Preventing The Disabilities of Later Life.* (Duplicated, 1962).
[12] *The Field of Work of the Family Doctor* (1963), p. 48.
[13] During the previous year G.P.s reported 5·86 consultations per man aged 65 or over as against 3·39 consultation for all males, and 6·41 for old women compared with 4·08 for all females. W. P. D. Logan and A. A. Cushion, *Morbidity Statistics from General Practice* (London: H.M.S.O., 1958), p. 27.

275

3. MEDICAL AUXILIARIES

In 1961 63 per cent of all visits made by *Home Nurses* were made to old people; the service is particularly relevant to the house-bound but the total number of visits was only equivalent to less than three per old person per year, or a regular daily visit to less than 1 per cent of all old people. In 1961 there was only about one home nurse (full-time equivalent) to every three general practitioners.[14] But the distribution is very uneven; in some areas there is one to each G.P., while in other areas G.P.s apparently seldom see a home nurse. Liaison between home nurses and G.P.s is bad.

A much lower proportion of the visits of *Health Visitors* are paid to old people; the service is used mainly for visiting mothers and young children. Health visitors at present visit relatively few isolated old people – but the service could be especially useful for detecting old people living alone and eating an insufficient or inadequate diet, or suffering from other obvious, yet untreated, ailments. The number of health visitors (full-time equivalent) has hardly increased since 1948. Yet Dr. Williamson in his article on unmet medical need writes: 'The health visitor service was started to meet the crisis of high infant and child morbidity which is now a thing of the past. Instead our society faces an equally serious crisis of ill-health and disability at the other end of life.'[15] An obvious solution is for more health visitors to receive geriatric instruction and to be attached to general practice. This should also solve the problem of the present bad liaison between health visitors and G.P.s.

It should be possible to divert health visitors from child to geriatric work. But with home nurses, since most of their time is already taken up on old people, there must be a major expansion. Home nursing is apparently popular with nurses because compared with hospital nursing it offers independence and more convenient hours. Home nursing only employs about 4 per cent of all working nurses. Many trained nurses who left the work to get married do not wish to rejoin the 170,000[16] whole-time

[14] Ministry of Health, *Health and Welfare: The Development of Community Care* (1963), p. 17.
[15] J. W. Williamson, I. H. Stoke *et al.*, 'Old People at Home: Their Unreported Needs', *The Lancet* (23 May 1964), p. 1120.
[16] Ministry of Health, *The Health and Welfare Services*, year ending December 1963, p. 145.

nurses working in hospitals. It should be possible to recruit some of these nurses into home nursing and meanwhile to train more. Only in this way, especially in view of the severe general shortage of nurses, can the medical needs of old people be effectively served by group practices.

The findings about old people's unmet need for attention to their hearing, sight and feet, make clear that if G.P.s referred all the old people in need of such treatment, it would be necessary to train substantially more specialized personnel. There is an obvious shortage of chiropodists. However, since about half of practising chiropodists have either had no training or have been trained primarily through a correspondence course, it should be no insuperable problem to train more chiropodists to the present, or to a somewhat higher, standard.

4. HOUSING

The Community Care 'Plan' said : 'The basic need of the elderly is for a home of their own where they can enjoy privacy and comfort . . .' By the end of 1962 local authorities had built over 300,000 'single-bedroom dwellings suitable for elderly people'. In the one year of 1962 more than a quarter of all local authority dwellings completed were homes of this sort.[17] However, because of the relative decline of the local authority sector in house building, this was less than 10 per cent of all homes built in 1962 – while people aged 65 and over in 1962 made up 12 per cent of the population. In the four-area survey 13 per cent of the socially isolated were already living in special one-bedroom homes, but another 21 per cent wanted to move into such accommodation.

The scale of variation between regions cannot possibly be justified on any conceivable grounds of objective need. The Royal College of Physicians of Edinburgh noted that while one Scottish local authority in the period 1945–62 had devoted 42 per cent of its home building effort to special homes for old people, at least two Scottish local authorities had built none at all and a number of others had built a negligible proportion.[18]

Moreover, these one-bedroom dwellings are only 'suitable for

[17] Ministry of Health, *Health and Welfare: The Development of Community Care* (1963), p. 15.
[18] Royal College of Physicians of Edinburgh, *The Care of the Elderly in Scotland* (1963), p. 24.

old people'; in fact some people living in them are well below the age of 60. The actual number of people over 65 living in local authority one-bedroom dwellings is unknown.

It is widely believed that many of these dwellings have a warden in attendance. In fact, wardens are quite rare. In the four-area sample not one person was interviewed who lived in a local authority one-bedroom home with a warden available. By the end of 1962 less than one in a thousand old people in Britain lived in such dwellings with wardens. Of all the 'single-bedroom dwellings suitable for elderly people' built by the end of 1962 only just over 1 per cent had a warden.[19]

A Ministry of Housing study was published in 1962 about the experience of ninety-nine old people living in six different flatlet schemes with wardens. The average age of these people was 75. Just over half were described as having unlimited mobility outside the building; 10 per cent were housebound. The majority of these old people were women (86 per cent), most were widowed (71 per cent), and all the rest single. In all of the six schemes a common-room was available; 44 per cent of the old people had used the common-room in the last fortnight and only 23 per cent 'never' used it at all. In all six cases the warden was a married woman aged between 30 and 55; four out of six had previous nursing experience. The wardens performed a wide variety of services for the old people varying from nursing and cooking for those in ill-health, to cleaning, shopping and writing letters. Most of the flatlets had electric bells which rang in the warden's home, and the wardens all had telephones. The wardens' husbands looked after the central heating. The survey reported a number of complaints from the old people but the general response was of strong approval.[20]

The great advantage of this type of housing provision is its flexibility. There is no need for an old person to feel that a warden threatens her independence – most large blocks of flats have caretakers. But the warden is available if required; and with the assistance of a home help and a home nurse – and any other services required – it should be possible for old people to continue living in their own home, even without the presence

[19] Ministry of Health, *Health and Welfare: The Development of Community Care* (1963), pp.15–16.
[20] Ministry of Housing, *Grouped Flatlets for Old People* (1962).

Housing

of children, into quite an advanced state of physical incapacity.

Apart from the lack of wardens, perhaps the most regrettable feature of many 'single bedroom dwellings suitable for elderly people' is the low level of design. The Ministry of Housing has issued a good deal of information to local authorities, based on work by the Building Research Station and other sources, as to the features which old people want in their homes. Despite this, even in such obvious details as the design of bathrooms and the placing of cupboards, little attention has been paid to old people's requirements. The most glaring deficiencies are in the matter of heating. In the words of V. Hole and P. G. Allen, 'old people with central heating find it both effective and acceptable.' But many local authorities still persist in providing only open fire-places. Frail old people are thus exposed to the physical problems involved in keeping open fires burning – and the fire hazard. This lack of imagination and planning in the long run saddles the local authority with the prospect of installing central heating in the future at greater cost.

Many local authorities are at present building only one type of one-bedroom housing for old people – low blocks containing from six to twenty flats – without central heating, common-rooms or wardens. However, research indicates a demand for a wide variety of different sorts of housing. Bungalows are extremely popular; but 80 per cent of old people who live in high blocks of flats (with lifts) find their flats 'highly satisfactory'.[21] The small low block of flats goes only half-way to the effectively 'sheltered' concept of the block with a warden which is suitable, if necessary, for quite severely incapacitated old people. This compromise approach places the old people next to other old people without giving them the facilities – such as a common-room – which makes social contact easier. But less formal sorts of provision are also required – such as groups of perhaps half a dozen small flats in tall blocks, provided with lifts and adequate sound insulation; another type of housing provision for old people is the conversion of existing houses into three or four self-contained flats, on the pattern pioneered by the Abbeyfield Society. Such 'informal' provision is less visible and

[21] V. Hole and P. G. Allen, 'Dwellings for Old People', *The Architects' Journal*, 9 May 1962.

279

Social Policy

carries less architectural prestige, but it offers flexibility and enables some old people to live close to their own children or other relatives, and yet to remain independent.

At present often the major motive for building one-bedroom dwellings is to provide for old people living alone in houses, and thus to make the houses available for families with children. S. K. Ruck wrote in 1960: 'If smaller units of accommodation were available, and if old people could be persuaded to move into them, the country's whole housing problem would be virtually solved overnight.'[22] This argument must not be used as an excuse for bullying old people out of their familiar homes or bundling them into so-called 'special' housing which is inconveniently designed and jerry built. One old woman in Harrow reported that the housing department would not put her on the waiting list because, living only in rented rooms, she had 'nothing to offer'. This means that old people living in the most insecure situation are the least likely to get the security of a small council dwelling. S. K. Ruck notes that councils are reluctant to force 'over-housed' old people into smaller homes, but he goes on:

> Short of this, persuasion is used, and at least one authority makes a practice of telling the over-housed tenant they consider he should move, then sending a family on the waiting list along to the dwelling concerned. Actual contact with unhappiness which the sitting tenant could relieve is often found to be the most eloquent sort of persuasion.[23]

Eloquent indeed. One can imagine a frail old woman, whose husband has recently died (leaving her 'over-housed'), gaining the impression that she has no choice but to move. What is (perhaps) intended as only gentle persuasion may be interpreted by an old person as a harsh command to leave her familiar home.

To what extent is special housing intended to vacate houses for families to live in, and to what extent is it meant simply to house old people? At present local authorities appear to select old people for special housing on the basis of widely varying criteria. More thought must be given to deciding what priorities should be adopted.

[22] S. R. Ruck, 'Housing the Old: A Reconnaissance', *The Builder*, 4 March 1960.
[23] ibid.

Housing

As Hole and Allen have written: 'A study of a more fundamental nature is required which would challenge present
assumptions concerning the needs of old people and view them
in the general context of the life-cycle.'[24] Housing does not
consist of baths, cupboards and doorknobs alone, although these
are important. Especially for isolated old people, housing is the
major part of the environment.

But the lack of satisfactory information about old people's
housing needs cannot obscure the unsatisfactory nature of the
current situation. Only 40·1 per cent of old people living alone
have their own kitchen, bath and inside toilet (national). Three-
fifths of all old people living alone – about 750,000 individuals –
lack these basic requirements.

The problem of the 'under-occupied' housing of old people is
concentrated among owner-occupiers[25] – contrary to popular
belief. Because they own a house, these old people are usually
not interested in, and do not qualify for, subsidized special flats
or bungalows built by the local council. But private commercial
builders are not greatly attracted to building small dwellings for
old people, presumably because of the risk, lack of familiarity
with the market and doubts about the economic resources of old
people and their difficulties in getting mortgages. Yet many old
people would undoubtedly be willing to sell their present three-
or four-bedroom houses and to buy one- or two-bedroom homes
if these were available in the right locations, such as near to
their children[26] or other relatives, or in the same area – so that
they need not leave the 'familiar' district. Local authorities
have strong planning powers. These should be used immediately
to require all private developers to include some small bungalows or flats – perhaps 15 per cent – in all private building
developments beyond a certain size. Experience and research
could be used to vary the precise percentage as required. In

[24] V. Hole and P. G. Allen, 'Dwellings for Old People', *The Architects' Journal*,
9 May 1962.
[25] 52·3 per cent of old people under-occupying housing were owner-occupiers,
against 38·5 per cent who paid rent (national). 'Under-occupation' defined as
one-person household in 4+ rooms or two-person household in 5+ rooms.
'Rooms' defined as bedrooms, living-rooms and kitchen (if used for eating hot
meals).
[26] An example of an old person in such circumstances is Mr. Warner, Interview
No. 8, above, pp. 171–176.

Social Policv

time when private developers experienced the demand for this type of housing, planning compulsion might be no longer necessary.

More thought about old people's housing is required in other directions. Many single or widowed old people would be eager to take in a lodger, but do not know of a suitable person. On the other hand many frail old people would be more happy living as lodgers with, and being looked after by, younger people – rather than living in an institution; a Welfare Department could subsidize such a frail person to a realistic level and still provide cheaper (and more satisfactory) accommodation than in an Old People's Home.[27]

The major requirement is for a radical expansion in the provision of dwellings for old people – both by local authorities and by commercial developers. This must be supported by more imaginative planning, research, and social work in the field of housing. A greater variety in design and location is needed, as are higher standards of design and building.

5. HOME HELP SERVICE

Table 14.2 shows that although 4·4 per cent of old people get the home help service, another 5·7 per cent have an unmet need for it. Nine per cent of the socially isolated get the service but another 8 per cent need it. The home help service was at first largely intended for expectant mothers, but by 1953 old people were already accounting for over half of its work and in 1962 about three-quarters; however, priority is usually still given to expectant mothers. Thus an old person cannot rely upon her help always coming, because illness may at any time cause a home help to be switched from an old person to someone deemed to be in greater need. For instance in Fulham in the bad weather of early 1963 half of the old people having home helps found the service 'interrupted . . . for periods ranging from three days to three weeks.'[28] At the old person's time of greatest need, the home help is least likely to come.

No general criteria govern this service. In some areas, old

[27] Lewisham Old People's Welfare Committee are pioneering along these lines with a 'boarding-out' officer.
[28] From a report summarized in Sally Sainsbury, 'Home Services for the Aged', *New Society*, 2 April 1964.

Home Help Service

people only get home helps for short periods during time of illness. A number of authorities will not provide a home help to an old person who has a daughter living in the local authority area; thus a daughter may be forced to give up work to do her elderly mother's cleaning, while the regulation does not apply to a daughter who lives just down the road, but in the next borough. Other authorities are willing to employ and pay a woman as a home help to look after her own mother. The tasks performed also vary greatly. Most home helps are discouraged from cleaning windows. Some are encouraged to cook meals, others not. In general there is a narrow definition of housework which tends to rule out 'spring-cleaning'.

The rate of expansion of the home help service was very rapid after 1945 but in the 1950's it was much slower and at present the service is only expanding at about the same rate as the population aged over 75 – the group who use home helps most. A major reason for this is the unattractiveness of the job. There is a huge turnover of labour – nearly half each year. Despite the expansion of the service between 1953 and 1962 the absolute number of *full-time* home helps actually declined.[29]

Most of the work is done by part-time home helps. In cities where there is a big demand for cleaners, the home helps' rate of pay is only about two-thirds of the best market rate for cleaning offices or private homes. An extreme example of this is provided by Stepney where 'the attractions of much better paid jobs in the adjacent City of London make it extremely difficult to recruit and retain sufficient numbers of home helps.'[30]

Home helps already provide more than a simple cleaning service in some cases. For instance, of old people receiving meals-on-wheels more were originally referred to the service by home helps than by hospital almoners.[31] Some doctors are eager that the role of the home help should be expanded:

A home help service, if it is to become a real social service, must be able to attract women who are balanced and mature enough to handle the elderly with patience; who have enough intelligence and understanding to relate their behaviour to the

[29] Ministry of Health, *Health and Welfare: The Development of Community Care* (1963), p. 18.
[30] L.C.C. Public Health Department, *Review of the Domestic Help Service* (1957), p. 11.
[31] Amelia Harris, *Meals on Wheels for Old People* (1960), p. 18.

283

Social Policy

process of ageing, and who can provide comfort and security as well as competent help.[32]

This means more pay, and at least a minimum amount of training. There is an obvious need for some instruction about contacting doctors or other social agencies. If the service is expanded to include more cooking, instruction will also be needed in cooking meals suitable for the elderly.

Better pay and some training would be of great significance in other ways. At the end of 1963 a full-time home help organizer was running a team of about eighty, mainly part-time, home helps;[33] much of the organizer's time is taken up in dealing with the huge turnover rate instead of getting to know more about the needs of the people for whom the service is provided. The home help service undoubtedly relieves social isolation – and raises old people's level of social contact. But where there is a succession of new home helps only staying for a week or two, the service may have the additional effect of adding to an old person's feeling of loneliness.

There is a clear need for major expansion of the home help service. The home help organizer is already the most important welfare worker involved in providing domiciliary care for the elderly. The pay system must be fixed with a more realistic regard to the local labour market. The functions of the service must be expanded to include cooking of meals where necessary. The whole service also needs to be expanded beyond the present 'daily help' concept – which is based on the middle-class image of the daily charlady.

The home help service must provide for such jobs as small carpentering tasks and decorating; crumbling dirty wallpaper is a major worry to some incapacitated old people. One or two 'handymen' should be attached to each home help organizer.

6. MEALS

The national survey shows just over 1 per cent of all old people in Britain receiving meals-on-wheels,[34] while five times as many

[32] C. H. Wright and L. Roberts, 'The Place of the Home Help Service in the Care of the Aged', *The Lancet*, 1 February 1958, p. 255.
[33] Ministry of Health, *The Health and Welfare Services*, year ending December 1963, p. 107.
[34] Peter Townsend and Dorothy Wedderburn, *The Aged in the Welfare State* (1965).

284

'Meals on Wheels' for Old People

again have an unmet need for it (Table 14.2). Once more the service is highly suitable for the more frail, or housebound, socially isolated people. About three-quarters of the meals-on-wheels schemes were operated by the Women's Voluntary Service – 72 per cent of those receiving the meals were living alone'[35] but in 1963 only about one in thirty of all old people living alone were receiving the meals. Once again there was a very uneven distribution between areas – one important factor being the availability of the voluntary workers who run the service.

About half of all recipients of meals-on-wheels are bedfast or housebound, but the other half say they are 'able to get to shops'. There is a very big unmet demand for this service but there are, of course, other alternatives. Just over half of meals-on-wheels recipients do not have home helps,[36] so the possibility of meals being cooked by them depends upon a big expansion of the home help service.

Another alternative is to provide 'luncheon clubs' where old people can go to get meals. Harrow has several of these lunch clubs – where meals are provided, as with the meals-on-wheels service, at a subsidized rate of around one shilling. The number of these lunch clubs has increased recently but the total of meals served is only a small fraction of the meals served by civic restaurants in 1945.

The demand for a five-fold expansion of the meals-on-wheels service – indicated in the national survey[37] – would probably also apply to the luncheon clubs (or old people's clubs serving lunches). An expansion of these two types of meals provision plus allowing home helps to cook meals would then enable the old people to choose which they preferred. Co-ordination between the services would permit an old person to switch from one to the other. For instance, an old person who could get to a lunch club in the summer, but was prevented from doing so in the winter (due to bronchitis perhaps) would, at that time of year, get a steady supply of meals at home.

[35] Amelia Harris, op. cit., pp. 3, 26.
[36] ibid., p. 61.
[37] Peter Townsend and Dorothy Wedderburn, op. cit.

285

Social Policy

7. CLUBS FOR OLD PEOPLE

Of all socially isolated old people 10 per cent had been to an old people's club in the last week; but another 12 per cent of the isolated said they would like to attend such a club. Most old people's clubs meet once a week or fortnight in borrowed or rented premises. The meeting is usually for two or three hours in the afternoon, the big event being cups of tea and light refreshment. The clubs are mainly organized by voluntary groups – over a third by the W.V.S. and most of the rest by Old People's Welfare Committees, the Red Cross and the Salvation Army. Many clubs meet in church halls or have some connection with a church or chapel. As with other old people's services, there is usually a local authority subsidy – and some clubs are run direct by the local authority.

However, neither the local authorities nor the voluntary organizations who run the clubs have thought out clearly exactly how the clubs are supposed to contribute to old people's welfare. The most obviously needy group of old people are the housebound, but there is little indication of the clubs taking any interest in them. In the four-area survey some housebound old people had been out for car rides, to church or to visit relatives, but none had been recently to attend an old people's club.

The clubs seem to be run in the interests of existing members, and in particular the more physically vigorous members. There is no standard procedure for visiting club members who are temporarily sick. Only a small minority of clubs have any transport for collecting members from their homes. However, coach trips are an almost universal feature of clubs; summer coach trips are often made, not always to the nearest seaside resort but often to a town 100 miles away. Paralleling the idea of one or two long day trips in summer – or week's holidays – is the big Christmas dinner.

There is a strong argument for appealing more to the frail, the isolated, the recently widowed and the housebound. With more money, better premises and improved organization, old people's clubs could undoubtedly appeal to more than the mere 6·6 per cent (national) of all old people who attend weekly.

The most obvious requirement is meals. This would attract some old people to whom the idea of merely sitting and talking

Clubs for Old People

over a cup of tea does not appeal. In turn the provision of a midday meal would require more elaborate premises. Old people could eat a nutritious and subsidized meal – and even in winter get home before dark. A club with even one mini-bus would be able to collect a number of the more frail members during the morning. The mini-bus could also be used for frequent short trips. For instance, many old people have never seen any old people's housing – and they could be taken to see such things in the immediate locality. Modest trips would appeal to at least some housebound old people.

A few areas in Britain already have large Day Centres for old people. Many more of these are required, with or without medical services on the premises. Perhaps the ideal solution would be a large Centre, open all day and every day with a number of smaller clubs or branches in the vicinity – the latter could concentrate on providing meals and a few simple facilities. The Centre would have a kitchen from which heated food could be taken to the branch clubs; the meals-on-wheels service could also operate from the Centre kitchen. The Centres would not all need to be the same; but they should contain facilities for recreation, reading rooms, and perhaps a bar to appeal to the old men. Such Centres should in no sense be thought of as an alternative to more and better domiciliary services. Indeed the Centre should also house the offices of the home help service. Any club member – whether in the Centre or the branch club – should be provided with advice on financial, health, legal, housing and other problems. If the particular office – for instance the National Assistance Board – was not in the same building, club organizers should ensure that any old person who so wanted would in fact see an N.A.B. officer.

Present old people's clubs are mainly run on very small budgets. There is a constant urge to raise small sums of money by raffles, bring-and-buy sales and the like. With adequately financed clubs a member should be able to attend a club for an hour or two without feeling that he needs to spend any money and without having to sit in silence staring at a newspaper – like so many old men in public libraries. The clubs should also make some provision for children, and relatives or friends of the old people to attend as associate members.

Such a club would obviously require some full-time staff,

including at least one person with social work training, who would presumably be employed by the local authority which provided the finance. But the maximum amount of power should be given to an elected committee of members.

Such renovated, expanded, and better financed clubs would also be able to make a methodical and sustained attempt to reach the isolated, the lonely, the recently widowed and the housebound. Full-time club organizers or committee members could visit them in their own homes and offer to show them round the club. A continuing programme could be maintained to visit members who suddenly stopped attending – to see if they were ill or otherwise in need of help.

At present old people's clubs are discouraged from making serious recruiting drives for more members because they lack the space in their restricted premises. Some clubs have waiting lists. The first essential is, then, a major increase in financial support.

8. VOLUNTARY VISITING

Regular friendly visiting can do much to help the elderly who are lonely or housebound. It is often combined with practical help inside or outside the home, such as letter-writing or shopping, and can frequently lead to other services, statutory or voluntary, being called upon when needed. Visiting services are particularly suitable for voluntary provision. Much is being done, in particular by the 1,350 local committees linked to the National Old People's Welfare Committee, but still further expansion will be necessary.

Despite these large claims and large hopes in the Ten-year 'Plan'[38] the four-area survey shows only about 1 per cent of all old people and 2 per cent of the socially isolated having had a voluntary visitor in the last week.

The clergy, on the evidence of the four-area survey, do very little visiting – apart from visiting some old people who still regularly attend church. There is also little sign of the clergy detecting need among old people and alerting the social services. For instance, of old people receiving the meals-on-wheels

[38] Ministry of Health, *Health and Welfare: The Development of Community Care* (1963), p. 20.

288

service only 2 per cent of the recommendations for the service came from clergy.[39]

In several areas there are schemes for organizing youth club members or school sixth formers to visit old people in the locality. The difficulty about these schemes lies in assessing what proportion of the teenagers do indeed make regular visits and what the old people think about them. No study of such a scheme has been conducted to date. In one scheme a record was kept of specific jobs done for 130 old people over a two-month period. Most of those jobs are small – such as delivering harvest festival parcels – but some are bigger, such as decorating rooms. It is further stated that another 500 old people have been 'regularly' visited. One is left with the impression that the organizers themselves have little clear information about these visits; the specific jobs listed could have been done by the paid organizers themselves in the two-month period without the help of any schoolchildren. Of course the teenagers may be paying regular visits and the old people may be enjoying them. But the records of this organization give a general impression of amateurish administration and provide no hard evidence to support the large claims made.

Most visiting schemes are run by Old People's Welfare Committees, the W.V.S., and other voluntary organizations. Some local authorities organize visiting schemes direct. A study is available of a scheme organized by the Old People's Welfare Association in Hornchurch, Essex.[40] The study was conducted by Stephen Baran, a social worker from New York who came to Britain on a Fulbright scholarship to study services for old people. Hornchurch was chosen because it appeared to have an unusually vigorous voluntary visiting programme and the organizers were willing to co-operate. However, Baran's report on this scheme is not encouraging. It was officially claimed that fifty-six members of the visiting scheme were paying regular visits to 402 housebound people; Baran concluded that these claims were exaggerated. He found record-keeping and organization to be haphazard and unreliable. Visitors knew little

[39] Amelia Harris, op. cit., p. 18.
[40] Stephen Baran, 'A Friendly Chat is not Enough', *New Society*, 25 February 1965; Stephen Baran, 'An Examination of a Voluntary Visiting Program for Old People in a British Community' (Unpublished), 1963.

Social Policy

about the social services and did little to refer those in need to the appropriate agency. Half of the visitors exhibited 'a smugness and sense of superiority towards the old people'. Only a fifth of the old people were receiving weekly visits lasting as long as an hour. Baran concluded:

> On the whole Hornchurch Old People's Welfare Association visiting of old people seemed to be of mediocre quality in its conception, in its execution and its end result . . . Substantial numbers of those visited denied being lonely, were not living alone, were physically able, and had numerous social contacts during the day. Many were indifferent or antipathetic to visitors who nevertheless continued to go to see them. There seemed to be little follow-up once visiting had begun to see it was doing good.

One of Baran's main criticisms is the lack of specific criteria by which visiting could be judged. There was no decision as to which categories of old people should be visited, and little idea of what should take place in the visits. The assumption seemed to be that the mere presence of the visitors – who tended to be middle-class married women aged about 50 – would automatically be beneficial to the old people. However, Baran's evidence from Hornchurch is that only just over half of the old people receiving visits had a generally positive reaction while 14 per cent were actually hostile. If the approval of the old people were adopted as a major criterion some of these visits would not have been paid. In the schemes for young people to visit old people, it is explicitly stated that the visiting will benefit the young people. However, nothing is said about what happens when the interests of the young person and the old person clash.

It is difficult to generalize from Baran's study in Hornchurch. But at present there is no systematic evidence in Britain of voluntary visits being received and positively *welcomed* by more than one in about every 200 old people. What of the Ten Year 'Plan' statement that 'still further expansion will be necessary . . .'? Before such expansion takes place it might be well to decide what voluntary visiting is meant to achieve and to discover more about old people's views on the subject.

Voluntary Visiting

9. LACK OF CO-ORDINATION AND PLANNING

Services for old people suffer from fragmentation, both between and within the three major groupings dealing with old people – the medical world, the local authorities and other statutory offices at the local level, and the voluntary agencies.

Medical services for the old are split between the hospital, the general practitioner, and the medical auxiliaries – such as home nurses, health visitors, chiropodists, and oculists. This lack of co-ordination is especially evident, for instance, in the absence of effective follow-up when an old person is discharged from hospital (including mental hospitals), or the fact of some old people who regularly see their family doctor but nevertheless fail to get necessary treatment of such an obvious kind as chiropody.

Statutory services for the old suffer from lack of co-ordination nationally between the Ministries of Health, Pensions, Housing, and Labour, and the National Assistance Board, and at the local level between the Public Health, Welfare and Housing departments in the Town Hall and, for instance, the National Assistance Board.

Voluntary organizations are even more numerous and overlapping. In some areas there is sharp competition between them, and a proprietary attitude to old people with whom they are dealing. Old People's Welfare Committees now exist in many areas with the prime purpose of co-ordinating voluntary services. Judging by Kathleen Slack's description of these Committees in the London area in 1958–9 co-ordination has sometimes been rather imperfect.[41] Some O.P.W.C.s have quite inadequate premises, and lack proper records.

Between these three main groups of agencies co-ordination is often even worse. A prime example is the split between hospitals under Regional Hospital Boards and Old People's Homes under local authorities – resulting in what the Royal College of Physicians of Edinburgh call a 'no man's land' in between.[42]

Lack of information was dramatically shown in a case reported in a Ministry of Health survey – the existence of a

[41] Kathleen Slack, *Councils, Committees and Concern for the Old* (1960).
[42] Royal College of Physicians of Edinburgh, *The Care of the Elderly in Scotland* (1963), p. 74.

Social Policy

long-established Old People's Welfare Committee was unknown
to the Medical Officer of Health in one county borough. Another example is reported by Kathleen Slack; at the time of her
study in London, Old People's Welfare Committees each had
representatives from ten to fifty bodies – but the great majority
had no representative from the Ministry of Pensions.[43]

Referrals between services operate on a most haphazard basis.
District nurses are referred to patients almost entirely by general
practitioners and hospitals. G.P.s also play a big role in referring
home helps. But in the case of meals-on-wheels only 12 per cent
of the referrals come from doctors; home helps refer 10 per cent
and 'friends and relatives' refer another 10 per cent. The
National Assistance Board, despite paying regular home visits to
quite a large proportion of isolated and housebound old people,
appears to do very little referring to other social services. For
instance, for meals-on-wheels only 4 per cent of the referrals
come from the National Assistance Board.[44]

Contracting in as a means of selecting old people to receive the
domiciliary services is clearly ineffective. Self-reporting of illness is also unsatisfactory. The failure of many old people to
apply for national assistance is another example. Old people are
also expected to take the initiative in getting their names on to
the waiting lists of local authority housing departments. The
failure of the contracting-in principle further applies to old
people's clubs. As the Royal College of Physicians of Edinburgh
comment: 'The aged are generally not an articulate group in
making their demands. Ignorance and apathy as well as incapacity may be responsible for a real and often undivulged
want.'[45]

Criteria indicating what a service is intended to achieve are
generally lacking. Little thought is given to basic questions such
as whether it is better to spread the home help service widely, or
to concentrate the help on a comparatively small number of
highly incapacitated old people. Or to take another example,
the development of some specific criteria as to what housing
provision for old people aims to achieve might make it easier to
forecast the future demand.

[43] Kathleen Slack, op. cit., p. 139.
[44] Amelia Harris, op. cit., p. 18.
[45] Royal College of Physicians of Edinburgh, op. cit., p. 40.

292

Lack of Co-ordination and Planning

In a number of spheres decisions have to be taken which involve weighing the requirements of old people against those of young people or children. A G.P. in an emergency may have to decide whether to pay his first visit to an old person or to a maternity case. Health visitors see mainly small children and old people. Old people's housing needs have to compete with those of families containing young children. Even at the National Assistance Board the old rub shoulders with unmarried mothers and young unemployed people. Little thought has been devoted to how these choices should be made, or how the situation is likely to be perceived by old people.

Another basic but inadequately considered question is the extent to which old people's expressed wishes should be taken into account if they conflict with the social agency's view of the old person's need. For instance, in old people's clubs – how much power should be allocated to elected committees of the elderly members to run the club as they choose and how much power should be reserved by non-elected organizers in the interests of 'efficiency' or of extending the facilities of the club to old people who are not yet members?

The lack of any *comprehensive inventory* of all the old people in the locality means that those who run social services for old people are often powerless to do anything about needy people who may live down the street from the office, but do not come forward to ask for help. At present there is not even a complete list of all old people in a locality who are already receiving at least one social service. But a mere pooling of names between doctors, the N.A.B., clubs, the meals-on-wheels and so on would be inadequate. The Royal College of Physicians of Edinburgh believe that 'only a complete register of old people would be satisfactory'. They think that old people would not regard this as an intrusion into their privacy. 'We consider that such an estimate of the probable attitude of old people is incorrect. In our experience, the great majority of elderly people like to be visited.'[46]

The present writer agrees that comprehensive local inventories of all old people should be established – based on the information already possessed by the Ministry of Pensions or the

[46] Royal College of Physicians of Edinburgh, op. cit., p. 47.

293

Social Policy

local executive councils of the National Health Service, or both. The names, marital status, age, household composition and physical capacity of all old people would be made available to all social agencies recognized by the medical profession and by local authorities.

The scope and value of *voluntary work* is an issue which cannot be avoided in any discussion of the fragmentation of old people's services. Voluntary workers involved in the meals-on-wheels service work on average ·two hours and twenty minutes per week.[47] The other important use of voluntary workers is in the old people's clubs, and here again the average worker probably works for a similar time, per week or fortnight. The availability of voluntary labour affects the likelihood of services being provided. Before 1962 the areas of highest social status were four times as likely to have a meals-on-wheels service as were the lowest status area.[48] (However, since 1962 local authorities have increasingly provided this service.)

Voluntary work in the provision of services for old people is merely part of the evidence of these services at present being given a low priority by society. If there is to be major development and a more professional spirit in the future, voluntary and untrained workers will inevitably play a smaller role. The voluntary organizations themselves are tending to employ a nucleus of full-time paid personnel.

The local authorities' powers are at present not being used to the full. Quite apart from the very low level of the services in many areas some services do not get provided at all. Local authorities have powers to provide special laundry services for incontinent old people. Incontinence is an important precipitating factor in old people being admitted to geriatric hospitals – and a more thorough and effective provision of this service is necessary. In the provision of holidays few councils have a substantial programme – Oldham is an authority which uses to the full its powers in this direction. The power to assist old people in meeting the cost of house removals is seldom used; the cost is a major disincentive to some old people, who might otherwise be eager to move out of large or inconvenient homes. Moreover, local authorities are not using their latent powers in other

[47] Amelia Harris, op. cit., p. 79.
[48] ibid., p. 67.

294

Lack of Co-ordination and Planning

directions – such as planning control over the type and size of homes in new private developments.

Transport is a key issue in the welfare of old people. A major factor in social isolation is the physical distance between some old people and their relatives or friends. Social contact as well as medical care, club attendance, meals-on-wheels, social visiting, and the home help service all involve either moving someone to the old person's home or moving the old person to the service. More fundamental thought and research is required on transportation and mobility. An obvious example is the question of delivering meals to infirm people as against taking infirm people to the meals. Do cars, taxis, mini-buses, or ambulances provide the best solutions? One possibility in reducing the current fragmentation of services is to have a transport pool for all the old people's services.

10. CO-ORDINATION AND CONSUMER-ORIENTATION

Administering all services for old people through one source is unlikely to be practical in Britain. However, two main foci are a more real possibility. One main focus would be the general medical practitioner in a group practice with health visitors and home nurses attached, plus an adequate secretarial staff to maintain continuous and effective liaison with the providers of care for feet, teeth, hearing and sight – in addition to hospitals and Welfare Homes. The second main focus would be a Centre for old people from which would be administered the home help service, and a variety of meals services. This Centre would presumably be attached either to the local authority Health or Welfare Department, or to a new combined department. It would require adequate staff to maintain effective and continuous liaison with the Ministry of Pensions and the National Assistance Board, the Council Housing Department and the voluntary organizations. A vital requirement would be to maintain active co-operation between the medical and welfare foci; co-operation between the two foci would involve establishing a common inventory of all old people in the locality.

Perhaps even more vital is the need for a change to consumer-oriented services. At present the services tend to be production-oriented – based on Hospital, Home, Welfare Department,

295

doctor's surgery, or church hall. Efficient marketing companies in the commercial world have redefined their functions in terms of the consumer and been prepared to subordinate factory and production considerations to what market research says the customers want. Providers of old people's services must cease defining their sphere of operations as being merely a home help, a home nurse, a National Assistance Officer, or a W.V.S. helper; they must all redefine their function as serving old people. This means a major and continuing programme of research to discover what old people want and the establishment of clear criteria by which the effectiveness of the services can be measured. In particular a customer-orientation would involve making it easier for old people to know about, use, and experiment with, the available services.

The new consumer-orientation will in turn involve training and re-training senior Civil Servants and administrators, doctors and the relevant types of social workers, including home helps. It will also require the employment of new managerial skills in the social services. The marketing manager of an efficient food retailing firm would be able to make major improvements in the meals-on-wheels service, if given the opportunity.

Where possible in the provision of social services, the old person should be able to choose. For instance an old woman whose arthritis prevents her from cooking should be able to choose between having mobile meals delivered, or having her home help cook them, or being transported to a club or Centre to eat the meals there; she should also be able to choose a combination of the three. Such requirements make flexibility vital – to meet a variety of local needs and the changing demands of new generations of old people.

II. RETIREMENT AND LEISURE

In the past, advocates of better social services for old people have pointed to retirement as the key problem of old men. This has led to demands that men be allowed to continue in work past 65; others argue on behalf of 'sheltered workshops' where old people are given work to do for a small 'wage'. In 1963 only forty-two of these schemes existed in Britain, and some signs of disillusionment with them were becoming evident. Obviously the old people are well aware of the 'sheltered' and subsidized nature of these workshops – the problem of diminished status associated with retirement is not adequately tackled.

Another possibility is to encourage people to prepare in advance for retirement. Many appear to have thought little about the problems they will face in retirement – the drop in income especially. There are already evening classes and lectures about retirement, but these may only involve preaching to the converted.

Few old people retain much contact with their fellow workers – even when they continue to live near the place of work. There is usually nowhere for such contacts to take place. The company which has employed a man, as well as the trade union to which he has belonged, must accept some responsibility for him after he retires. In this field Britain has much to learn from many American companies – and from trade unions such as the United Automobile Workers. A social club close to or within the company buildings enables retired men to mix with their former fellow workers on familiar ground. If current employees of the firm also use the club, the work atmosphere is automatically retained. Trade unions must either negotiate such facilities for retired workers or must provide adequate facilities direct.

At present clubs specifically for old people are attended slightly less by old people than are clubs unrestricted by age. Therefore one must not minimize the importance of women's groups, working men's clubs, British Legion and the like. Although the provision of club facilities and other channels for social activity can be greatly improved these will probably never appeal to more than a minority. Especially for the socially isolated, newspapers, radio and television will continue to be of great importance.

Old people like a wide variety of programmes and there are already a few programmes directed primarily at them. Obviously the major media already possess from their normal audience and readership research a good deal of information about old people's preferences. What is required now is a rather more imaginative approach. Much of the information that reaches isolated old people comes from the media, and yet the old people are often ignorant of many simple pieces of useful knowledge – about pensions, and national assistance, and about the whole range of services available to them. They may, perhaps, be no more ignorant than are other age-groups, but such knowledge is potentially of more central relevance in the lives of old people. The mass media surely should be doing something to bridge this gap in knowledge. One possibility would be radio or television serials along the lines of *The Archers* – which is already very popular with old people – and laced with hard information, not about farming matters, but about things that would be useful to all old people. There could be record programmes for old people, with an elderly disc jockey. Another obvious possibility would be an historical programme dealing with the events of fifty or sixty years ago and based on edited reminiscences of old people. This type of programme would be particularly suitable for the television regions or for local radio. Local newspapers also could be more imaginative than merely using the inevitable pictures of groups from old people's clubs.

12. FURTHER RESEARCH

Research, research and yet more research is needed. A good deal of this should be basic work, from which it will be possible to build comprehensive theories of the psychology and sociology of old age in all its aspects. After the great outpourings of research about childhood over the last fifty years, we now need a flood of research about the other end of the life span.

In social medicine we need to follow up the pioneering studies of recent years. It is extraordinary that we are only just beginning to realize the huge extent of the unmet medical needs of old people. The Royal College of Physicians of Edinburgh comment: 'We believe that the need for care in all areas is greater than is generally realized, and consider that painstaking surveys are necessary to determine exactly how far we are failing to meet the misfortunes of the elderly.'[49] This research needs to cover, not only the actual physical and mental ailments of the elderly but also the medical profession and such medical auxiliaries as health visitors, home nurses and chiropodists.

The Ministry of Pensions and the National Assistance Board

[49] *The Care of the Elderly in Scotland* (1963), p. 41.

Further Research

pay out over £1,000 million annually to old people but until very recently have shown a marked lack of further interest in the old people. We need to know more about how old people spend their money. There is a strong argument for a special cost of living index for old age pensioners.

To take one more example, we at present have very little systematic knowledge about old people's housing. A great deal more detailed research is required on the practical physical details of the home itself. More sophisticated investigations are needed into old people's housing needs; about the dilemmas old people are placed in, for instance at widowhood; about the social implications of living in special groups of flats or bungalows; about preferences in living next to younger or older neighbours. Above all housing must be viewed as a social process. How do old people come to put their names on Council housing lists? How does the administrative procedure function? How do old people first learn about special housing? Why do so many old people say they want to live in bungalows?

In the whole field of provision for old people the social process of administration itself needs to be studied. Although the Ministries responsible should be doing much more to find out what is happening to their expenditure, not all of this research can be conducted by the official agencies. Studies of the working of the National Assistance Board, the relations between home nurses and home helps, or the precise kinds of 'persuasion' used by local housing departments to get lone old people to vacate houses – all these are subjects best studied by outside bodies, such as universities. The universities, where presumably the more basic theoretical research would also be done, could thus help to achieve a balance.

A good deal of future research needs to be on a continuing or longitudinal basis. Just as panels of babies are studied as they grow up to adolescence, so middle-aged people need to be studied and re-interviewed as they enter old age. Such studies will in turn require research on problems of method like how to retain a high proportion of the sample as co-operating respondents over a series of interviews.

Another major reason for continuing and repeating research projects is the very development of social services discussed in this chapter. If major changes are made in Institutional provision, domiciliary services, and the level of social security financial provision – this will change the general social circumstances of the elderly population. More research will then be necessary.

13. FINANCE

Expenditure in 1963–64 on the three main domiciliary services to old people – home helps, home nursing and health visiting was about £16·7 million for England and Wales. If other services such as old people's clubs and the meals-on-wheels service are included the total expenditure was probably about £19 million.[50] (The Ministry of Pensions paid out £990 million to retirement pensioners in 1963.)

If the expenditure on services to old people were increased by 300 per cent from £19 million to £76 million this would still only be about £12 for each old person in the population. Such an increase on services to old people of course would enable money to be saved by keeping some old people out of Homes and Hospitals.

[50] This excludes the Welfare expenditure, mainly on Residential Homes.

Selected Bibliography

G. F. Adams and E. A. Cheeseman, *Old People in Northern Ireland* (Belfast: Northern Ireland Hospitals Authority), 1951.

C. M. Arensberg and S. T. Kimball, *Family and Community in Ireland* (Cambridge: Harvard University Press), 1940.

Stephen Baran, *An Examination of a Voluntary Visiting Program for Old People in a British Community* (London: Unpublished), 1963.

Stephen Baran, 'A Friendly Chat is not Enough,' *New Society*, 25 February 1965.

Wendell Bell, 'Anomie, Social Isolation, and the Class Structure,' *Sociometry*, Vol. 20, No. 2, June 1957, pp. 105–16.

James E. Birren, *The Psychology of Aging* (New Jersey: Prentice-Hall), 1963.

Zena Smith Blau, 'Structural Constraints on Friendship in Old Age,' *American Sociological Review*, Vol. 26, No. 3, June 1961, pp. 429–39.

Ernest W. Burgess (ed.), *Aging in Western Societies* (University of Chicago Press), 1960.

Isabel Cary-Lundberg, 'On Durkheim, Suicide and Anomie,' *American Sociological Review*, Vol. 24, No. 2, April 1959.

Marshall B. Clinard (ed.), *Anomie and Deviant Behavior* (New York: Free Press), 1964.

Dorothy Cole, *The Economic Circumstances of Old People* (Welwyn, Herts., Codicote Press: Occasional Papers in Social Administration), 1962.

Charles Booth, *The Aged Poor in England and Wales* (London: Macmillan), 1894.

Elaine Cumming and William E. Henry, *Growing Old: The Process of Disengagement*. Foreword by Talcott Parsons. (New York: Basic Books), 1961.

Bleddyn Davies, 'An Index of Variation in "Need" of County Boroughs for Old People's Homes', *Sociological Review*, Vol. 12, No. 1, March 1964, pp. 5–38.

Dwight G. Dean and Jon A. Reeves, 'Anomie: A Comparison of a Catholic and Protestant Sample,' *Sociometry*, Vol. 25, No. 2, June 1962, pp. 209–12.

Bibliography

Emile Durkheim, *Suicide* (London: Routledge and Kegan Paul), 1952 edition.

A. R. Emerson, *A Survey of Elderly People* (Nottingham: duplicated), 1958.

Meyer Fortes, *The Web of Kinship among the Tallensi* (Oxford University Press for International African Institute), 1948.

H. J. Friedsam, 'Older People in Disaster' in George W. Baker and Dwight C. Chapman, *Man and Society in Disaster* (New York: Basic Books) 1962, pp. 151–84.

Peter Gregory, *Deafness and Public Responsibility* (Codicote Press: Occasional Papers in Social Administration), 1964.

Paul Halmos, *Solitude and Privacy* (London: Routledge and Kegan Paul), 1952

P. From Hansen (ed.) *Age with a Future* (Copenhagen: Munksgaard), 1964.

William H. Harlan and J. Singh, *The Social Status and Attitudes of Old Men in an Indian Village* (Paper at International Congress of Gerontology), 1963.

Amelia Harris, *Meals on Wheels for Old People* (London: National Corporation for the Care of Old People), 1960.

Amelia Harris, *Health and Welfare of Older People in Lewisham* (London: Government Social Survey, duplicated), 1962.

V. Hole and P. G. Allen, 'Dwellings for Old People,' *The Architects' Journal*, Vol. 135, No. 19, 9 May 1962.

Trevor H. Howell, *A Student's Guide to Geriatrics* (London: Staples Press), 1963.

Robert W. Kleemeier (ed.), *Aging and Leisure* (New York: Oxford University Press), 1961.

Bernard Kutner *et al.*, *Five Hundred Over Sixty* (New York: Russell Sage Foundation), 1956.

S. M. Lempert, *A Survey of the Aged in Stockport* (Borough of Stockport), 1958.

Marjorie Fiske Lowenthal, *Lives in Distress* (New York: Basic Books), 1964.

Marjorie Fiske Lowenthal, 'Social Isolation and Mental Illness in Old Age,' *American Sociological Review*, Vol. 29, No. 1, February 1964, pp. 54–70.

Peter Marris, *Widows and their Families* (London: Routledge and Kegan Paul), 1958.

Dorothy L. Meier and Wendell Bell, 'Anomia and Differential Access to the Achievement of Life Goals,' *American Sociological Review*, Vol. 24, No. 2, April 1959, pp. 189–202.

Bibliography

Robert K. Merton, *Social Theory and Social Structure* (New York: Free Press), 1957 edition.

H. C. Miller, *The Ageing Countryman* (London: National Corporation for the Care of Old People), 1963.

Ephraim H. Mizruchi, 'Social Structure and Anomie in a Small City,' *American Sociological Review*, Vol. 25, No. 5, October 1960, pp. 645–54.

Ephraim H. Mizruchi, *Success and Opportunity* (New York: Free Press), 1964.

Clark E. Moustakas, *Loneliness* (New Jersey: Prentice Hall), 1961.

National Corporation for the Care of Old People, *Chiropody for the Elderly*, 1961.

National Council of Social Service, *Loneliness*, 1957.

National Labour Women's Advisory Committee, *Care of the Elderly: Domiciliary Services*, 1964.

National Old People's Welfare Council, *Leisure in Later Year* (London: National Council for Social Service), 1963.

Gwynn Nettler, 'A Measure of Alienation,' *American Sociological Review*, Vol. 22, No. 6, December 1957, pp. 670–7.

Talcott Parsons, *Essays in Sociological Theory* (New York: Free Press), 1964 edition.

Talcott Parsons, *Family, Socialization and Interaction Process* (London: Routledge and Kegan Paul), 1956.

Suzanne Reichard, Florine Livson and Paul G. Petersen, *Aging and Personality* (New York: John Wiley), 1962.

I. M. Richardson, *Age and Need: A Study of Older People in North-East Scotland* (University of Aberdeen), 1963.

Alan H. Roberts and Milton Rokeach, 'Anomie, Authoritarianism and Prejudice: A Replication,' *American Journal of Sociology*, Vol. LXI, No. 4, January 1956, pp. 355–8.

B. Seebohm Rowntree, *Poverty: A Study of Town Life* (London: Macmillan), 1901.

B. Seebohm Rowntree, *Old People* (Oxford University Press), 1947.

Royal College of Physicians of Edinburgh, *The Care of the Elderly in Scotland*, 1963.

S. K. Ruck, 'Housing the Old: A Reconnaissance,' *The Builder*, 4 March 1960.

S. K. Ruck, 'A Policy for Old Age,' *Political Quarterly*, Vol. 31, No. 2, April/June 1960, pp. 120–31.

Sally Sainsbury, 'Home Services for the Aged,' *New Society*, 2 April 1964.

P. Sainsbury, *Suicide in London* (London: Chapman and Hall), 1955.

303

Bibliography

Ethel Shanas, *The Health of Older People* (Cambridge: Harvard University Press), 1962.

J. H. Sheldon, *The Social Medicine of Old Age* (Oxford University Press), 1948.

B. E. Shenfield, *Social Policies for Old Age* (London: Routledge and Kegan Paul), 1957.

T. S. Simey, *Social Contacts in Old Age* (Liverpool University Press), 1953.

L. W. Simmons, *The Role of the Aged in Primitive Society* (New Haven: Yale University Press), 1945.

Kathleen M. Slack, *Councils, Committees and Concern for the Old* (Codicote Press: Occasional Papers in Social Administration), 1960.

Douglas R. Snellgrove, *Elderly Housebound* (Luton: White Crescent Press), 1963.

Leo Srole, 'Anomie, Authoritarianism and Prejudice'. Letter to the editor of *American Journal of Sociology*, Vol. LXII, No. 1, July 1956, pp. 63–7.

Leo Srole, 'Social Integration and Certain Corollaries.' *American Sociological Review*, Vol. 21, No. 6, December 1956, pp. 709–16.

Erwin Stengel, *Suicide and Attempted Suicide* (Harmondsworth: Pelican), 1964.

Y. Talmon, 'Aging in Israel: A Planned Society,' *American Journal of Sociology*, Vol. LXVII, No. 4, November 1961, pp. 284–95.

Clark Tibbitts (ed.), *Handbook of Social Gerontology* (University of Chicago Press), 1960.

Clark Tibbitts and Wilma Donahue (editors), *Social and Psychological Aspects of Aging* (New York: Columbia University Press), 1962.

Peter Townsend, *The Family Life of Old People* (London, Routledge and Kegan Paul), 1957.

Peter Townsend, 'Social Surveys of Old Age in Great Britain,' *Bulletin of the World Health Organization*, 21, 1959, pp. 583–91.

Peter Townsend, *The Last Refuge* (London: Routledge and Kegan Paul), 1962.

Peter Townsend, 'The Timid and the Bold', *New Society*, 23 May 1963.

Peter Townsend, 'The Place of Older People in Different Societies,' *The Lancet*, 18 January 1964, pp. 159–61.

Peter Townsend and Dorothy Wedderburn, *The Aged in the Welfare State* (London: G. Bell), 1965.

R. J. Van Zonneveld, *The Health of the Aged* (Assen, Holland: Organization for Health Research), 1961.

Bibliography

Emily E. White, *The Over-60's Club and the Community* (Derbyshire Old People's Welfare Committee), 1964.

J. Williamson, I. M. Stoke *et al.*, 'Old People at Home: Their Unreported Needs,' *The Lancet*, 23 May 1964.

Peter Willmott and Michael Young, *Family and Class in a London Suburb* (London: Routledge and Kegan Paul), 1960.

L. A. Wilson, I. R. Lawson and W. Brass, 'Multiple Disorders in the Elderly,' *The Lancet*, 27 October 1962.

C. H. Wright and Llywelyn Robert, 'The Place of the Home Help Service in the Care of the Aged,' *The Lancet*, 1 February 1958.

M. Young and H. Geertz, 'Old Age in London and San Francisco,' *British Journal of Sociology*, Vol. 12, No. 2, June 1961, pp. 124–41.

Official Publications:

Central Health Services Council, Standing Medical Advisory Committee, *The Field of Work on the Family Doctor* (H.M.S.O.), 1963.

London County Council, Public Health Department, *Review of the Domestic Help Service* (Report of Departmental Working Party), 1957).

Ministry of Health, *Health and Welfare: The Development of Community Care:* Plans for the Health and Welfare Services of the Local Authorities in England and Wales (H.M.S.O.), 1963.

Ministry of Health, *The Health and Welfare Services* (H.M.S.O.), 1964.

Ministry of Housing and Local Government, *Flatlets for Old People* (H.M.S.O.), 1958.

Ministry of Housing, *More Flatlets for Old People* (H.M.S.O.), 1960.

Ministry of Housing, *Some Aspects of Designing for Old People* (H.M.S.O.), 1962.

Ministry of Housing, *Grouped Flatlets for Old People* (H.M.S.O.), 1962.

Appendix 1

Method

The author joined the project in November 1962, and started by interviewing thirty old people in Ilford. After this it was decided to develop a screening interview with a second follow-up interview for those who were isolated, lonely, single, recently widowed or housebound; forty-eight screening interviews and fourteen follow-up ones were completed in Walthamstow. On the basis of this experience and a reading of the existing literature, a planning paper of about 20,000 words was written. Then the screening and follow-up questionnaires were revised. Most of the short screening questionnaire is used to give the old person a social isolation score. The longer follow-up questionnaire includes further questions on social relationships and on retirement, health, leisure, housing and finances. Some of these questions were adopted direct from the national survey. But there are also in the follow-up questionnaire sections aimed at the lonely, single, recently widowed and housebound; these tend to be of a more open kind.

The next problem was to select areas in which to conduct the survey. Three urban areas were chosen on the basis of the following statistical information – the intention being to get a group which together would be fairly representative of urban England:

THREE OUT OF A TOTAL OF 157 BRITISH TOWNS'[1]

	Oldham		Northampton		Harrow	
	Value	Rank	Value	Rank	Value	Rank
Population						
Population (1,000)	121	42	104	63	219	18
% of pop. aged 65 and over	11·1	64	12·2	34	8·8	132
Females per 1,000 males	1,124	60	1,121	63	1,126	56
% Population change 1931–51	−13·6	149	8·2	88	127·1	11
% Population change 1951–58	−2·4	110	−3·6	127	−2·4	110
Households and Housing						
% one-person h/holds	12·4	35	10·3	65	6·6	138

	Oldham Value	Rank	Northampton Value	Rank	Harrow Value	Rank
Persons per room	0·76	57	0·68	128	0·7	106
% overcrowded h/holds	6·3	70	4·5	121	4·9	112
% h/holds in shared dwellings	3·8	148	11·9	83	15·7	63
% h/holds with W.C.	86	147	97	72	98	39
Total new housing rate 1945–58	31	126	48	80	22	145

	Oldham Value	Rank	Northampton Value	Rank	Harrow Value	Rank
Economic Character						
Occupied as % of population	69·1	1	62·7	54	61·4	68
% if women in labour force	40·3	4	35·2	39	32·7	75
% in manufacture	60·6	19	51·5	53	31·4	110
% in all service industries	28·3	124	33·8	100	52·5	37
Commuting ratio	51	79	26	135	78	48
Social Class						
% in social classes I and II	12·0	130	15·8	78	29·5	20
% in social class IV and V	32·4	35	20·1	124	14·5	150
Voting						
1951 % voting left	49·1	86	53·7	54	39·6	126
1955 % voting left	48·8	79	52·7	53	38·3	120
Health						
Mortality rate 1957 lung cancer	120	68	98	116	126	53
Mortality rate 1957 bronchitis	221	3	92	99	72	134

	Oldham Value	Rank	Northampton Value	Rank	Harrow (Middlesex) Value	Rank
Services for elderly[2]						
No. of *Home Helps* per 1,000 population aged 65 and over	8·0	10	2·7	112	3·6	80
No. of *Home Helps* per 1,000 pop. aged 65 + planned for 1972	16·6	1	2·9		3·5	
Health Visitors per 1,000 population	0·15		0·03		0·11	
Social Workers per 1,000 population	0·16		0·02		0·06	

[1] C. A. Moser and Wolf Scott, *British Towns: A Statistical Survey of social and economic differences* (London: Oliver and Boyd), 1961.
[2] Peter Townsend, 'The Timid and the Bold', *New Society*, 23 May, 1963.

Appendix

South Norfolk was chosen in a more arbitrary fashion, and it undoubtedly differs markedly from many other rural areas – especially hill farming areas. It does, however, have a very strongly rural character and is well away from the conurbations of London or the North of England.

Once the areas had been chosen, the next move was to approach doctors. The co-operation of four general practitioners from each area was required. A list of about twenty doctors in the area was drawn at random from *The Medical Directory*. The addresses of their surgeries were plotted on a map. These addresses were then split into four groups of equal number by drawing a North–South and an East–West line on the map; from each quadrant one doctor was chosen at random (to avoid the possibility of all four doctors being bunched up in one geographical section of the area). Letters were then written to the chosen doctors explaining the purpose of the study and asking for their co-operation. Some doctors were no longer in general practice, had retired, or were dead. Of those who were in general practice four refused to co-operate; thus twenty functioning G.P.s were approached before sixteen agreed to co-operate.

The writer visited each doctor, usually after his morning surgery, and explained the study further. Then with the doctor's permission names of people born sixty-five years ago or earlier were extracted from the surgery records; in a single practice every *fifth* name was taken, in a double practice every *tenth* name and so on. Altogether the names extracted came from the records of twenty-seven doctors. There is, of course, a good deal of difference between the patients of different doctors. For instance, one doctor was a single woman in practice on her own (a second woman was in partnership with her husband); this doctor had a low proportion of old men, and a high proportion of elderly spinsters as patients.

Three of the four doctors who refused to co-operate were in Harrow, which may have been because the Harrow doctors were approached in February – likely to be a busy month for G.P.s. But apart from the possible exception of Harrow, this method of sampling probably provides a reasonably good cross-section of those $99 \cdot 8$[3] per cent of old people in domestic households who are registered with doctors.

[3] Figure from national survey for which the sample was drawn from electoral registers.

Appendix

The screening interviews in the four-area survey (after the pilot stage) were all conducted by specially recruited interviewers. These were people living in or near the areas concerned. Advertisements for interviewers produced a big response – in one area alone there were forty-six applicants for the job. In the four areas a total of six interviewers were used. Nine out of ten screening interviews were conducted by women aged between thirty and fifty. Two-thirds of the interviews were conducted by married women. Six out of ten interviews were conducted by people with social science degrees or diplomas; the remainder were done by people with extensive interviewing experience. Half of all the screening interviews were carried out by people who had both experience of interviewing in a survey on old people and who also possessed social science qualifications.

The screening interviewers had no direct supervision; they worked from a list of the old people's names, addresses and age. However, the interviewers were told that some of the old people would subsequently be re-visited by the author. The screening interviewers were encouraged to be careful and thorough; they were not paid by the interview and no standard was laid down of what constituted a normal day's work. In the event the median time taken to complete the short three-page screening interview was 25 minutes; three quarters of the total were between 20 and 30 minutes.

Of the 538 old people with whom screening interviews were completed, 195 were re-interviewed because they came into one or more of the categories of socially isolated, often lonely, single, widowed within the last five years, or housebound for six months or longer. All of these 195 follow-up interviews were conducted by the author; this interview, in the great majority of cases, was between a week and a month after the screening interview. The median duration of follow-up interviews was 1 hour 45 minutes. 73 per cent were between 1 hour 15 minutes and 2 hours 15 minutes. 2 per cent were under 1 hour and 11 per cent lasted 2 hours 30 minutes or longer. After completing the follow-up interview the author dictated a commentary (for subsequent typing) into a tape recorder; this was almost always later on the day of the interview. Ten of the commentaries in somewhat abbreviated form are included in the text of this book. Most of the commentary is in indirect speech.

Appendix

However from the outset it was decided to select key sentences for verbatim recording. In the commentaries these sentences appear in direct quotation.

The follow-up interviewing began in Northampton in July 1963, continued in Norfolk and Harrow and ended in Oldham in June 1964. Thus although the findings for individual areas may be biased by the weather and time of year, this should not be a factor in the four-area survey as a whole.

A total of 696 names were drawn from the doctors' lists in the four areas. Some of these names were of people not in fact available for the following reasons:

Dead	11
Under 65	8
Removed from address	31
Not known at address	27
In hospital, Home or other institution	16
	93

In a number of cases the old person had left the address, or died, some years earlier, which is, of course, an indication that general practitioners' records are often somewhat out of date.

This left 603 old people, 10·8 per cent of whom were not interviewed:

Screening interview failures

Too ill	0·5
Too deaf	0·8
Non-contact	7·0
Refusal	2·5
	10·8
Total	100
Number	603

Only 2·5 per cent were actual refusals by the old people. Some of the non-contacts probably were in effect refusals. If a relative said the old person did not want to be interviewed this was categorized as 'non-contact'. Some old people refuse to answer the door to anyone. But probably some of the 7 per cent of non-contacts in fact were not old people available for interview. The screening interviewers made a minimum of three calls, and sometimes four or five.

At the follow-up stage the failure rate was 10·1 per cent.

Follow-up interview failures

Too ill	1·4
Too deaf	0·5
Non-contact	2·8
Hospital	1·4
Refusal	4·1
	10·1
Total	100
Number	217

This is slightly inflated by the inclusion of old people in hospital, whom there was no possibility of interviewing at home. For those who were 'too ill' or 'too deaf' there had in each case been a proxy interview at the screening stage. Proxies were accepted at this stage for old people who were too ill or deaf to answer; it was assumed that any household member would be able to give fairly accurately the information required for the usually frail old person. However, at the follow-up stage no proxies were accepted, since the attitude questions could hardly be answered in this way.

The category of 'refusal' at the re-interview stage includes some old people who were willing to talk for a few minutes but not for longer – sometimes on the assumption that the second interview would be as short or shorter than the screening interview.

The decision not to accept proxies at the second stage affected the housebound group especially. Half of the follow-up failures (11 out of 22) were housebound old people. Other groups – the single, recently widowed, the lonely and the socially isolated – do not, however, bulk especially large among failures at the follow-up interview.

Including the pilot stage of the survey, the author personally interviewed 273 old people.

Appendix

313

Appendix

Significant Correlations

Level of
Significance

Table 4.3	P. <	·01	Significant difference in loneliness between married and widowed.
Table 4.4	P. <	·01	Significant difference in loneliness by degree of incapacity.
Table 5.2	P. <	·05	Significant difference in high anomia between the non-manual and manual social classes.
	P. <	·05	Significant difference in high anomia between clerical workers (3 non-man) and skilled manual workers.
Table 5.3	P. <	·05	Significant difference in high anomia between those who went to a club last month and those who did not, and between those who went to a church last month and those who did not. (Difference not significant at ·05 level between those who saw neighbours and friends last week and those who did not or between isolated and non-isolated or between lonely and never lonely.)
Table 5.4	P. <	·05	Significant difference among widowed women in high anomia between recent and long-term widows.
Table 7.1	P. <	·05	Significant difference among widows in age by duration of widowhood.
Table 8.2	P. <	·01	Significant difference in proportion sharing household with children between housebound old women and all old women.
Table 11.2	P. <	·01	Significant difference in proportion of old men and old women having been to old people's club in previous week.
	P. <	·05	Significant difference in isolation between old men and old women who went to any kind of club last month.

314

Appendix 2. Questionnaires

A. *SCREENING QUESTIONNAIRE*

1. Name: Dur wid ....

2. Address: H bound.................

3. Date of birth: Lon ....

4. Household composition: Soc i ....

Relationship to subject (ring HoH)	Occupation	Sex		Age	Marital status				No. of years widowed
		M	F		mrd	sng	dve	wid	
A Subject									
B									
C									
D									
E									
F									
G									

5. *Ask men and single women subjects:* In what occupation and industry have you been most of your life?

   Ask married or widowed women subjects: What was your husband's occupation and industry most of his life?
   Occupation:
   Industry:

6. Have you been housebound during the last month?   Yes   1
                                                       No   2

   If Yes: (a) for how long have you been housebound? ....

   (b) for how long do you expect to remain housebound?......

7. How many of the last 7 days did you go out of the house (for shopping, walk, visit to friend or club etc)? ....

Appendix

8. Do you go out to paid employment?   Yes   1
                                                   No   2

If Yes: (a) how many hours per week?   ....hrs p/wk
            (b) in this work, do you normally
                   talk to other people?   Never   0

Seldom   1

Sometimes   2

Fairly often   3 *one*

Often   4 *code*

9. Have you any children alive?   Continually   5 *only*

	Eld-est	2nd	3rd	4th	5th	6th	7th	8th	9th	10th
Son or daughter										
How many times did you see him/ her last wk (or mnth)?										
Ditto his/her spouse										

10. Have you any brothers or sisters alive:

	Eld-est	2nd	3rd	4th	5th	6th	7th	8th	9th	10th
Brother or sister										
How many times did you see him/ her last wk (or mnth)?										
Ditto his/her spouse										

316

Questionnaires

11. Have you seen any other relatives within the last week or month – such as nieces or nephews, grandchildren, cousins?

	Last week	*Last month*
....	.... times	.... times
....	....	....
....	....	....
....	....	....
....	....	....
....	....	....
....	....	....

12. Have you seen any neighbours – next door or down the street or lane – within the last week or month?

	Last week	*Last month*
....	.... times	times
....	....	....
....	....	....
....	....	....

13. How often have you seen friends (other than neighbours)?

	Last week	*Last month*
....	.... times	.... times
....	....	....
....	....	....
....	....	....

14. Have you seen any of these within the last week or month?

	Last week	*Last month*
Doctor	.... times	.... times
Home help	....	....
Meals on Wheels	....	....
Health visitor, Home nurse	....	....
Vicar, Minister	....	....
Voluntary Visitor	....	....

15. Do you eat your meals alone, or with other people? ....
During the last week, how many of these meals have you eaten with others?

Mid-day meals: .... eaten with other(s) present

Tea/evening meals: .... eaten with other(s) present

16. We've been talking mainly about the last week. Has the last week been unusual for you, because of illness, holidays, or some other reason?

317

Appendix

If unusual : Work   ....
Seeing children ....
Brothers & sisters ....
Other relatives ....
Friends, neighbours ....
Meals with others ....
Other (specify) ....

17. Are you often alone, seldom alone, or never alone?
     Often alone 1
     Seldom alone 2
     Never alone 3

18. Do you go to any sort of club or society?   **Yes** 1
                   No 2
  If yes : (a) What *type* of club? ....
     (b) How many times did you go
       last week (or month)? ....

19. Do you go to church or any other place or worship? **Yes** 1
                   No 2
  If yes : How many times did you go
   last week (or month)? ....

20. Apart from staying with children or relatives at their homes, have you
  been away on holiday or to a convalescent home in the last 12
  months?   **Yes** 1
                   No 2
  If yes : (a) How long for? Number of weeks ....
     (b) Did you go away with somebody you knew
       and if so, who was it?
            Went on own (no one known) 3
            Went with (specify) ....

21. With whom did you spend last Christmas Day?
  (Exclude anyone with whom less than one hour spent)

Alone	1	Other relatives	4	*Code all*
With spouse	2	Friends	5	*that*
With children	3	Others (specify)	6	*apply*
		....		

22. Would you say that you are lonely often, sometimes or never?
  One code only   Often lonely 1
  running prompt   Sometimes lonely 2
          Never lonely 3

Questionnaires

23. The following are some things that people sometimes say. Do you agree (definitely) or disagree?

(a) "There's little use writing to public officials because often they aren't really interested in the problems of the ordinary person." — Agree 1, Disagree 0

(b) "Nowadays a person has to live pretty much for him/herself and let tomorrow take care of itself." — Agree 1, Disagree 0

(c) "In spite of what some people say, the life of the ordinary person is getting worse, not better." — Agree 1, Disagree 0

(d) "It's hardly fair to bring children into the world with the way things look for the future." — Agree 1, Disagree 0

(e) "These days a person doesn't really know whom he can count on." — Agree 1, Disagree 0

Length of Int.   *Date:*   *Interviewer:*

B. FOLLOW-UP QUESTIONNAIRE

1) Name: *Date:*

2) Address: *Duration:*

3) Household composition:

Relationship to subject	Occupation	Sex M	Sex F	Age	Marital status mrd	sng	dvc	wid	No. of years widowed
A Subject									
B									
C									
D									
E									
F									
G									

4) Does anyone else live in the house, but not household?

5) How many miles away from here were you born? ......miles
   (b) How long have you lived in this district? ......years
   (c) How long have you lived in this house/flat? ......years

6) Did you do any paid work last week? Yes ....
   No ....
   If Yes, what?

TO ALL THOSE WHO HAVE GIVEN UP WORK COMPLETELY

7) *Occupation* immediately before retiring ....

8) *Industry* immediately before retiring ....

319

Appendix

9) How many years ago did you last do any paid work? ......years
During the year before you stopped working for the last
time, how many weeks did you work? ....weeks
How many hours a week? ....hours.

10) Is there anything in particular you miss now you have stopped
working?

    Do you miss any of these things? :–

the feeling of being useful	....
Enjoying the job itself	....

PROMPT

Money	....
Company	....
Miss nothing	....

11) Do you feel able to do some sort of paid work now?

    Yes   ......
    No   ......
    D.K.   ......

If *Yes*, is there any kind of work you would like to do?

12) Have you been to an employment exchange recently?

13) Why did you retire from work?

14) Did stopping work make much difference to your life?

15) Do you still see anyone you used to work with?

16) Do you still see as much of your friends and family as when you were
working?

Questionnaires

17) Here are some things that quite a few people over 65 have difficulty in doing without help.

IF DIFFICULTY

Do you or would you have difficulty in:	No difficulty	Difficulty	Can you do it on your own, even with diff? Yes No	Do you usually have someone to help you with it? (Who?)
(1) Going out of doors on own				
(2) Going up and down stairs on your own				
(3) Getting about house on your own				
(4) Getting in and out of bed				
(5) Washing or bathing yourself				
(6) Dressing yourself and putting on your shoes				
(7) Cutting own toenails				

Appendix

18) Here are some activities which you may or may not do for yourself, but could you do without difficulty:

(1) Do light house-work like washing up, dusting, tidying				
(2) Do heavy cleaning, like washing floors, cleaning windows				
(3) Make a cup of tea				
(4) Prepare a hot meal				
(5) Collecting pension				
(6) Shopping				
(7) Heavy washing				
(8) Shaving/haircut				

TO ALL HOUSEBOUND

19) How long is it since you've been outside the house (apart from in a car or ambulance)?

...............years   ....weeks

20) Are you ever taken out in a car? How often in the last year?

.... times.

21) What prevents you from getting out?

Questionnaires

22) Can you do the following for yourself, even with difficulty?

	Yes	No	If *No*, who helps you?
(1) Stand up			
(2) Walk without aid			
(3) Comb own hair			
(4) Feed self			
(5) Read			
(6) Attend to own toilet			

23) Do you manage to get out of the house/flat into a garden?
24) What is the worst thing about being unable to get out?
25) Are there any compensations in being unable to get out?
26) Do you think enough is done for people who can't get out in this area?
27) Do you think the Government does enough for elderly people who can't get out?

TO ALL

28) How often do you see your doctor? ....

In the last year	No. of times	Is this as often as you would like? Yes No Comments
(1) Been visited by your doctor		
(2) Visited your doctor's surgery		
(3) Been to hospital as an out-patient		
(4) Been visited by health visitor or dist. nurse		
(5) Been treated by a chiropodist		

323

Appendix

29) Have you been a hospital in-patient during the last 5 years?
If *Yes*, how long for in the 5 years? .... weeks
What was wrong with you? ....

30) (a) How many times have you been in bed at home during the last 5 years? ....
(b) Roughly how long altogether in 5 years? ....
(c) What was wrong with you? ....
(d) If you were ill in bed at home during the last year, did your doctor visit you the last time you were in bed?

Yes ....
No ....   Not ill ....

If ill during last year

(e)	(f)	(g)
Who got most of your meals?	Who did most of your shopping?	Who did most of the housework while you were in bed?

(Specify)

31) Do you get any meals brought by the 'Meals on Wheels' service?

Yes ....
No ....

(a) If *Yes*, how many meals do you get a week? .... a week.
If *No*, would you like to have them? Yes ....
             No ....
(b) Do you think the Meals on Wheels are good to eat?

32) What did you have to eat for these meals yesterday?

Breakfast	....
Mid-day meal	....
Tea	....
Supper	....

33) How many hot meals have you had during the last week? ....
What did you have at the main meal yesterday?

	Meat	....
	Eggs	....
	Cheese	....
PROMPT	Fish	....
	Green veg.	....
	Fruit	....
	Milk	....
	Puddings	....
	Custards	....
	Potatoes	....
	Soup	....
	Bread/butter	....
	Other	....

Questionnaires

34) Did anybody give you assistance *last week* in either buying food for, or cooking, meals? If so, who?

	How many times in the last week?	Who gave help?
Buying food	....	....
Cooking	....	....

35) How many meals did you eat alone last week and how many did you eat in the company of other people or another person?

Number of meals eaten alone ....
Number eaten in company ....

36) Do you have anyone coming in to help with the housework? (Who does it as a job.)

Yes ....
No ....

If *Yes*, how many times does she come? .... times a week.

Is she from the Council?

If *No*, do you need to have someone to come in and help with the housework?

Yes ....
No .... How many hours?.........hours.
D.K. ....

37) Do you think home helps are good at housework?

38) What sort of people are the home helps?

TO THOSE WHO HAVE HOME HELPS

40) How many different home helps have you had in the last 2 years?

41) What does your home help do at present?

Heavy cleaning ....
Light cleaning ....
Shopping ....
Washing clothes ....
Washing subject ....
Other ....

42) About your present home help.
(a) How old is she? ....
(b) Does she understand an old person's needs? ....
(c) Does she do the work cheerfully? ....

43) How long ago was it that the home help organizer last called? What did she say?

Appendix

44) Do you wear glasses?
        Yes   ....
        No   ....
        Totally blind   ....
        Reg. blind   ....
        Reg. partially
           sighted   ....

45) Do you have any difficulty in seeing, even with glasses?
        No difficulty   ....
        A little diffy.   ....
        Lot of diffy.   ....
        Totally blind   ....

46) Do you have a hearing aid?
        Yes   ....
        No   ....
  If *Yes*, do you use it regularly?
        Yes   ....
        No   ....

47) Do you have difficulty in hearing ordinary conversation, even with a hearing aid?
        No difficulty   ....
        A little difficulty (admitted)   ....
        A lot of difficulty (admitted)   ....
        Difficulty observed (unadmitted)   ....

48) Does this town (area) do enough in the way of making facilities available for older people – entertainment, transport and other services?
        Enough   ....
        Too much   ....
        Too little   ....

  (b) Does the Government do enough for young families in the way of children's allowances and services for children?
        Enough   ....
        Too much   ....
        Too little   ....

  (c) Does the Government do enough in the way of pensions for old people and helping them financially?
        Enough   ....
        Too much   ....
        Too little   ....

Questionnaires

49)

	Dead? Age at death	Sex of child	Marital status	How long hrs/mins away	Frequency seen usual	Grandchildren	Seen	
Eldest								
2nd								
3rd								
4th								
5th								
6th								
7th								
8th								
9th								
10th								

50) Have any of your children come to stay with you (apart from those in h/h) during the last 12 months, or have you stayed with them?

Child	Visit	Duration
....	....	....
....	....	....
....	....	....
....	....	....

51) Do any of your children help you with money, shopping, cooking, or anything else?

52) Do you help any of your children or grandchildren with housework, looking after the children, presents, etc.?

Appendix

TO ALL WITH SIBLINGS

53)

(Ring sub- ject)	Dead? Age at death	Brother, sister?	Marital status	How long hrs/mins away?	Frequy. usually seen	Their children	Seen
Eldest							
2nd							
3rd							
4th							
5th							
6th							
7th							
8th							
9th							
10th							

TO ALL

54) Have you seen any other relatives, such as cousins, during the last month?

	Yesterday	Within 7 days	Within month
....	....	....	....
....	....	....	....
....	....	....	....
....	....	....	....

55) During the last week or month have you talked to (more than just a few words) any people who live in the house but not the same dwelling as yourself, or next door, or in this street?

(Specify proximity)	Yesterday	Within 7 days	Within month
....	....	....	....
....	....	....	....
....	....	....	....
....	....	....	....

Questionnaires

56) Have you exchanged more than a few words with any friends during the last week or month? Please say how you came to know them – from school, through work, through relatives or other friends, at a club or church, or through previously being neighbours.

(Specify how met)	*Yesterday*	*Within 7 days*	*Within month*
....	....	....	....
....	....	....	....
....	....	....	....
....	....	....	....

57) Do you find that time passes slowly for you?

Often ....

Sometimes ....

Never ....

If *Often* or *Sometimes*, when does it pass slowly?

58) (a) What is the main thing in life out of which you get pleasure?
    (b) What activity occupies most of your time? ....
    (c) What activities did you engage in last week?

No. of days last week

Paid work	....	
Shopping	....	
Seeing relatives	....	
Watching television	....	
PROMPT Radio	....	
Cooking	....	
Cleaning	....	
Washing	....	
Gardening	....	
Read newspaper	....	Which paper(s)......
Read magazines	....	
Read books	....	
Sew, knit	....	
Smoke	....	
Walk in park, etc.	....	
Attending club	....	
Other (specify)	....	

59) Some people belong to clubs or associations most of their life. Have you done so for a long period?

Yes ....

No ....

If *Yes*,

Type of Club, Association	*Years belonged*	*Last went*
....	....	....
....	....	....
....	....	....
....	....	....

What appeals to you in this type of organisation?

Appendix

60) Do you belong to an Old People's Club?

Yes ....

No ....

Is having clubs especially for old people a good idea?

61) Have you been to an old people's club in the last month?

Yes ....

No ....

If *No*,   (a) Why not? ....

          (b) Would you ever go to such a club regularly?

If *Yes*, (went to an O.P. club in last month)

          (c) What about the club appeals to you?

          (d) What did you do last time you went to the club?

                    Talk   ....

                    Dominoes, etc.   ....

PROMPT   Cards   ....

                    Entertainment   ....

                    Drink tea   ....

                    Eat meal   ....

          (e) How many people were there at the last club session?

          (f) Were they mainly men or women?

          (g) Do you have a special friend at the club?

          (h) Do you learn anything new at the club?

          (i) How did you first start to go to this club?

62) Do you go to church or other place of worship?

Yes ....

No ....

If *Yes*, what sort? ....

          (b) When were you last there? ....

          (c) Is there any reason why you don't go more often?......

63) Have you been away on a holiday in the last 12 months?

          (a) For how long?   .... weeks

          (b) How far away?   .... miles

          (c) With whom?

          (d) Where did you stay (hotel, child's home, etc.)?

          (e) What time of the year?

64) With whom did you spend last Christmas Day?

65) Have you written or received any letters in the last month?

Correspondent	Number of letters	
	Received	Written
....	....	....
....	....	....
....	....	....
....	....	....

Questionnaires

66) (a) Can you use a telephone?
   (b) Do you have a telephone in the house?
      With whom have you talked on the phone in the last month?

Person phoned	Number of calls	
	Received	Called
....	....	....
....	....	....
....	....	....
....	....	....
....	....	....

67) (a) Did you go out of the house yesterday? ....
   (b) How many times did you go out of the home yesterday?
      .... times   How long altogether?

68) Do you (or your husband) own this house/flat, pay rent, or is it free?
   If *rented*, (a) How much do you pay in rent? .... a week
              (b) If rates paid separately, how
                  much a year?   £...............

69) How many rooms do you have (excluding bathroom and kitchen,
   unless you use kitchen as the main living room)?
                  Number of bedrooms   ....
                  Total number of rooms   ....

70) Do you have the following domestic facilities?
                  Sole use of kitchen   ....
                  Use of fixed bath   ....
   PROMPT   Piped water supply in
                  the dwelling   ....

71) Do you have a W.C. for the sole use of this household, do you share
   a W.C., or is there no W.C.?
                  ....
   If has W.C.
                  (a) Do you have to go outside the house to get to it?
                  Yes   ....
                  No   ....
                  (b) In relation to the room in which you spend most of the
                      day, is it:
                  On same level   ....
   PROMPT   Upstairs   ....
                  Downstairs   ....

72) Do you have any of the following?
                  Radio   ....
                  Television   ....
   PROMPT   Washing machine   ....
                  Refrigerator   ....
                  Car   ....

331

73) Is there anything about this dwelling which you dislike or find inconvenient?

Yes ....

No ....

If *Yes*, what sort of thing? ....

74) Is your present home too large?

Yes ....

No ....

75) Would you like to move from your present home?

Yes ....

No ....

If *Yes*, (a) Supposing it was available in the place you wanted, what kind of housing would you like?

(b) Under the conditions that actually exist, where would you like to move to?

76) Would you like to move into a small block of new flats specially built by the local Council for older people?

Yes ....

No ....

(b) Is there anything about such accommodation which worries you?

	Stairs/lift	....
	Small size	....
PROMPT	High rent	....
	Distant location	....
	Other	....

77) What is your present home like in cold winter weather?

(b) In mid-winter, for how many hours a day do you have a fire/heater on in the room you are in?

.... hours a day

(c) Is there any heating in your bedroom?

Yes ....

No ....

TO ALL WIDOWED WITHIN THE LAST FIVE YEARS

78) How was it that your husband/wife died?

79) Who came the funeral?
Relatives :
Others :

80) Have you moved house since the death?

81) Has anyone come to live here temporarily or permanently?

82) Have you been separated from any of your children since the death?

83) Do you see anything of his/her family?

84) Do you go out more or less since he/she died?

85) Have you kept contact with any of his/her friends?

86) Has your attitude to religion altered at all?

Questionnaires

87) Do you sleep less well or better?
88) Has your health been less good or better?
89) Has your interest in people altered?
90) Did you do as much for him/her as you would have liked?
91) Do you have any especially vivid memories of him/her?
92) Can one get over grief?
93) Do you think there is anything that can be done for widowed older people which is not being done at present?
94) Do you think that widowhood is different for older people from what it is like for younger people?

TO ALL SINGLE

95) Does being single affect what happens to you when you are ill?
96) Does being single affect the ordinary social life of an older person?
97) Are there any compensations for not being married, such as that you're more independent?
98) Would you have liked to have children, or do you think you are better off without them?
99) Are you pleased or sorry you never married?
100) How was it that you did not marry?
101) Was there somebody you were engaged to or nearly married?
102) Does not being married have anything to do with your parents or with being the eldest or youngest child?
103) Is a single person treated differently from a married person when in mixed company?

TO ALL LONELY OFTEN OR SOMETIMES

104) Do you feel more lonely now than when you were younger?
105) At what times do you feel (a) Most lonely ....
     (b) Least lonely ....
106) Is the winter or summer the worse for loneliness?
107) Do you feel lonely for someone :–
     (a) Who is no longer alive?
     (b) Who is still alive?
     (c) For nobody in particular?
108) Does going out to work affect loneliness?
109) What is the main cause of any loneliness you feel?
110) Is there anything you can do to make yourself less lonely?
111) Do you think people become more lonely as they get older or not?
112) Does going to a club make any difference to loneliness?
113) Are you more lonely when by yourself or when with other people?

333

Appendix

114) Some people say that National Assistance is charity; others say everyone has a right to it. What do you think?

115) Have you received any National Assistance in the last 12 months?
> Yes ....
> No ....

If *Yes*   (a) How much N.A. do you get per week?
         (b) Is that what you've had all the last 52 weeks?
         (c) Have you received any special payment to cover items such as clothing, bedding, etc.?
         (d) When did you last have a visit from a N.A. officer?
         (e) What happened at that meeting?

116) Do you receive any of the following?
         (a) Contributory Retirement Pension.
         (b) Employer's Pension.
         (c) Dividends.
         (d) Rent.

117) Since you have been 65 have you used up any of your savings?

118) What is your annual income?

119) Do you have any special difficulty with any of the following? :–
> Food   ....
> Clothing   ....
> Rates   ....
> Fuel   ....

SUPPLEMENTARY QUESTIONS

1) How old were you when your parents died?
> Age at father's death   .... years
> ,, ,, mother's ,, ... years

2) Did you look after them in their later years?

3) What kind of life have you had in general?

4) What was the happiest time in your life?

5) What was the unhappiest time?

6) How long do you think people should expect to live?
> And you? What would you like? ....

7) Is there anything you need very badly?

8) Do you think there is anything more that can be done **for** older people?

Appendix 3

Scoring Social Isolation

As explained in Chapter 3 the system of scoring social isolation is a modification of that used by Peter Townsend in *The Family Life of Old People*. The modified system was laid down in the planning paper before the four-area survey was begun. Townsend's unit of 'social contact' was used. The system was intended to emphasize daily or near daily contact – in particular with the primary groups of close kin and at work (for those still engaged in paid work). However, it is still possible to score a large number of contacts with neighbours or friends, or in clubs.

In the four-area study the scoring system was devised to produce a somewhat bigger group of socially isolated than the 10 per cent Townsend found in Bethnal Green. Under the new system about 17 per cent of Townsend's Bethnal Greeners aged 65+ would be isolated – against 15 per cent for Northampton and 21 per cent for the four areas as a whole.[1]

In the revised system greater flexibility is introduced. Contact with household members and contact at work both remain important, but whereas on the Townsend system the old person scored 14 contacts for each individual with whom he shared the household and 20 contacts for full-time work, on the revised system a household member can produce a score varying between 0 and 21, and full-time work from 10 to 20 (or more if overtime is worked).

The old person scores 7 contacts if he lives with his spouse. For any other household member, he scores one contact for each of the last seven days on which he had a social contact with this person.

---

[1] The cases quoted by Townsend (*Family Life of Old People*, pp. 167–9) would all fall from 54 to about 47, 124 to 93, 69 to 61 and 18 to 10 respectively. Townsend's 10 per cent of socially isolated would rise to about 16 per cent. But Townsend included women aged 60–64; if those are excluded, the socially isolated would probably rise from 16 per cent to 17 per cent.

335

Appendix

To emphasize further prolonged social exposure to some household members a new score is introduced for *meals*. For each midday or evening meal eaten in company during the last week the old person scores a contact, with a maximum meals score of 14. A married old person who eats all meals with his spouse thus scores $7 + 14 = 21$. An old person who lives in the same household, but has little contact with his spouse, scores less. It also enables an old person who spends all her time with her daughter, but returns home to sleep in the house where she 'lives alone' to score a maximum (if she sees the daughter every day and eats all main meals with her) of $7 + 14 = 21$. Meals can of course be eaten in silence, but this meals score is included as a convenient indicator of social exposure.

Another effect of the meals score is to emphasize prolonged exposure to one person, as opposed to less frequent exposure to a large number of people. For instance an old person who has a meal with five people will score only one extra contact – in addition to the 5 for social contacts with each of the five individuals.

Children in the new system only score if they are aged six or over. This is not to deny that old people may enjoy seeing small children, or grandchildren – the intention is to reduce the inflation effect caused, for instance, by a daughter who briefly visits her elderly mother accompanied by her several small children. If two of the children are under and two are over six years, on the Townsend system an old person would score 4 contacts, but on the revised system only 2 contacts.

Work is also treated in a somewhat different manner in the revised system. Old men working as nightwatchmen or old women cleaning an office or shop may work in complete isolation. On the revised system such work produced only half the number of social contacts compared with work in which the old person 'continually' talks to other people.

The *time-span* of the revised system is slightly different; only weekly or monthly contacts are counted. Townsend's system of including less frequent contacts is not adopted.

Club visits and church-going continue to score two contacts per visit during the last week. Cinema visits, however, are excluded on the ground that no social contact is automatically involved.

336

Scoring Social Isolation

The following questions from the screening questionnaire provide the social contact score:

Q.4   If the subject shares the household currently with his spouse he scores 7 contacts. (Other household members are scored in the appropriate question, e.g. child, sibling, friend, etc.)

Q. 8   An old person working forty hours scores a minimum of 10 contacts; if he talks to other people at work 'seldom' he scores 12, if 'sometimes' 14, if 'fairly often' 16, if 'often' 18, and if 'continually' 20. A person who worked twenty hours last week scores half this – from 5 to 10, according to how often he talked to people. A person who worked ten hours scores from $2\frac{1}{2}$ to 5, and so on.

Q. 9   If the child was seen once last week this scores 1 social contact. The maximum is 7 for each child and 14 for each child plus child-in-law. The minimum is $\frac{1}{4}$ contact for a child (or child-in-law) seen once last month.

Q. 10   Siblings are scored similarly to children.

Q. 11–13 So are other relatives, neighbours and friends.

Q. 14   Contacts here are always counted, even if they are very brief. Again the maximum is 7, e.g. for a home help who comes every day. The minimum is $\frac{1}{4}$, e.g. for a minister who called once in the last month.

Q. 15   The maximum for each meal is 7, for both meals 14. Eating a meal 'with' another person is defined as another person being in the same room at the time, even if that other person is not eating.

Q. 18–19 One visit to a club or to religious worship last week scores two contacts. Minimum score is $\frac{1}{2}$ contact for one visit in last month; three club meetings last week scores 6 contacts.

These are the only questions for which contacts are scored.

INDEX

339

Index

Index

341

Index

Ministry of Health, Community Care 'Plan', 270, 277, 288, 290
Ministry of Housing, 278, 279
Ministry of Pensions, 293–4
Mizruchi, Ephraim, 101, 107
Mobility, physical, 24, 29–30, 36, 41, 88, 113, 119, 124–5, 156–66, 172, 176, 278
Mobility, Residential, 78–80, 115–16, 144–6, 294
Money, 12, 26–27, 28, 34, 169, 170, 198, 199–206, 269
Mortality rates, 153, 158
Moustakas, Clark, 19

National Assistance, 28, 34, 44, 57, 116, 117, 123, 129, 169, 175, 180, 182, 186, 194, 199–206, 260, 270, 287, 292
Negroes, 243
Neighbours, 22, 26, 32, 36, 37, 43, 65, 78, 80–85, 101–2, 115, 121, 127, 128, 149, 157, 162, 163, 164, 165, 166, 173, 177, 178, 179, 183, 185, 193, 203, 221, 225, 232, 237
Nephews, nieces, 32, 43, 114, 121, 128, 164, 165, 178, 179, 193
Newspapers, 26, 32, 38, 43, 114, 121, 128–9, 173, 178, 185, 190, 194, 195, 196, 197, 298
Non-literate societies, 249–52, 256, 260, 269
Norfolk, 54
Norfolk, South, 5, 8, 80, 83–84, 93, 94, 97, 106–7, 134, 135, 137, 152, 155, 162, 165, 191, 194, 196, 197, 200, 203, 225, 270–1
Northampton, 5, 7, 80, 93, 106–7, 131, 135, 137, 139, 140, 147, 148, 149, 150, 151, 152, 192, 202, 205, 213, 215, 220, 224, 270–1, 307–8
Nottingham, 54
Nurses,
— Home Nurses, 61, 162, 213, 273, 276–7, 278

Old age, definition of, 2, 229–30, 249
Old People's Welfare Committees, 286, 289, 291–2
Oldham, 5, 7–8, 62, 80, 94, 95, 96, 106–7, 131, 134, 135, 136, 137, 139, 140, 148, 149, 150, 151, 164, 191, 192, 196, 202, 211, 213, 215, 222, 270–271, 294, 307–8
Orpington, 53–54
Outings, Club, 220, 222, 286

'Over-housed' old people, 280, 281
Owner-occupiers, 281

Parents of old people, 28, 34, 39, 45, 96, 116, 117, 123, 129, 132–3, 134–5, 138–9, 140, 175, 180, 186–7
— parents-in-law, of old people, 96
Parsons, Talcott, 18, 237, 247, 252, 255, 257–61
Peasant society, 252–5, 256, 269
Pensions, occupational, 28, 101, 175, 180, 182, 199–200, 201, 256
— state, 2, 28, 34, 39, 57, 62, 116–17, 123, 138, 180, 186, 199–200, 205, 260, 269–70
— state, attitudes to, 25, 37, 43, 114, 120, 127, 172, 175, 178, 180, 183
— state, effects of, 257, 269
Personality, 13, 133, 171, 229–46, 248, 261
Pets, dogs, cats, birds, 95, 115, 140, 170, 179, 181, 185, 194
Political attitudes, 27, 38, 174, 178
Poor Law relief, 62, 269
Population, proportion of old people in, 2, 59, 262
Poverty, 3, 204–6, 236
Power of the old, 250, 253–5
Public Transport, use of, 8, 37, 178
Pubs, 97, 171, 179, 184, 185, 189, 192

Radio, 34, 38, 58, 94, 115, 121, 129, 164, 173, 178, 189, 190, 194, 196, 197, 297–8
Referrals for social services, 283, 288–9, 290, 292
Refusals, for interviews, 243, 245
Reichard, Suzanne, 235–7, 238, 242–3, 244
Religious Ministers, 208, 217, 288–9
— religious services, 101–2, 107, 125, 136, 179, 189, 217, 286
Re-marriage, 28, 154
Reminiscing, 245
Rent (and rates), 27, 32, 38–39, 115, 122, 179, 180, 186, 200–1, 204–6, 212
— rent control, 60, 114–15
Research on old people, 2, 245–6, 261
— research method, 4–6, 8–9, 64–67, 241–3, 245–6, 307–12
— research, report writing, 9–10
— research required, 245–6, 296, 298–300

342

Index

Retirement, retired, 2, 3, 18, 19, 22, 23, 35, 36, 40, 97, 99–101, 105, 106, 107, 108, 111, 113–17, 118, 122, 124, 139, 149, 171–6, 181–7, 201, 231–2, 235–41, 244, 248, 256, 261, 296–8
Riesman, David, 20
Rivers, W. H. R., 249
'Rocking chair' pattern, 234, 236, 238
Roles in old age, 232, 237, 238
— role loss, 232, 239
— 'role' as a sociological concept, 262
Rose, Arnold, 233
Rosenmayr, Leopold, 53, 262–3
Rowntree, Seebohm, 58–62
Royal College of Physicians, Edinburgh, 273, 277, 291, 292, 293, 298
Ruck, S. K., 280
Rural-urban differences, 80, 83–84, 106–7, 108

Salford, 55
Sampling, 5, 307–10
Savings, 34, 39, 180, 199–200, 201, 206
School, attended by old people, 23, 29, 119
'Self-hater' pattern, 234, 236, 237
Sex, 154–5
Sexes, social differences between, 47–48, 51, 66, 67–68, 72, 74, 82, 83, 86–88, 92, 101, 105, 108, 111, 130, 152–3, 156, 157–9, 197–8, 201, 218, 221, 232, 236–7, 249, 250–1, 278
Shanas, Ethel, 4
Sheldon, J. H., 2, 20
Shopping, 24, 29–30, 36, 41, 56, 61, 94, 113, 119, 126, 138, 160, 164, 165–6, 173, 177, 182, 185, 190–1, 198, 214
Siblings, 26, 37, 43, 56, 70–72, 114, 121, 130, 132, 138, 139, 144, 148, 165–6, 172, 178, 184, 205, 232, 241
Simmons, Leo, 249–52, 260
Single, 1, 9, 10, 11–12, 35–40, 49–50, 57, 62, 72, 78, 84, 88, 101, 103, 105, 108, 111, 112, 113–17, 130–41, 189, 214, 229, 254, 260, 278, 282
— single men, 84, 88, 111, 130, 138–9, 218
— single women, 35–40, 50, 88, 93, 94, 111, 113–17, 130, 142, 143, 164, 218, 254
Sister, 22, 29–34, 96, 97, 116, 117, 128, 140, 145, 172, 176, 178, 184, 221
Slack, Kathleen, 291–2

Sleep, 25, 38, 147–9
— sleeping on ground floor, 33, 126
Smoking, 44, 173, 179, 185, 186, 189, 198
Social class, 53, 55, 78, 80, 83, 84, 92, 99–100, 105, 106, 107, 108, 158, 209, 214, 220, 243, 248–9, 261
Social contact score, 10, 19, 29, 35, 64–85, 113, 118, 124, 138–9, 163–5, 335–7
— social contact, high, 29–34, 64–85, 86–87
Social policy, 3, 13, 57–58, 61, 112, 229–30, 260, 269–300
Social participation, 80–82, 85, 101–2, 107, 108
Social Services, 12, 207–25
— Social Services, attitudes to, 25, 37, 42–43, 160, 172, 178, 209–210, 216–17
Socialization in old age, 231–5
Socially isolated, social isolation, 1, 3, 4, 8, 9, 10, 11, 17–19, 21, 22, 40–45, 64–85, 86–88, 96, 97, 101–2, 105, 107, 108, 111, 112, 113–17, 130, 138–9, 142–4, 147, 152, 164–6, 169–70, 171–6, 176–80, 181–7, 188–98, 199–206, 207–25, 218–19, 222–3, 225, 229, 231–3, 236–7, 240, 244–6, 260–2, 269, 275, 276, 281, 282, 284, 285, 286, 288, 295, 297
— socially isolated, extremely, 23–28, 67, 72, 82–84, 138–9, 165, 240
Social participation, 18, 99
Sociological theory, social theory, 3, 13, 229–30, 247–68
Sons, 26, 51, 55, 70, 74–77, 120, 124, 127–8, 147, 165, 172, 174, 184, 187, 193, 251, 252–4, 257
— son-in-law, 22, 31, 76, 146
Spectacles, unmet need for, 31, 42, 127, 171, 177–8, 183, 211, 213, 271, 274, 277
Srole, Leo, 21, 98–99, 234
Status, loss of, 232, 237, 249, 297
Stengel, Erwin, 18
Stepney, 283
Suburban areas, 60
Suicide, 18, 21
Sunday, alone on, 93
Surveys, four areas and national compared, 4, 5, 46, 86, 131, 145, 156, 158–60, 162, 208, 218
— institutional survey, 4–5

343

Index

For Product Safety Concerns and Information please contact our EU
representative GPSR@taylorandfrancis.com
Taylor & Francis Verlag GmbH, Kaufingerstraße 24, 80331 München, Germany